THE
OLD SOUTH

STRUGGLES FOR DEMOCRACY

By

WILLIAM E. DODD

•

NEW YORK
THE MACMILLAN COMPANY
MCMXXXVII

Copyright, 1937, by
WILLIAM E. DODD.

All rights reserved—no part of this book may be reproduced in any form without permission in writing from the publisher, except by a reviewer who wishes to quote brief passages in connection with a review written for inclusion in magazine or newspaper.

Set up and electrotyped. Published October, 1937.

FIRST PRINTING

PRINTED IN THE UNITED STATES OF AMERICA
BY THE STRATFORD PRESS, INC., NEW YORK

From a Contemporary Portrait

SIR EDWIN SANDYS

Preface

THE EVOLUTION AND COLLAPSE OF THE OLD SOUTH IS less known and understood than the history of other sections of the United States, although in recent years a great deal of interest in its problems has been revealed in all parts of the country. I have given special attention to the basic subjects and conducted seminars in the University of Chicago more than twenty-five years, and when I accepted appointment as Ambassador to Germany in 1933, ten of the following fourteen chapters had been written. During the four succeeding years I was able to revise the work and write the concluding section. The kindly loan of the *British State Papers* by the Prussian State Library and similar assistance generously granted by the Library of Congress and the Virginia State Library enabled me to do this work at so great a distance from our chief sources of information. Of hardly less value, however, had been the years of co-work with hundreds of graduate students at the University of Chicago, where so many excellent young scholars were preparing themselves for the teaching and writing of real history in all parts of the United States. Although I can not name all those whose theses were most helpful and suggestive, it is my wish thus to express genuine thanks.

I wish especially to thank R. D. W. Conner, President of the National Archives, Wilmer L. Hall, Virginia State Librarian, Thomas C. Colt, Jr., Virginia Museum of Fine Arts, Earl G. Swem, William and Mary College, D. D. Wallace, Wofford College and Joseph L. Wheeler, Enoch

PREFACE

Pratt Free Library for kind assistance in securing appropriate illustrations for the early Southern settlements. In addition to these helps the New York Public Library, Miss Helen C. Calvert, Morris K. Barroll, Edward F. Rines and Frances Johnston have generously assisted in the use of portraits and photographs.

The subject of this first of the four volumes, which I hope to complete ere long, indicates the motives which moved nearly all Europeans to cross the stormy North Atlantic during the seventeenth century. The letters and documents in the *British State Papers* have been at times quite surprising when they reveal the resolute ideals of the early settlers of Virginia, Maryland and the two Carolinas. European emigrants, unemployed at home, showed themselves willing to risk their lives on hundred-ton boats in order to settle upon small land-grants where religious freedom and simple self-government were basic objectives. It was the beginning of the Old South, many of whose people were to grow rich and then to lose about all they and their ancestors had accumulated in two hundred years.

During the first hundred years of our colonial history the terrible struggles of the English people for a more liberal system of government, and the terrific wars on the continent of Europe greatly influenced the North American settlers. There was even then no such thing as economic isolation. The Virginians were almost ready to join the Dutch in the war of 1672 in their struggle for free trade; and not one of the four Southern colonies could seriously enforce the Navigation acts of Charles II, when European rivalries and conflicts supplied all American coasts and harbors with privateers and pirates ready to pay about twice as much for colonial products as England was in the habit of paying. In view of the fact that conditions in the different colonies had to be described and compared there are a number of repetitions which I hope are not puzzling to readers.

Thus free homesteads, freedom of religion, self-government and free trade have been the major subjects of the following chapters, covering a period of some seventy years. In the next volume of my *Old South* book I shall seek to describe and explain the great changes which took place between 1690 and 1754. The title will be *The First American Social Order,* and the object will be to describe the emergence of Negro slavery and its effects upon the system which Sir Edwyn Sandys and John Locke had hoped to see established in far-off North America.

W. E. D.

Contents

CHAPTER	PAGE
1. SOIL AND CLIMATE	1
2. THE FIRST ENGLISH SETTLEMENT	16
3. THE BEGINNINGS OF THE TOBACCO PLANTATIONS	36
4. VIRGINIA VS. MARYLAND	53
5. THE DUTCH REPUBLIC AND EARLY CHESAPEAKE BAY SETTLERS	72
6. A COHERENT SOCIAL ORDER	89
7. THE DREAM OF SIR EDWIN SANDYS	118
8. THE ASYLUM FOR TROUBLED CONSCIENCES	136
9. STUART ECONOMIC NATIONALISM	162
10. THE FIRST AMERICAN "RECOVERY"	183
11. THE ALBEMARLE OVERFLOW	208
12. THE FIRST AMERICAN CIVIL WAR	235
13. CHARLES TOWN	255
14. THE EMERGING CAROLINAS	276
INDEX	299

THE OLD SOUTH
STRUGGLES FOR DEMOCRACY

I

Soil and Climate

> "The land about us, very sandie and low, so full of grapes as the very beating surge of the sea overflowed them—in all the world the like abundance is not to be found."—J. F. Jameson's *Narratives of Early American History.* I, 228.

I

THE LOW, IRREGULAR AND STORMY COAST THAT stretches from the Chesapeake Bay to the mouth of the Saint John's River, broken with shifting sand bars flung out to sea, and indented with hundreds of shallow, treacherous inlets and sounds, marks the front of what was once the most important, is now the most romantic, port of the United States. It is a mild, gentle shore in fair weather, long-legged herons picking fish and crabs out of the shallow waters; it is one of the roughest of all American regions when the storms of spring and autumn sweep the waters of the Atlantic far inland, turning the floods of the rivers over the wide marshes and sand ridges—a coast that mariners know and dread all over the world. Behind this coast there are hundreds of rivers and creeks, some of them pouring ten thousand cubic feet of silt-laden water into the ocean every second, the ten thousand feet increasing to three or four hundred thousand feet a second at times of flood, all of them following their tortuous courses from the hills and mountains a hundred to three hundred miles inland.

When the English explorers first traversed this "sweet-scented" coast, it was covered with dense undergrowth, vine-clad oaks and pines along its northern, palmettoes and moss-covered sweetgum and cypress along its southern stretches. Trees and shrubs overhung the rivers and inlets, trees laden with delicious grapes in season. A few miles inland the surface rose imperceptibly to sand ridges and plains, across which the rivers and creeks had worn their ways, depositing fertile silt and decaying refuse from the uplands in arbitrary patches or wide valleys, dominated here and there by bluffs which fronted the streams. Everywhere there was timber in abundance, tall long-leaf, evergreen pines dropping their needles unceasingly upon the ground. As one left the coast, the pines grew so thick that all smaller growth tended to disappear, making a vast evergreen forest, the trees rising to a height of sixty to a hundred feet, with a cluster of branches at the top. On open spaces where the Indians had burned away the trees for their corn, or on the banks of streams, there were green bay bushes with their sweet odors and scrubby dogwoods covered in season with white blossoms—a profusion of forest and vines and shrubs that moved the explorer to write of the "new paradise."[1]

Above the falls of the rivers, fifty to a hundred miles inland, toward the hazy, blue mountains, there was a long stretch of country from the site of Washington City of today to the sources of the Savannah River, forty miles wide at the upper end to a hundred and fifty at the lower, a region seven hundred miles long from northeast to southwest, a reddish loam, covered with dense forests of rosemary pine, of poplars, chestnuts and sycamores, sometimes three or four feet in diameter and from fifty to a hundred feet tall, woods as valuable for commercial purposes as could be found anywhere in the world—the region on which Richmond, Raleigh, Columbia, Augusta,

---

[1] Samuel A. Ashe, *History of North Carolina*, Vol. 1, 2, quotes report of Philip Amadas and Arthur Barlow, first English explorers of the Virginia coast, to this effect.

Greenville, Charlotte and Danville now stand.[2] The more southern parts of this area expanded into wide rolling prairie where deer and buffalo abounded and from which the latter, feeding upon the native bluegrass as they went, strayed late in the autumn to the higher altitudes of what is now North Carolina and Virginia.

The higher mountain area which composed the third important part of the terrain of the Old South extended from the wild country about the present city of Wheeling to the Savannah River, from Danville and Charlotte to Bristol and Knoxville, a vast complex of elevated ridges and towering peaks, six hundred miles long and from one to three hundred miles wide. In northwestern Virginia and western Maryland the Indian or the buffalo crossed ten or more ranges of mountains, from one thousand to three thousand feet above sea level, parallel ridges of living or decayed rock densely covered with chestnut, oak and locust trees. But if the explorer went farther southwest, the heart of the Appalachians appeared at what is now Hot Springs, Virginia, or the Greenbrier White Sulphur Springs, West Virginia, where the forest-covered mountains rose almost to the timber line. From these regions all the way to northern Georgia the aspect of the open grass plots on the mountains and the snows that linger from October till April reminded one of Switzerland.

This great stretch of lofty mountains was then as now broken by two main valleys. The more important of these was the valley of the Shenandoah, thirty to sixty miles wide, extending from the Potomac at Harper's Ferry and Martinsburg of our day to Staunton and Lexington, a region covered three hundred years ago with magnificent oaks and walnuts. As one mounted the valley toward Staunton and passed beyond, the second valley or high-

[2] Ernest Brunken, *North American Forests,* New York, 1899, Ch. II gives some suggestive facts.

land plateau began, a similar strip of country twenty or thirty miles wide and extending southwest to Bristol and Knoxville and on to Chattanooga. Some miles to the north of Bristol there was an easy pass through the western or Cumberland range of the Appalachians into what is now Kentucky. From the southwest as well as from the west the Indians and the buffaloes entered these highlands. If they went north they passed into Pennsylvania by the Cumberland valley that extends from the Potomac to the upper Susquehanna; if they went southwest they crossed the Blue Ridge range in the region of the Peaks of Otter or the passes farther southwest and found their way over the richer uplands of the Carolinas already mentioned. Wherever the soil in these highlands was very fertile, the natives seem to have repeatedly burned off the undergrowth of the forests, which caused the bluegrass to flourish, giving much of the region a park-like appearance.

These varying stretches of country, seacoast, upland and mountains compose some two hundred and fifty thousand square miles. The soil was in the beginning and still remains very fertile over large sections of the country; it was quite unproductive, almost barren, in other sections: in the middle region of Maryland and northern and western Virginia the tough, red, rocky lands were then, and are now, almost as productive as the black lands of Illinois; along the coast all the way to Florida there are alternate ridges and plains on which pines and scrubby oaks grow and rich, deep soils, composed of decayed vegetable matter brought in by the streams, and on which luxuriant crops have been grown for two centuries; in the higher, rolling uplands from middle Virginia to upper South Carolina there are some areas exceedingly fertile, while there are other sections barely worth the cost of clearing off the scrubby trees. Of particular importance were the valleys of the rivers that fell into the Chesapeake Bay and into the South Atlantic. The rivers wind about in serpentine fashion, and at high water sweep over valleys sometimes a mile or even two or three miles wide.

In the so-called tidewater Virginia, the region which lies between the Rappahannock and the James Rivers and reaching toward the uplands, fifty to a hundred miles, there were many small rivers now called the Po, the North Anna, the Pamunkey and the Chickahominy, and numberless creeks, runs and backwaters, all inviting tired, war-worn Europeans to their secluded shores. On either side of these streams there were fit places for numberless plantations, bluffs or elevated banks on one side or the other overlooking broad waters or wide expanses of land. However, only a small proportion of the area under consideration was composed of river bottoms fit for large-scale agriculture. The greater part of the section was made up of sandy levels of ridges rising a few feet above the water in the streams or gradually sloping upward toward the west. The thin soils of the ridges were fit for the small farms of less enterprising folk.

South of the James River the wilderness stretched toward the mountains of North Carolina. But below what we call the Dismal Swamp there appeared another network of rivers and smaller waterways emptying their burdens into the Albemarle and Pamlico Sounds, from the Nottoway in southern Virginia to the Neuse in North Carolina, scores of larger or smaller streams flowing into these or into the great Roanoke halfway between. Here again there was a region the size of Belgium, cut into hundreds of valleys with inviting sites for plantations, with water communication to the Atlantic, although the shifting sands at the mouths of the rivers or the outlets of the sounds made traffic in vessels of more than eight-foot draft most dangerous. Here as in Virginia the river bottoms were fertile, although subject occasionally to inundations from the rivers or from storms at sea that swept high tides into the bays and streams far inland.

The ridged and small plateaus between the rivers were of light sandy texture, except in certain areas where decaying vegetation in swamps or on natural levels had through the ages laid down a rich black earth that invited ambitious plantations.

But from the Cape Fear country about Wilmington, North Carolina, to the lazy bottoms below Beaufort, South Carolina, there was the most wondrous of all these regions captured in the long ages from the Atlantic. The Pedee, the Santee, the Cooper, the Ashley and multitudinous other streams, big and little, that fall into these and others on to the Coosawatchie, a little north of modern Savannah, drain a country of thirty or forty thousand square miles. They are very large rivers, with wide sandy-loam soils along their courses, very crooked, and with here and there beautiful promontories for settlements and plantations. On the smaller streams or deep inlets from the Georgetown, the Charleston and Beaufort Bays there were many, very many inviting areas awaiting the exploitation of the white man. The whole region bore something of a tropical aspect. The larger rivers ran almost on a level with the surrounding country, and presented a little of the appearance of the Mississippi. In the drier seasons the salt water of the ocean was carried by the tides forty or fifty miles inland; in winter and spring the rivers spread gently over vast stretches of country and carried their debris far out to sea. The triangular areas between the rivers were alternating bottoms and sand ridges where scientific drainage and clearing of forests would offer both plantations for large undertakings and little farms for less ambitious. The outlets to the ocean were like those of Virginia and North Carolina, perhaps more difficult, except at Charleston, where there was a quiet, deep and for the time, ample, harbor, as there was in fact at the mouth of the James River. And as one went south along the coast, there ap-

SOIL AND CLIMATE 7

peared a network of fertile islands where animal and vegetable life was most abundant. In all of these attractive if complicated regions the front was toward the ocean, as if to beckon Europe. However, west of the lowland, fifty to a hundred miles inland and beginning in middle North Carolina, there was an extensive strip of rolling sand hills where the vegetation was meagre and which formed for a long time a barrier to the spread of the settlements to the west.[3]

II

Multitudes of rivers and streams suggest heavy rainfall or melting snows. The climate of the Old South, like that of the present United States, is erratic. The winters of the high mountains from western Virginia to northern Georgia were and are almost as severe as those of the middle region about Philadelphia and New York, although they are not so long. From November till March the prevailing winds, laden with moisture from the Atlantic, beat upon the high ridges of the eastern Appalachians and precipitate snows that cover the piedmont hills and the highlands a foot, sometimes eighteen inches, deep. Even the low-country is sometimes wrapped in snow a few days in each winter. In the upper regions these snows are frequent, and the temperature runs so low that the land is often covered a foot deep for months at a time, the earth frozen underneath to a depth of two feet. From Wheeling to Asheville and Knoxville, ice is harvested in winter quite as regularly as in New England, every important farmstead with its pond and storage facilities. In the mountains the drifts are many feet deep, ingress and egress most difficult, the higher ridges and peaks

[3] Hugh H. Bennet, *The Soils and Agriculture of the Southern States;* Charles C. Colby, *Sourcebook for the Economic Geography of North America.*

covered with snow on their northern and western sides half of each year, thus feeding innumerable streams that supply the rivers of the lowlands.

But while the great mountain area presents so much of the appearance of a harsh northern climate, the section of the Old South between the Saint John's and the Cape Fear Rivers and as far west as Augusta and Columbia offers a remarkable contrast. The sun is visible nearly every day from December till April, the winds are gentle and caressing and the atmosphere invigorating, although the rainfall is frequent and heavy. Snow falls very rarely south of Charleston and east of Augusta. But there are frequent and terrible rain and wind storms that sweep upward from the southeast and inland for many miles, devastating farms and plantations, sometimes so sudden and so violent as to carry destruction over large areas.

Nothing illustrates this better than the account of the tornado of 1761 preserved in the family records of the well-known Baptist preacher, Oliver Hart, of Charleston:[4]

> On Monday, 4th of May, 1761, at half-past two P.M. and an hour and a half after new moon, a most violent whirlwind passed down Ashley River and fell upon the shipping in Rebellion Road. It was first seen coming down Wappoo Creek with great swiftness into Ashley River. The quantity of vapor which composed the impetuous column and its prodigious velocity ploughed the river to the bottom and laid the channel bare. Many boats, schooners and sloops dry and at a distance from the shore were carried into the bay. Then suddenly the storm was reinforced by another from the northwest and with terrific roar joined the former, ploughed into the sea, and within three minutes five sea-going vessels were sunk outright. Many, both white people and negroes, were killed or hurt; the cattle lay dead in the fields, and along its course from the southwest where every tree and shrub was torn up, chimneys

---

[4] *The Charleston Yearbook*, 1885, 389-392. This quotation is compressed from detailed account by an eye-witness.

and houses were blown down. But by four o'clock the wind was fallen and the sun shone clear and serene. We could scarcely believe that such a dreadful scene had been exhibited but for the sunken vessels and the melancholy proofs.

Farther north and west, from Wilmington to the Chesapeake Bay and from the low country of North Carolina to the foothills of the Blue Ridge at Lynchburg and Danville, the winters are mild, if rainy, with occasional snows and skating on the rivers. At Richmond men formerly gathered ice from the eddies in the river or from ponds created for the purpose. Even at Brandon and Westover, the famous colonial plantation houses, there were ice houses. The Potomac at Georgetown freezes over solid once in three or four years; and once in half a century the Cape Fear at Fayetteville is covered with ice. All of which means that the fierce blizzards from the Alleghanies or directly from the north occasionally sweep as far south as the James River, sometimes as far as middle South Carolina.

If the winters offer so much variety, the summers are less capricious. From May to October in all but the highlands the sun shows little mercy to the outdoor worker; and the atmosphere is laden with moisture which in the middle and lower counties makes the climate oppressive. Along the coast and inland some forty or fifty miles the heats of midsummer are ameliorated by friendly sea breezes, while at many points where the sand bars project out to sea there are delightful resorts, as at Fort Monroe, Wrightsville, at the mouth of Cape Fear, and on the islands off Charleston. But over the great area that lies inland, from Georgetown and Alexandria to Augusta and Savannah, the long heats of summer are anything but delightful, although it is rare that the present generation of white workers, indoors or out, ceases its toil. This applies more to the white than to the black population, contrary to the view that the latter loves a scorching sun.

In summer the highlands offer seasons as cool as those of most northern resorts, and they continue delightful till the middle of October, although at Asheville or the White Sulphur Springs the midday sun is glaring and the atmosphere sometimes moisture-laden. But the nights are cool. Fires are regularly kindled on open hearths almost everywhere before the end of August, and double blankets always lie at the foot of one's bed. These differences in each twenty-four hours are due to the more direct rays of the southern sun by day and the cooling effects of rains and mists that hover about the mountain peaks, as well as to the elevation above the hot plains below.[5]

The climate of the South, then, in winter as in summer, varies more sharply than in more northern communities as the lower and elevated regions likewise vary more widely. And this varying climate produces like variety of crops, wheat thriving everywhere but in the very low lands; tobacco and cotton flourish over the lowlands and the hills to the edges of the mountains; and forests burnt off or cut away by lumbermen quickly reappear under favorable attention. But everywhere the precipitation is great: the snows of the highlands being as heavy and as frequent as in New York, the rains of the low country and piedmont more heavy and more frequent than in any other part of the United States, although in this there are contrasts. At times there are drouths that continue from early summer till autumn, withering seasons which dry the rivers and springs and give the country a parched and dreary appearance, blights that sometimes threaten famine. But after these dry, hot seasons there are apt to come terrible storms with rainfall in such torrents that the crops are ruined and the soil carried into the streams.

[5] R. De C. Ward, *Climatology of the United States.*

Thus erosion of the best lands in the piedmont region of the South goes steadily on where the forests have been cleared away or where grasses do not protect the ground against the sudden rainfall. One of the storms of the upper South as early as 1667, as described by an eyewitness, gives a vivid impression of the terrors of nature as well as the damage wrought upon men, animals and crops: [6]

In April we had a most prodigious Storm of hail many of them as big as Turkey Eggs which destroyed most of our younge Mast and fruit, and forward English grain; broke all the glass windowes and beat holes through the tiles of our houses, killed many young hogs and cattle. (Then) It fell to raining and continued for forty days together which spoiled much of what the hail had left of our English graine. But on the 27th of August followed the most dreadful hurricane that ever this country groaned under; it lasted 24 hours, began at North East and went round southerly till it came to West and so on till it came to South East where it ceased. It was accompanied with a most violent rain but no thunder. The night of it was the most Dismall tyme that ever I know or heard off, for the wind and rain raised so confused a noise mixt with the continual cracks of falling houses and the murmur of the waves impetuously beaten against the shores and by the violence forced and, as it were, crowded up into all Creekes, Rivers and Bays to that prodigious height that it hazarded the drowning of many people who lived not in sight of the Rivers, yet were then forced to climb to the top of their houses to keep themselves above water. It was wonderful to consider the contrary effects of that storm, for it blew some ships from their Anchors and carried them safe over Shelves of Sand where a Wherry could could difficultly pass, and yet Knocked out the bottom of a Ship belonging to Col. Scarburgh (ready to sail for England) in eight foot water more than she drew, but when the morning came, and the Sun risen it would have comforted us (or any else) after such a night had it not withall lighted us to ruins of our Plantations, of which I think

[6] From a letter of Secretary Thomas Ludwell to the Secretary of the Board of Trade, early September, 1667.

not one escaped. The nearest computation is at least 10000 houses blown down all the Indian Grain laid flat upon the Ground, all the Tobacco in the fields torn to pieces and most of that which was in the houses perished with them, the fences about the corn fields either blown down or beaten to the ground by trees which fell upon them.

Thus the rivers of the South, due to topography, to climate and rainfall, are the largest of the eastern United States. The Potomac takes its rise in the mountains of Pennsylvania and western Virginia, traverses a distance of three hundred miles, drains twenty thousand square miles of territory, and empties into the Chesapeake Bay at high flood four hundred thousand cubic feet of water per second, at low flood only one thousand! The Cape Fear, whose springs are in southwestern Virginia and western North Carolina, is four hundred miles long, navigable for light craft at least seventy miles, drains an area of twelve thousand square miles, and empties into the sea at Wilmington; at high water two or three hundred thousand cubic feet of water, at low water two or three thousand feet. It is not different with the Great Santee or the Savannah, although the volume of water carried is greater in each case and the length of the navigable stretches longer.[7]

III

There was an active life of beast and man in the midst of this wild, beautiful country at the close of the sixteenth century. From the northern end of the long coastal lowland to its extremity in Florida there were tribes of red men, a few hundred some times in one neighborhood, a few thousands in confederated neighborhoods,

[7] *Report of the Chief of Engineers,* United States Army, Part 1, 507 and succeeding pages, for accurate account of the rivers of the South.

who lived upon the best soils or fished at the falls of rivers or took oysters and herring from the teeming sealife—now hunting deer and turkeys and bears in the forests, now chasing hostile tribes off their hunting grounds; now engaged in the dull, vegetating life of their little wigwams; a people who had developed a crude, tribal social order and who were seized at times by fears of evil spirits, worshipped a common master in the skies and danced weird cadences in his honor around blazing nightfires in the forests; but they were withal a hardy, resolute race, proud of spirit, brave as the best of Europeans, clad in rude garments made of the skins of animals, driving boats burnt out of dead trees, and accustomed to throw a feathered arrow with great dexterity; men who held themselves to be the owners and masters of the continent they inhabited, yet hospitable folk, bringing their best meats to the famished stranger and ready to show the country to any who sought to explore it—giving up their own crude beds of skins to the pale-faced visitors from Europe.

Such, in brief, were the natives who first welcomed Englishmen to Virginia and the Carolinas. And what has been said of those tribes lodged along the river banks and upon the sandy coasts of the South might also be said of other and sometimes greater bands who roamed the valleys of the Potomac and the Shenandoah or hunted bears and buffaloes among the highlands of the southern Blue Ridge and Alleghanies. The Delawares of northern Virginia, the Tuscaroras of eastern North Carolina, the Cherokees of the high mountains and the Creeks of southern Georgia were all so nearly of the same habit, attitude and character that one needs hardly to differentiate for the purposes of general history. There were perhaps a hundred thousand native red men on the two hundred and fifty thousand square miles of the Old South, men who knew enough of the country to assist the early settlers. They smoked tobacco, grew Indian corn, wore delicately constructed moccasins, gormandized in autumn and winter upon the fat carcasses of bears and deer and starved in late spring and early summer upon roots and the tender buds of plants.

It was an interesting, wild life that won the attention of the naturalists of Europe, from the gentle Arthur Barlowe, 1584, to the famous John James Audubon of the early nineteenth century. All over the region deer abounded, the most beautiful and active animals, multiplying in the most favorable of habitats in such numbers that venison became a common diet with the earlier generations of southerners. Of hardly less importance was the deerskin, a large, soft hide, easily converted into breeches and moccasins by the newcomers or packed in bundles and shipped to Europe, one of the important economic influences in the settlement of the Old South. If the deer was important in early colonial economy, the bear was hardly less so. A small, black animal of some two or three hundredweight, fat more than half the year, slow, pilfering of cornfields and chicken roosts, covered with a soft, hairy skin that made the warmest of covers for a winter's night or a long journey. Moreover, the bear made good food for strong appetites, and he was to be found in every part of the South.

While buffaloes occasionally wandered over the uplands of the South, they played no part in the development of the region comparable to the part played by the same animal on the western plains two hundred years later. But there were wild turkeys, opossums, raccoons, foxes, squirrels and rabbits that abounded everywhere and which furnished both the Indians and the early settlers a good part of the necessary meats for their crude tables. A land teeming with animals of so useful a character the more readily invited settlement. Nor were the beasts, little and big, all that lent advantage to the region.

The rivers, the shallow sounds and quiet inlets of sea water were all stocked with fish of many varieties, and at certain seasons one might take cartloads of shad and mullets with but the simplest of traps and seines. So, whether the newcomers dwelt near the coast or penetrated far inland, nature itself was ready to meet half the cost of living.

Of remoter value and influence, the rivers, in their descent from the mountain plateaus to the lowlands, poured for miles over rapids or precipices and gave the basis of immense water power. All the way from the foothills of the Blue Ridge to the fall line at Richmond, Fayetteville and Columbia there were and are sites for power plants, the mills necessary for the cutting of the lumber and the manufacturing of the raw materials of the South—power just now harnessed to the wheels of industry. Thus the area of the Old South, as large as modern France, offered at the beginning of the seventeenth century a fertile soil and a salubrious climate, great natural advantages and positive animal foodstuffs of most substantial value; and withal the sea front and its network of rivers and harbors gave promise of easy communications and a ready contact with Europe. And if these pictures of a rich new world, so industriously advertised by English travelers and propagandists, appealed to hard-pressed country and town populations, there were other and imperious influences operating to drive men across the rough Atlantic to try anew their uncertain fortunes.

2

The First English Settlement

> "The poor being thrust out of their houses go to dwell with others."—Sir Simon D'Ewes, *Journal of the House of Commons*, 1601, p. 674.

I

THE TANGLED EUROPE FROM WHICH THE BRITISH emigrants of the 17th century departed from 1584 to 1640 was largely the creation of Martin Luther, the bold monk of Wittenberg, who risked his life for twenty years in the hope of reforming the great, corrupt Catholic Church. The German people were thus beginning to emerge from the cruel, thousand-year mediaevalism under which they had suffered; and in many towns there was an actual struggle for democracy, religious and political. But Charles V, the Netherlands-Spanish heir to the discoveries of Columbus and would-be dictator of all Europe, forced the enthusiastic Lutherans into a compromise between 1540 and 1555. However, their influence had spread northward to Sweden and westward through the Netherlands even as far as England. There were probably a million Protestants who maintained a certain religious freedom, educated their children as young people had never been educated before, and proclaimed themselves ready to die rather than surrender their ideals.[1]

In the little country of Switzerland, where men had fought and died for liberty and self-government for three hundred years, there appeared in Zurich about 1520

[1] Smith, Preserved. *The Age of the Reformation.*

THE FIRST ENGLISH SETTLEMENT 17

one of the first democrats of western Europe—Ulrich Zwingli. He reformed the corrupt church of his city, denounced the custom of forgiving men's sins for gifts of money and caused the endowments of useless cloisters to be applied to the education of young folk. With a fairly free press, this work spread over Switzerland and parts of southern Germany. In 1536 the more famous John Calvin made even more drastic religious and social reforms in the border French city of Geneva, which was a little later annexed to Switzerland, and soon became the greatest of all reformation centers in Europe. The stern Calvinist religious and educational influence quickly spread northward along the borders of western Germany into France and the Netherlands and thence *via* Scotland into England. A new and marvellous age was beginning.

Parallel to these activities of Luther, Zwingli and Calvin, there was the influence of Erasmus, of Rotterdam, and Thomas More, of England. With an emerging free press, Erasmus wrote *Moriae Encomium* and other classic books in which he ridiculed kings and popes, princes and bishops; and More the famous *Utopia*. For a hundred and fifty years after the deaths of these men their books were translated and reprinted in all the languages of western Europe. Since all these men were in danger of being executed throughout their mature years, their books were highly prized in any area where they could be had.[2] *Utopia*, a picture of idealistic democracy, was read in all the early American colonies, its author beheaded by Henry VIII in 1535. With religious reforms and literary activity intermingling and spreading as never before or since, even the masses of common folk were coming slowly into an attitude of self-respect and freedom unknown even during the better decades of Roman republicanism.

About the time Luther's influence began to decline and

[2] Blok, P. J. *History of the People of the Netherlands.*

Calvin was just emerging, Ignatius Loyola, of Spain, emerged as the organizer of the Society of Jesus, whose purpose was to save Europe from the "calamity" of the Reformation and, if possible, bring all mankind into a reformed Catholic Church. Never before had there been such an organization as that of the "Jesuits." Their leader considered himself a general; he was to be acknowledged as an absolute master; the organization was to be regarded as everything, the individual nothing; the sacrifice of intellect to one's superior was regarded as the highest grade of obedience to the general, even to God Almighty. As Luther, Erasmus and Calvin passed away and the Netherlands and England seemed to *emerge* as new and half free religious realms, Philip II lent the aid of the Spanish empire to the spread of Jesuitism and to the maintenance of Catholic absolutism. For more than half a century Catholic propaganda and relentless war, aided by enormous quantities of gold and silver from Latin America, were applied to all the Protestant parts of Europe. Distress, amazing brutalities and economic disaster put both Catholic and Protestant populations into a worse plight than they had known since the Hundred Years' War and the Black Death.[3]

Towards the end of the 16th century there emerged from this long-drawn struggle two of the most influential peoples of modern history: the United Netherlands of William of Orange, two millions strong, having won the great war with Spain and compelled free trade with Latin America; and the England of Queen Elizabeth, with hardly three million inhabitants, whose seamen balked the great Armada in 1588 and were exploring the dangerous coasts of North America before 1600. These two peoples were emerging from feudalism, applying the doctrines of Luther and Calvin, beginning even to adopt here

[3] Merriman, Roger B., *The Rise of the Spanish Empire.*

THE FIRST ENGLISH SETTLEMENT 19

and there the idea of democratic self-government.[4] And no less men than Shakespeare and Descartes were developing literary and philosophical groups which were to reach cultural heights never since surpassed. In London and Amsterdam there were freedoms, intellects, energies and commercial activities which put ships upon every sea of the world and gradually made North America and Asia so well known that thousands of poor but enterprising folk were ready to make themselves homes in these distant realms. Such were the conditions of Europe which gave the Thirteen Colonies of North America their beginnings.

II

However, before the British struggle with Philip had reached the critical moment of the great Armada, Sir Walter Raleigh, of lively and imperious imagination, inveigled two-score men upon ships bound for the shores of what is now North Carolina. They landed safely, 1584, on a sandy island off the mouth of what was later called Albemarle Sound and began the search for mines that might rival those of Philip. They found no gold, and, after wandering about the low, semi-barren island and shores of the mainland, they returned in 1585 to England. The next year other ships and a hundred colonists landed upon the same island and made the beginnings of a settlement only to be lost in the mysterious forest and never to be heard from again. The Armada of 1588 drew even the most ardent of explorers into the heroic defense of the country, and for a time the appeal of American colonization lost its urge.

As the Spanish monarch relaxed his grip upon his far-

[4] Read, Conyers, *Secretary Walsingham and the Policy of Queen Elizabeth;* and M. Creighton, *The Age of Elizabeth.*

flung American empire, the cupidity and the ambitions of the rising peoples of the north were aroused to intense activity. The Dutch were perhaps the rightful heirs to the colonial possessions of their declining enemy. But Englishmen had no thought of yielding so rich a harvest to their economic rivals and religious brethren at Amsterdam. London tradesmen turned their ambitions for a moment to Muscovy and the East Indies. Single ship owners, like the Drakes and the Gilberts, cruised the South Atlantic to fight the Spaniards or the Dutch and bring back cargoes which yielded a hundred to two hundred percent profits. The Dutch held their own and accumulated capital which went into better and greater ventures. To overcome the sharp competition of the Dutch in the East, Thomas Smythe, Thomas Campbell, William Romney and a score of other hardly less wealthy men united in the autumn of 1600 to form a stock company to which each contributed a share or shares of capital. The organization was quickly effected, and the Queen granted one more charter to a great monopoly. The company built ships and armed them as for war; it sent out the best trained seamen and the sharpest witted tradesmen that could be found; and in five years members of the new company had reaped new fortunes or enlarged old ones in India, China or the Indian Ocean and held high heads in London. Soon after James I became King of England, Sir Thomas Smythe was made head of the India Company; and in a little while he was sheriff, then mayor of London, and finally the pretentious ambassador to Russia. Thomas Campbell was not less lucky, and at his death he was able to leave the unprecedented legacy of forty-eight thousand pounds to needy causes in London, father of all the philanthropists. William Romney ran a similar course and became Sir William Romney and master of a great estate. Thus the India Company quickly proved its power in the East,[5] and it did much to bequeath the mysterious association of peoples, called India, to the British crown. The greatest nobles were glad to associate themselves with tradespeople who put scores of ships upon the ocean and hundreds of thousands of pounds into men's pockets.

Other companies sought charters; and the glowing accounts of Virginia trees laden with grapes and Virginia streams filled with shining ores, which Philip Barlow sent to Walter Raleigh, reminded men of the fortunes which the Spanish had steadily drawn from Mexico. In 1606 the London Company received a charter to explore and to colonize the shores of Virginia. Sir Thomas Smythe became treasurer of the new organization, without resigning the presidency of the East India Company. The Earl of Southampton gave his name and his fortune to the cause. William Cecil, the son of Lord Burghley and Earl of Salisbury, William Cavendish, high sheriff of Derbyshire and later the earl of Devonshire, and the famous brothers, Robert and Richard Rich, nephews of the tragic Earl of Essex, lent their names and their money. How could such a company fail? But the greatest man who had a share in the new company was Sir Edwin Sandys, a leader of the House of Commons and a student and writer whose books had been gathered up and publicly burned at the doors of the Royal Exchange the year before. It was the hope of these merchants and landlords to found two colonies, the one in northern, the other in southern Virginia. James I gave hearty approval in April, 1606; crossing the Atlantic in fifty-ton ships was, however, a dangerous adventure in those days. In some cases both ships and men were lost at sea; at other times the Spaniards captured men and ships, and on still other

[5] William Robert Scott, *The Constitution and Finance of English, Scottish and Irish Joint Stock Companies to 1720*, Cambridge, 1910, Vol. II, Ch. 5, for history of India Company.

occasions remnants of parties returned to tell the most dismal tales about contagious diseases. But on the last day of December, 1606, Captain Christopher Newport, Captain Bartholomy Gosnold and Captain John Radcliffe, with a hundred and twenty men mostly of the "common sort" on board, set sail on three ships, the *Susan Constant,* the *Goodspeed* and the *Discovery,* the largest of a hundred tons burden, the smallest twenty-five tons. They went slowly down the Thames, lingered long for favorable winds at the mouth of the river and on the eighteenth of February, 1607, set their prows toward the West Indies, the heavy winds bearing them swiftly on:

> "To get the pearl and gold,
> And ours to hold
> Virginia,
> Earth's only paradise."

After resting their tired men and taking water and wood in the West India islands, the little ships turned their noses on May 6, 1607, into the Chesapeake Bay. They now opened their precious chest and drew therefrom the orders of the company in London by which Edward Wingfield was made governor and Christopher Newport, John Smith, George Kendall and others became an advisory council, a miniature government of England in the new land.

The natives proved unfriendly, but the ships explored the banks of the beautiful, winding river, henceforth to be called the James, after the new monarch at home, seeking a sheltered place where both native Indians and the threatening Spaniards might be held at bay. The settlers finally landed, May 24, on a little peninsula projecting from the north shore of the river, thirty miles from the ocean.[6] Crude cabins and flimsy frame houses were built,

[6] Alexander Brown, *The First Republic in America,* Boston, 1898, 24-27.

THE FIRST ENGLISH SETTLEMENT 23

patches of the dense forest cleared, each man given a ladle of barley meal and brackish water for his daily ration, gentlemen finding that hard axe handles rubbed the skin off their tender fingers. But there was always the eager expectation of a gold mine to renew one's hope. Heavy rains soaked the earth. A hot sun and a sticky atmosphere made beads of perspiration stand upon one's brow; dark-visaged natives peered wonderingly and with hostile mien from behind huge trees. The planting season passed before the value of Indian corn was duly learned. The outlook was not bright. But the two larger ships in which the colonists had come returned to Plymouth, the smaller one being dismantled in the fear that "evil-disposed persons" might seize it and return to England. The policy of the company is revealed in the fact that all letters to friends and kinspeople at home for the next few years were censored and all publications duly edited.[7] On September 10, forty-two of the hundred and twenty gentlemen and peasants were dead and buried in the oozy, unhallowed soil of what was called Jamestown. The Virginia paradise!

Captain John Smith, a soldier of fortune, but a gifted leader of the forlorn colony, sailed up and down the rivers and along the shores of the great bay, sometimes fighting, sometimes coaxing the natives into selling their own winter's supply of corn, the only means of relief for the starving settlers. When Smith brought his supplies into the pest-ridden camp at Jamestown early in January 1608, only thirty or forty of the colonists were alive. Happily, Captain Newport came again from England on January 14 with seventy other settlers and some foodstuffs. The day of his arrival a fire broke out among the cabins, consumed about all the corn Smith had brought and left the colonists half-naked, with small stores of

[7] *Calendar of State Papers* (1574-1660), *Colonial,* III, 68; also Charles Poindexter, *Captain John Smith and his Critics,* Richmond, 1893, 43.

food, the rigors of an unexpected winter closing about them. Once more the child-like natives divided corn with the white men who had come to take their country from them. With hunger half relieved, the weakened men turned to loading Newport's ship with bright yellowish sand, the precious gold at last! Ten days after the ship returned to England, its worthless sand on board, Captain Francis Nelson anchored his ship *Phoenix* near the peninsula and unloaded forty more colonists. It was the end of April, 1608, about a hundred men, new and old comers, holding doubtfully to their brave adventure. It was planting time again, though little ground was put to English wheat or Indian corn; the natives were restless and threatening. After bitter quarrels and some murders, John Smith was placed in charge, an autocrat whose stern will was thought to promise better times. The Councillor Newport came a third time, bringing seventy poor men, coaxed away from the poverty of their homes to the Virginia "paradise." Newport also brought complaints from London that the colonists had done badly, found no gold and planted little wheat.[8] To improve Indian relations, Smith was ordered to crown Powhatan, the greatest of the Indian chiefs in the region, an emperor, seek once more the elusive gold and send a company of explorers off two hundred miles south in search of the hundred and eight men whom Raleigh had left in the wilderness of North Carolina twenty years before!

Thus the dismal story goes from folly to calamity till June, 1609, nine more ships sailed from Falmouth, England, with six hundred fresh settlers, swept into the vessels by the promises of a new and enchanted land. After storms and adventures beyond belief, with Sir Thomas Gates on board for governor of the colony, a remnant of the six hundred, on two vessels improvised after shipwreck in Bermuda, reached Jamestown on May 23,

[8] Alexander Brown, *The First Republic*, 55-59.

From an old engraving

CAPTAIN JOHN SMITH

From an old portrait. Photo by H. P. Cook

WILLIAM CLAIBORNE

1610. "Out of the ruins of the place there tottered sixty wretches, more like ghosts than human beings, to tell their sorrowful story." [9] A little later, four hundred more of the Falmouth expedition arrived, their provisions spoiled on the way and some of the newcomers in the grip of deadly disease. It was a dismal business, but the leaders of the London Company had no thought of surrendering to the decrees of an adverse fortune. They picked a peer of the realm, Thomas West, Lord De La Warr, as he is known in history, for governor under the new charter of 1609, and that high dignitary arrived at Jamestown on June 20, 1610, with one hundred and fifty colonists, soldiers, mechanics and the "necessary gentlemen of quality." First and last a thousand Englishmen had landed at Jamestown, but that autumn there remained less than two hundred alive of all the devoted adventurers, hunger and mysterious disease having done the fatal work, a disease which I cannot avoid thinking had been brought from the West Indies, as most of the expeditions persisted in stopping among those islands on their way to Virginia—yellow fever? What was the use to run away from misery in England to a plague-ridden swamp in America?

But De La Warr bestirred himself. He sought the fabled gold mines far in the interior and stirred the Indians to renewed anger and attack. He sent expeditions to fish at Cape Charles, to purchase bacon in the Bermudas, even to fish on the banks of Newfoundland. A pious man himself, Lord De La Warr repaired the church at Jamestown, supplied a handsome walnut table for the communion service, and then undertook to cleanse and rebuild the dilapidated village. He fell ill and hurried off to England, leaving the settlement with only three months' supply of provisions and one hundred and fifty

[9] Samuel Purchas, *His Pilgrimages of the World*, London, 1905, IV, 1749.

forlorn settlers.[10] It was March 28, 1611. Sir Thomas Dale took the vacant governorship and applied, like Smith before him, the heavy hand of autocracy, permitted the settlers to scatter along the river but held the men at Jamestown to strenuous toil and a limited diet. Some of the colonists ran away. He captured them and burned them at the stake; others tried to slip away to England on a mere barge; they were caught and duly hanged. Gentlemen "born to estates of a thousand pounds a year" were subjected to the stern will of the master. A French settlement had been made at Mount Desert Island. Dale's assistant, Captain Samuel Argall, brought the rival settlers before the governor, who talked to them "of nothing but ropes." Then the governor sent an expedition to the St. Croix River, Nova Scotia, which made hasty work of a French settlement there. From 1611 to 1614 the autocrat held men to eleven months hard work each year in cornfields, or clearing lands. The twelfth month, apportioned through the year, the men were allowed to grow corn for themselves. Although fresh immigrants had come in from time to time, there were in 1616, when Dale departed, to the relief of all, only three hundred and fifty-one men, women and children in the colony; the cabins were falling to pieces, and the reputation of Virginia had grown so bad in England that new colonists were not to be had, except by force. The whole return of the best year of Dale's work amounted to three hundred pounds' worth. Nine years of dreary effort and eleven or twelve hundred deaths and misery unimagined made the story of "the Virginia paradise" sad reading. Now a strange thing happened.

[10] Brown, *The First Republic*, 136-138.

III

The Spaniards had learned long since the uses of tobacco. English explorers reported that they had discovered Indians in what is now Florida who carried the powdered leaves of a mysterious weed about them. They put the powder into pipes and lived upon the smoke of it for three days at a time. The story was told and believed in England. Since Spanish gentlemen smoked this powdered weed, it was considered highly proper for English gentlemen to smoke. Sir Walter Raleigh proved an apt and influential teacher. It became the fashion in London to smoke long before the first Jamestown expedition was set on foot; but the new King, James I, so disliked the habit that he issued a book, *A Counterblaste,* in 1604, against the *filthy weed.*[11] However, the Spaniards continued to sell tobacco all over Europe, Englishmen buying as much as two hundred thousand pounds' worth a year. And when Sir Walter Raleigh mounted the executioner's block in 1618, he paused a moment to finish his pipe and steady his nerves. There was little chance that an unpopular monarch would check the "pernicious" habit when unexpected influences, often so decisive in history, began to play. The savages of America were setting new thought-patterns for Europe.

Four years before the close of Dale's administration, John Rolfe planted some tobacco seeds in his garden. He sent the dried leaves to London in 1612. They smelt as good as Spanish tobacco, selling at five shillings the pound; and an acre of James River bottom would produce five hundred pounds a year! The King himself be-

---

[11] James I repeated his attacks as late as 1616: "A custom loathsome to the eye, hateful to the nose, harmful to the brain, dangerous to the lungs, and in the black stinking fume thereof nearest resembling the horrible Stygian smoake of the pit that is bottomless." From Andrew Steinmetz, *Tobacco: its history, cultivation, manufacture and adulterations,* p. 11.

gan to doubt the wickedness of smoking tobacco, and the King's friend, Sir Thomas Middleton, of the House of Commons, hesitated to repeat his attacks. Pamphleteers who, to please the King, had written:

> "Better to be chokt with English hemp
> Than poisoned with Indian tobacco"

wondered what to do with their tracts. W. Budd wrote to Lord De La Warr that *The Flying Horse,* a Dutch ship, had unloaded a great roll of Virginia tobacco at Plymouth in 1615, a Dutch trader to Virginia! Sir Francis Bacon, who was not a foolish man, wrote: [12]

> "Tobacco toppes the braine,
> And makes the vapors fire and soote,
> That man revives again—
> Nothing but fumigation
> Doth charm away all spirites."

The leaders of the company who had spent two hundred thousand pounds of their own money, and who of late had held little hope of ever receiving any return, thought James I might grant them a monopoly of the tobacco trade and that Virginia might supply tobacco in abundance. William Shipman said that five thousand pounds a year might be given a discreet nobleman at court if he would procure a patent from the King for the new business.[13]

James I hardly waited for a discreet noblemen to sue. Virginia was becoming a "gold mine." Peasants from the country and tradesmen from the towns stood ready now

---

[12] Alexander Brown, *The Genesis of the United States,* Boston, 1897, II, 679, 772.
[13] Brown's, *Genesis of the United States,* 679 for Bacon's, 772 for Shipman's statement.

THE FIRST ENGLISH SETTLEMENT 29

to take ship to Virginia. Before the end of 1619, twenty thousand pounds of tobacco had been shipped from the James River plantation, and hundreds of emigrants hastened across the Atlantic. There must be a new charter in place of the old one of 1609; a new arrangement with the crown; and new and better regulations for the patenting of lands and the organization of settlers. From a mere setting up of lotteries to coax contributions from rich Londoners, the Virginia Company now rivaled in interest the great East India Company. Sir Thomas Smythe, entertaining on occasion the French Ambassador and a hundred and twenty onhangers at his town house, wished now to control the offices of the Virginia Company and keep an eye upon the rules that Sir Edwin Sandys sought to apply on the banks of the James River. The charmed weed had wrought the miracle. It was to work many another in the long story of Virginia. But the colonists must eat as well as smoke.

In Virginia the natives cultivated on common fields a sturdy grass which, planted in April or May, produced "delectable ears" of corn in July and August. John Smith gave it the name of Indian corn as against wheat which was thereafter called English grain. Roasting ears became and remained the fashion of the Virginians. Rabbits and wild turkeys were easy to catch, and they made a better food than European peasants had enjoyed. Still other foods came easy in the wilderness. The natives knew how to take fish and oysters in season. The Virginians adopted the art. The Indians wore the skins of animals for protection in cold weather. The settlers quickly learned the value of deerskin moccasins for their feet, of buckskin breeches for their legs and bearskins for coverlets on their straw beds—white men whose ships traversed the Atlantic learned, before the King's fight against tobacco was over, to feed and clothe themselves somewhat after the manner of the simple native. The long, despairing Virginia endeavor was on the way to success; cabins and cornfields were now to be seen on both sides of the James River for miles, with increasing numbers of cows and hogs feeding in the swamps. Three hundred and fifty of the thousand or more immigrants who had arrived began to feel safe, hardly recognizing that they were soon to become the envied of rich and poor in England.[14]

IV

But the sudden prosperity of the Virginia Company and the distant colonists in the Virginia swamps was to prove quite as fatal as the preceding poverty and distress. James VI of Scotland, an unpopular monarch, of disagreeable manners and endured rather than welcomed in London, had mounted the throne of Elizabeth in 1603,[15] just as the valiant Queen herself was losing her grip upon her unruly subjects. For half a century war had made many English farmers and merchants rich, and more English cottagers and denizens of the towns poor; it was the beginning of the industrial age. The newly-rich farmers and merchants, once in the House of Commons or in the offices of great companies, with a hundred ships upon the seas, had no mind to submit to the wills of monarchs. Before Elizabeth was dead Sir Edward Coke, a great lawyer and a rich man besides, connected by marriage with the second Cecil, first Earl of Salisbury, set up in the House of Commons a determined opposition to the new monopolies, fattening upon the English public. James I (VI of Scotland) was not likely to curb such men as Coke when Elizabeth herself had failed. And there were

---

[14] Brown, *The First Republic*, Ch. XXIII.
[15] Samuel Rawson Gardiner, *History of England,* London, 1884-89, I, 48-49.

THE FIRST ENGLISH SETTLEMENT 31

many other ambitious men ready to join the recalcitrant group in parliament.

One of these was Edwin Sandys, son of the Puritan bishop of York and a student of the famous author of the *Ecclesiastical Party* at Corpus Christi College, Oxford, forty-three years old, the author himself of the *Religious State of Europe,* an orator of surpassing power and "a contemplative man" whom the King early came to dislike. Sandys headed the committee of the Commons to inquire into the wrong-doing of the monopolies in 1604; he was himself one of the principal organizers in 1606 of the Virginia Company, as we already know; and he was in 1614 made a member of the East India Company. But he never ceased to oppose the granting of monopolies; and he came gradually into the position, with Pym and Hampden, of persistent opposition to the King; he was called "a demagogue." [16] In 1619 Sandys and Sir Thomas Smythe, still the head of the East India Company, prepared the first democratic constitution that was ever applied in North America. Sir George Yeardley, governor under the new document, appeared in Virginia on April 19, 1619, to apply new remedies to the old ills. There was to be a governor and six councillors, appointed by the company, and twenty burgesses, or representatives of the people, to sit in a Virginia legislature in every essential like the House of Commons in England. There were to be two burgesses from each of ten "plantations" or "hundreds" along the banks of the river, chief of which were James City, Charles City and Henrico. The council and the burgesses sitting in one room were to compose the assembly. The freemen were to elect the legislators without references to the ownership of property. The land was distributed freely: every immigrant

[16] Frederick George Marcham, *Sir Edwin Sandys and the Growth of Opposition in the House of Commons,* dissertation at Cornell University, 1926.

who had come at his own expense was to have a hundred acres in fee simple and another hundred acres each for all who had owned as much as a share in the company. Further, everyone who had been brought to the colony by the company was to have a hundred acres at the expiration of his term of service; and new settlers were to have fifty acres each. There were large tracts reserved for such as Nicholas Ferrar and the Earl of Southampton, and whole peninsulas and bends on the river had been seized by favored leaders in the Virginia venture; the vast wilderness was thus, under the new dispensation, to be opened on most liberal terms to any who would clear away the trees, build a cabin and plant tobacco.

In the hope of hastening the development, Sandys permitted or encouraged the thought that men were to govern themselves in the new England.[17] The freemen were to be the rulers of the land; religion was to be untrammeled and hardly amenable to control of any sort. Even Anabaptists and Brownists were invited to emigrate and set up their chapels wherever they would. So free and liberal was the new régime reported to be that James I thought of Sandys as little better than an enemy of the royal authority, even before the fight between the crown and the parliament became intense.

At the election of officers of the Virginia Company in 1620 James I made his wishes known: "Elect the Devil treasurer if you will, but not Sir Edwin Sandys." The Earl of Southampton, Shakespeare's friend, was chosen —only another Sandys. The busy Spanish Ambassador needlessly informed the King: "Your Majesty had better look to the Virginia courts which are kept at Ferrar's house where too many of the nobility and gentry resort to accompany the popular Lord Southampton and the dangerous Sandys. These meetings will prove a seminary

[17] Lyon G. Tyler, *Narratives of Early Virginia*, New York, 1907, 277-78, also Brown, *The First Republic*, 262-63.

THE FIRST ENGLISH SETTLEMENT 33

or a seditious parliament." [18] Everybody was watching Virginia.

Emigrants continued to enter the new paradise, and the ships brought back more and more tobacco, fifty-five thousand pounds, as estimated for the year 1620. The King, ever in need of money and endeavoring to raise taxes without consulting parliament, laid a duty of a shilling a pound on the company's tobacco, but limited the amount to be imported. Nearly three thousand pounds of good money for the needy King, if he could collect his tax. But as the parliamentary party contended that the King could lay no lawful taxes without a vote of the Commons, Sandys shipped the whole crop of 1620 to Holland, and the King lost his expected income! It was war to the knife; and this matter with others became so acute that James I was compelled to call parliament in 1621. Every effort was made to have a majority of the King's friends returned.

Sandys offered in the borough of Sandwich against Sir Thomas Smythe, turned ardent champion of the King. Sandys made the monopolies the issue: "The East India Company is a pernicious matter to the Kingdom; I am against it." After a tumultuous campaign, Sir Edwin was chosen. He sat in the next parliament and fought the King's program at every turn: the monopolies, the divine rights of kings and the unlawful taxes. It was a stormy session. At its close, Sir Edwin and his friend, the great liberal lawyer, John Selden of London, were thrown into prison,[19] Sir Thomas Smythe, grown old and peevish, but always ready to lend the King his most loyal support.

There followed violent attacks upon the whole Virginia undertaking. Smythe charged that Sandys had been the cause of the loss of five thousand precious subjects of

[18] Brown, *The First Republic*, 439.
[19] Stephenson, Nathaniel W., gave an excellent picture of Sir Edwin Sandys in *William & Mary Quarterly*, Vol. XXII.

His Majesty in the swamps of the James River. "These men of discourse and contemplation and not of reason and judgement" would ruin the Kingdom. It was for His Majesty to vacate the charter of the company and take what part of the Virginia tobacco the government needed. The Virginians were so wroth that they changed the name of "Smythe's Hundred" to Southampton Hundred. The Earl of Pembroke wrote: "There is a great faction, the heads on one side Southampton, Lord Cavendish, Sir Edward Sackville, Sir Edwin Sandys and divers others; on the other Robert Rich, Earl of Warwick, Sir Thomas Smythe, Alderman Robert Johnson and many more."

But notwithstanding the bitter controversy, as many as three thousand fresh emigrants went to Virginia to become freemen, like "the freemen of Norfolk," to take lands for themselves and to grow tobacco, thousands of cattle and swine let loose in the woods to thrive and increase. It was not unlike the treks over the Alleghany Mountains two hundred years later. But suddenly the Indians, nursing ancient grievances and alarmed at the swarms of white men that penetrated the forests without let or hindrance, fell, on March 22, 1622, upon the unsuspecting settlers and murdered all but eight hundred and ninety-four of them. It was like a stroke of lightning, and, but for the desperate courage and valor of a few leaders, every man, woman and child must have fallen that day. No other American colony ever suffered so many calamities as early Virginia. What the King and his ablest partisans had despaired of doing might now be done with ease.

The next year Alderman Johnson carried a petition to James I begging a commission for the investigation of the colony of Virginia, about to be ruined under the administration of dangerous men.[20] The King asked the

[20] Brown, *The Genesis*, II, 1016; also Brown, *First Republic*, 517 and following.

THE FIRST ENGLISH SETTLEMENT   35

company to surrender its charter. Sandys fought desperately, but a commission was appointed. Some of its members went to Jamestown to study for themselves the dismal scene, more emigrants landing with the arrival of every ship, more tobacco planting than ever before. The Governor of Virginia and members of the council, in sympathy with Sandys, refused their records to His Majesty's commissioners, Virginians proving as unruly as the House of Commons. The commission returned and reported against the little democracy, in spite of a protest from Jamestown, called the *Tragical Relation*. In the midst of these commotions, the Virginia assembly, meeting yearly the while, declared in formal session: "The Governor shall not lay any taxes or impositions upon the colony, their lands or commodities other way than by the authority of the general assembly" [21]—proof enough that Sandys had done his work. One June 24, 1624, Sir Thomas Smythe was ordered by the King to take charge of Virginia; the charter was vacated. The next year James I himself died. Sir Thomas followed in a few months and was buried under "a superb monument in Hone Church, in Kent," the inscription running: "To the glorie of God and the pious memory of the honorable, Sir Thomas Smythe." Sandys was beaten, but the toilsome work of years was not so easily annulled. Virginia was and remained a true child of the company, a "dangerous seminary of sedition."

[21] Hening, William Waller, *The Statutes at Large, a Collection of all the laws of Virginia*, Richmond, 1809, I, 124.

3

The Beginnings of the Tobacco Plantations

> "Having groaned for six years under the oppression of unconscionable merchants, by the excessive rates of their commodities, we hope that through His Majesty's favour we may recover new life"—Governor, Council and Burgesses of Virginia, 1628, *Calendar State Papers,* Colonial, March 26, 1628.

I

SIR EDWIN SANDYS, "A MAN OF GENIUS AND A LEADER of enlarged mind," engaged to the last moment of his life in stern resistance to the increasing pretensions of the crown, went to his grave four years after the death of his great rival in both the India and the Virginia companies, and four years after his loyal and worshipful settlers on the James River had become the immediate and unwilling wards of the King.[1] But Sandys had contrived to secure for the distant Virginians a constitution and habit of self government as liberal as he and his friends had long endeavored in vain to secure for England. The death of the great and genial friend in the circles of high authority in London was deeply felt among the tobacco farmers on the border of the American wilderness. Still things had to go on. The older settlers contrived for themselves larger and larger holdings; the freemen clamored for the dispossession of the Indians; and the term-expired servant, more numerous than both the other classes, took his two suits of clothes, his axe and his new

[1] Alexander Brown, *The Genesis of the United States,* II, 992-994. Although Hume pronounced Sandys one of the two men of the "greatest parts and knowledge in England," there seems to be no biography.

THE TOBACCO PLANTATIONS 37

wife, when one could be found, and opened a clearing for himself. It was the beginning of the masses of American freemen who were to play so great a rôle in history.

The incoming groups of settlers to Virginia continued to bring with them pigs and cows and poultry. The forest was open and the weather not severe. There was abundance of grass, of reeds that remained green late in winter and budded early in spring, of acorns and pine mast, roots and worms, that would sustain cattle and hogs almost without attention from their owners. But the wild expanse of swamp and forest was open to the Indians who liked to kill pigs and drive off cattle for their own support. The more ambitious settlers thrust fences across the narrow points of the peninsulas [2] and bends of the rivers and creeks and thus at a small outlay enclosed great tracts of land which were thus somewhat protected against the marauders as well as against the straying of the stock. The tall trees were cut into ten foot lengths and these were split into rails which were easily laid one upon another, zig-zag fashion, and securely staked—the Virginia worm fence. The fence secure and the tract bounded by wide expanses of water, the owners of herds of cattle, of swine and goats, each made his mark in the ear or burnt his brand upon the side of his animals and set them loose to forage for themselves. Meanwhile father, son and servant, where there were such, cut down other trees, hewed two sides half smooth and notched them into fair walls for a cabin.[3] An opening was cut on the side next to the spring or improvised well of water, a log was laid down for a doorstep and a heavy door of oak or walnut was swung upon creaking hinges. Auger holes were bored

---

[2] Thomas J. Wertenbaker, *Virginia under the Stuarts*, 20-21. Princeton, 1914.
[3] Fairfax Harrison writes: "I have no reasonable doubt that log houses were built in Virginia before 1650."—Jan. 8, 1930. William G. Stanard: "The log house became so characteristic as to be called 'the Virginia house.'"

through the walls near the door and on either side of a crude stick-and-dirt chimney the better to espy and shoot prowling Indians. The roof was made of long boards riven from the straightest logs which were made fast in place by wrought-iron nails or by smaller logs laid transverse and weighted in place with heavy stones.[4] A broad fireplace accommodated huge pieces of wood, a rough crane swung pots and kettles on and off the blazing fire, singing squeaky cadences as it turned unwillingly on its pivot at the corner of the fireplace. Blocks of wood, sawed-off convenient trees, made stools for children who rolled them into place by the fire when evenings were cold; older folk propped themselves on split or leather-bottom chairs painfully worked out of whiteoak timber. But there was little time for parents or children to bask by the great luxuriant fires, albeit someone must ever keep a watchful eye upon the embers, lest the fire die down and someone have to walk two miles or more to fetch live coals to start it again.

The cabin in order and the housewife about her busy tasks, men and boys and servants again set themselves to the hard task of clearing off the huge trees, smaller undergrowth and brambles that stood almost impenetrable upon fertile bottoms. The work was done with crude axes, mattocks and briar scythes fashioned and hardened in England. It was no easy task for an English townsman to swing his axe and bring low a tree three feet in diameter, or to dig and pull stumps and roots out of the ground when the trunks of the trees were removed. Nor were the more numerous peasants from ancient manors in much better plight. It was a busy season from autumn till the warm spring sun put the work fairly past endurance. But at last the soil of spacious gardens, digged

---

[4] Hening, II, 76; Force, *Tracts*, III, *Leah and Rachel*, 18; Mary Newton Stanard, *Colonial Virginia, its People and its Customs*, New York, 1917, Chapter II.

and pulverized after the manner of the old country, was ready for the seeds of early vegetables, for collards which grew late and kept all winter, for turnips and beets.[5] Half a year's supply could be taken from a small well-tilled plat of ground. The garden prepared and a high, close pale set around it to ward off chickens, geese and ducks that cackled and squawked about every man's house; the cornfield was next taken in hand, Indian corn now being the alpha if not the omega of every self-sustaining settler. Eight or ten acres of forest and brambles, roots and stumps had to be removed before there was room to produce the needful crop. And here the Virginians early learned to imitate the Indians again by "belting" the larger trees in early spring, clearing off the underbrush and planting their seeds—leaving the tall trees to stand, like skeletons in the fields, shedding their huge limbs year after year and covering the earth with decaying bark and broken boughs.

Corn planted in April sprang quickly, yielded its fruit in August ready to be cooked with the squirrels brought in from the forests at the break of day by the man of the house. It early became the practice of housewives to carve the grains off the roasting ears and dry them on elevated platforms in the hot August sun, and thus add to the variety of foods for the winter. Before the ears were entirely dry on the stalks, the blades of fodder were stripped off, tied into bundles and stacked conveniently to be fed to the oxen that drew the sleds or the half-famished cows brought out of the forests in January to supply a modicum of milk for babies or delicate folk. In October the ears were dry. They were gathered and put into cribs built on stilts to give free circulation of air as well as to circumvent the rats that pestered men in the wilderness as they had done in the slums of London. Corn, soaked in salted water or lye made of oak ashes, softened so that

[5] Hening, *Statutes,* I, 126.

the husks fell off easily and left the grains ready to be beaten in wooden mortars and then boiled with fat bacon, the famous hog and hominy, still favorite items of food on remote Southern tables. Roasting ears, fresh squirrels and dried grain softened again and cooked with chicken or duck made better food than poor folk were accustomed to in England.[6]

But there were hogs to be managed. These were left in the forests to shift for themselves till the acorns and pine mast fattened them late in the autumn. Then a little corn was strewn at a chosen feeding place and the master called in a loud, lonesome whoop that might be heard a mile or more. In a few days the animals found the corn and learned their master's call. A little corn once a day flavored the meat ready to be killed. Then so many of the better ones as were ready were enticed into a pen, fed a few days more and converted into pork which, duly salted, was suspended from the joists of a tight-walled but open-roofed cabin, called the smokehouse, its door as sturdy as that of a jail in England. Here a little fire was kindled late in winter and special woods and shrubs were laid on for weeks at a time, smoking the hams, bacon and jowls and thus made ready for the hominy, or to be fried hard over the fire and served steaming for breakfast upon the family table. It was not a bad diet for men who cleared forests or for women who bore many children, scrubbed puncheon floors and brought the family water from distant springs. Thus the settlers began to adapt themselves to the new world and provided a wholesome food on which to rear a sturdy race.

Hog and hominy were not all. The cows roamed and multiplied in the woods, the better of them enticed by the call of the women or by the judicious placing of salt at milking places near the farm house. Here a pen was

---

[6] Edward Eggleston, *Household History of the United States and its People,* New York, 1888, appropriate chapters.

duly made, a little corn sometimes thrown into a trough and the cows milked. Evening and morning the women performed this task and prepared cream for dainties, sweet milk for children and buttermilk for grown-ups. And sometimes there was butter and cheese to ease the heavy diet of boiled pork or fried ham. When the wide cow-pens were thoroughly saturated with dung and urine, new enclosures were made for the milking, the trees cut down and the soil carefully prepared for turnips which were planted in midsummer and soon developed a luxuriant salad which was carefully clipped, washed and cooked with slabs of half-lean, half-fat bacon or jowl, a balanced food so often referred to by southerners in years to come as "bacon and greens, the proper food of gentlemen." [7]

Nor were these all the items of table fare in early Virginia. The hard, dry corn of the cob was shelled of evenings by sleepy urchins, ground in little mills, bolted to the corner of the house or a well-set post. From these back-breaking mills there came a coarse meal which was sifted, mixed with buttermilk or water and baked in little ovens, called "spiders" in that day. The result was a thick corn meal loaf, known even now in remote sections as corn pone. Sometimes slabs of this corn-meal dough were cast into the hot embers of the fireplace and cooked till a hard crust appeared and then taken out and washed and left to bake and dry by the fire. These were called ashcakes, dirty looking but not unpalatable. Roasting ears from the fields and fresh meats from the forests; smoke-cured hams and corn pone; turnip greens and hog jowl. These fairly completed the items of early Virginia fare, though deer and wild turkey abounded and a good marksman easily laid plentiful supplies upon his table.

Thus the first necessities of life were painfully supplied in the new region, the more enterprising already

---

[7] Force's *Tracts*, III, *Leah and Rachel*, 13; frequent references in the correspondence of John Randolph and Nathaniel Macon, 1800-1828.

making their cabins and their farms bountiful, if primitive, homes soon to become as dear to them as their ancient cottages in England. As the decades passed, larger houses and broader fields appeared along the river fronts and barns were built for the few horses that were later brought over from England, and the oxen that were used to drag timber from the forest to the wood pile or casks of tobacco to the wharves. On some fields a little English grain was grown, ten or twelve bushels per acre, and it was made into finer flour for such as could afford the luxury of European bread.[8]

II

The fundamentals were thus learned—the natural economy that provided shelter and bread. No gold had been discovered; and the company's efforts to smelt iron from the thin ores of the upper James river valley were disappointing. It was tobacco that set the new pace and taught the Virginians that they were rich, all Europe, in spite of princes and priests, beginning to smoke and chew "the noxious weed." And tobacco made James river bottoms valuable. The company, as we know, sought during its last fitful days to apportion the lands in the hope of stimulating contented settlement and more fruitful tillage. The King hastened to confirm the company's measures. Every householder who lived as long as three years in Virginia now received in fee simple the title to fifty acres of the soil; and for his wife and each child fifty acres more. That was the beginning of permanent holdings, but a cabin must be built on each tract. To those who brought large numbers of settlers great areas of land

[8] Bruce, *Economic History*, I, 330-50 gives detailed account of agricultural life.

were awarded, fifty acres for each servant or tenant; thus, during the twenties and thirties of the seventeenth century, there appeared in Virginia two scores of landlords with a thousand to five thousand-acre tracts, with frame or brick houses on some of them and private landings for ships. And as the demand for tobacco seemed for a time insatiable, there appeared some of the abuses which ever mark the course of development across a new country. An influential man with a patent for a hundred acres of land quietly changed the figures to a thousand. If the price of tobacco was high, officers of the company, or later of the counties, were too busy to protest. Were there not millions of acres all about? As time went on ship captains appeared at the wharves, left their seamen on board, went to the office of the secretary of the colony and procured a "head right" for each sailor, a claim for fifty acres of land; then he exchanged his head right for a warrant for as many times fifty acres of land as he had employés on board his ship. When tobacco sold well, he readily disposed of his warrants to those who wished to add to their holdings.

The Virginia fever spread far and wide in England. Men who hoped to make fortunes from tobacco persuaded cottagers and their poor kindred in the towns to migrate to the James River. The unemployed and the homeless were not loth to go. They were put on boats at London, Plymouth and Bristol, their little earthly goods bound up in old rugs or in little boxes. It cost six pounds of good money to pay the transportation of an emigrant to Virginia; and there was little space for extra baggage or worn-out folk. It was a toilsome voyage, besides, with disease taking a heavy toll of the adventurers ere they reached the Virginia capes. The hopeful immigrants were bound in legal bonds to serve those who paid their fare: terms three, four and sometimes seven or eight years after reaching the new country.⁹ They were to be supplied with some sort of a cabin, the fare of the country and rough clothing while they cleared off the forests and cultivated the precious tobacco of their masters. It was no light venture.

Not only were the cottagers and the poor of the cities coaxed in increasing numbers across the ocean to a new world, but the criminals of the prisons and the poor who lived upon the parishes were likewise bound to entrepreneurs or sold to ship owners and carried to Virginia to start afresh in life; nor is there evidence that these latter made bad citizens in the long run of the years. All served their places in laying the foundations of the America that was to be. Every indentured servant was promised at the end of his term freedom, the right to vote, fifty acres of land and a cabin, decent clothes to wear, and a few crude implements. He was to hold the fifty acres as a tenant for a term of years when he might patent a tract of fifty acres for himself, for there was always "scrip" for sale, or he might run away to the wilderness, make peace with the red men and hold as much land as one could make use of.[10]

Thus it was easy to procure land. The freemen took their tracts under the crown, which involved an annual fee, the well-known quit rent. Since the company lost all its rights to the king and the king was the feudal overlord of all the lands in America, every man was held to the payment of two shillings per hundred acres a year, a most important fee if all the lands of Virginia were granted. It was the business of the king's officers, particularly the receiver general in the colony the next hundred and fifty years to gather these fees from the increasing

---

[9] Bruce, *Economic History*, I, 552-60; Thomas J. Wertenbaker, *The Planters of Colonial Virginia*, Chapters III and IV.
[10] R. H. Tawney, *The Agrarian Problem in the Sixteenth Century*, London, 1912, Part III; James C. Ballagh, *White Servitude in the Colony of Virginia*, Johns Hopkins University Studies XIII, 291-306.

THE TOBACCO PLANTATIONS   45

number of landholders. It was all reasonable enough since the king protected the colonists against the hated Spaniard, and tobacco sold so high in the beginning, when the rule was adopted. However, as the price of tobacco fell almost every year the shilling tax was not exacted the first seven years. Men who took great tracts of land forgot their quit-rents entirely; smaller folk, as usual, imitated the greater. Besides, the king was a long way off. As the Stuart kings lost their hold on the people at home, quit-rents in Virginia came to be a grievance; "land belonged to him who improved it"—young America taking her own way.[11]

There was ebb and flow in Virginia. Some years great numbers of men ventured across the sea; other years even simple folk resisted the lure of the new land, though prisoners were generally ready to exchange a filthy cell for the open forests of the new world. Freemen with incomes were frightened by the tales of the wild uncleared wilderness and the hard toil of the tobacco fields. But boys and girls and idlers about the wharves were packed into ships against their protests and sold to the captains to be resold at Jamestown for what they would bring, as one may judge from the numerous ballads that came into common use:

> "When we came to Virginia . . .
> Where the captain he stands with a cane in his hand,
> And our aching hearts before him doth stand,
> With tears in our eyes in a foreign land,
> Was sold for a slave in Virginia." [12]

The process continued; cornfields, swamps, pastures and the game of the forests guaranteed a sustenance and tobacco even at a low price brought clothes, furniture for

[11] Beverley W. Bond, *The Quit-rent System*, Chapter VIII.
[12] C. H. Firth, *Ballads Relating to America*, 72.

better homes, a bit of lace for the housewife, guns and the needful ammunition for the chase. More tobacco, more land and more labor became the trinity of the new community. The required two acres of corn per capita might be cultivated with comparatively little labor. Not so tobacco. The best land must be selected; and the best land was covered with the greatest trees and matted with the biggest roots and the thickest brambles. Since tobacco grew best on fresh land, every farmer set himself each winter to felling trees, "deadening", as I have said, the greater ones. When the new field lay covered with logs of oak, pine and walnut, the neighbors gathered to put these into heaps for the final burning. Then the axemen turned to their mattocks, taking roots, little stumps and brambles off the surface to make ready for the tobacco, an acre or two as much as a pair of human hands could put in order in a season. At last little "hills" were carefully made three or three and a half feet apart in rows three feet wide, the fresh new earth pulverized and exposed for the first time to the warm sun. It was planting time.

Long before the new field was ready, a choice spot of mellow ground was chosen on the border of the forest, screened from the northwestern winds and exposed to the southern sun. Here the trees were taken out, the stumps painfully cleared away, every root removed and the soil pulverized in the most careful manner. The plot was fenced about to keep the pigs and cows at a distance. There early in March the tiny tobacco seeds were carefully sown and gently covered, a thin cloth spread over the bed to keep the myriad of early bugs and beetles off the plants when they appeared.[13] After the first rain, the precious little slips broke through the ground. They were nursed and watered till the middle of May, when they

[13] Ulrich B. Phillips, *Life and Labor in the Old South*, 112-114.

THE TOBACCO PLANTATIONS 47

were transferred to the hills in the larger field where the earth was stirred every week. In three or four weeks the first real enemies of tobacco were to be seen, late of evenings: beautiful yellowish beetles humming about the green, sticky leaves and depositing numberless eggs upon them. A few days later lusty green, horned worms appeared on the underside of the tobacco leaves, gnawing holes through them. Unmolested these miserable little vermin would ruin in ten days every stalk of tobacco in a five-acre field, and the painful work of a year would go for naught. There was urgent work for the farmer, the farmer's wife, and all the children, picking the nasty worms that hatched fresh every night. Six weeks or more the cultivation of the soil and the killing of the worms went on, every child dreading to pull off the worms and mash them under bare feet on the ground—hands becoming sticky, grimy and stinking, sometimes swollen from the poison in the green leaves. But tobacco sold for three shillings the pound in London till 1629!

In August the tobacco plants were two to three feet high. Then the top was pinched out, allowing eight to ten leaves per stalk which slowly broadened and thickened, suckers appearing at the crotch of each leaf. These were removed as often as they appeared in order to drive all the sap into the leaves as they ripened for the harvest. As the September days wore on the leaves became yellow in spots, then yellow all over; and the work of cutting began. The worms had ceased to pester. Then master, apprentices, women and children stripped the leaves from the stalks, fastened them to strings and stretched the strings under wide sheds where the tobacco, protected from the violent September sun and the equally ruinous showers, cured slowly for the final packing. When the damp November days came, the leaves of the tobacco were smoothed, worked into huge rolls or fastened together in bundles and carefully laid in crude hogsheads, made on the ground.[14]

Thus the world looked good in the early years of the royal administration of the colony, and the disappointed settlers forgave the King and his monopolists who had destroyed the company at the moment of its greatest promise. The Virginians would supply England with tobacco; the King would maintain a monopoly of the market by laying a duty of three shillings upon the importation of every pound of Spanish tobacco; the royal exchequer would be enriched by as much as ninety thousand pounds a year! The Virginia tobacco was to be received by agents of the Crown, prepared for the market and then distributed by special appointees of the government in the various towns of the country, the surplus to be shipped, "dumped", to the Netherlands for distribution on the continent. Everybody was to receive his share and the price was to be properly regulated.[15]

III

But the new system had hardly begun to work before the London buyers found that a great deal of the tobacco was inferior, thin sandy leaves plucked too near the ground, heavy dark leaves grown too near the water or on soils too deep and fertile. The inferior product was taken without compensation or thrown out altogether, after the manner of markets in all ages. It became necessary to regulate the harvesting of tobacco; and laws were made accordingly. The farmers were required to leave their poorer stuff in the fields and they must cease to plant doubtful lands. Even then there would be difficulty. Under

[14] *American Husbandry*, by an American, I, Ch. XV, description applies to a later date, but is very instructive; A. O. Craven, *Soil Exhaustion as a Factor in the Agricultural History of Virginia and Maryland*, 34-37.
[15] Hening, I, 134.

the best of conditions, some farmers made better, some worse tobacco and the packs were different. The London buyers continued to complain: they refused to take the inferior grades and indifferent packs, the market glutted half the time. The Virginia lawmakers made other and stricter laws. They built warehouses near the landing places and appointed inspectors whose business it was to test each crop that came in—all tobacco required now to be sold through public warehouses and packed in "hogsheads". It was the first standardization in American industry.[16] Each farmer received a slip of paper which indicated the amount of tobacco deposited, its quality and its condition. The policy of regulation and standardization was developed and fairly completed between 1624 and 1630. Here was stability at last. The farmer waited till the end of December each year when the ships came to bring indentured servants and the goods which paid for the year's crop, if anything was due after the payment of debts, fees and storage charges. The farmers gathered at the landings, accompanied the ship captains to the doors of the warehouses, bargaining and haggling as farmers have done through the ages. The price of tobacco declined from three shillings to three pennies the pound between 1629 and 1630; the price of London goods was high, three times as high in Virginia as in England! December–January was the time of the year for all reckonings, the payment of local debts in tobacco, the purchase of fresh servants from English parishes and jails, the distribution of new clothes to dependents who had served their terms, and the making of contracts with tenants for the next year. Would the settlement be a success? If prices could be more reasonable; men who had never owned land in their own right now talked of hundreds of acres; free laborers who had rarely handled more than a shilling at a time now received a shilling a day for their

[16] Hening, *Statutes*, I, 126, 141, 152; ibid.

wages; and everybody had meat on his table. Prosperity?

But there was another drawback. As we have noted the best grades of tobacco grew only on fresh lands. Five or six years successive planting showed an inferior tobacco, and inferior tobacco hardly paid the freight across the ocean. There must then be new clearings every year, more cutting of great trees, digging of stumps and roots, blazing fires marking the work of progress and destruction at the same time. It was work, endless work; and there was little chance of plows to lighten the burden of cultivation, though as the new farms were opened at a distance from the river landings a few draught animals were employed.[17] Lucky strokes for certain farmers, steady self-denial and persistent work for others and possible high prices for crops might enable men to increase the size and comfort of their houses. Frame dwellings with three or four rooms appeared here and there and, as families grew, annexes and "ells" on different levels and in different styles were added; and as the dead trees, stumps and roots disappeared from the fields the toilsome work with the mattock and spade yielded a little. When fields spread farther and farther from the houses and the eligible sites on the rivers, the term plantation came to be applied to the property of an individual as well as to the neighborhood. And there were more and better accommodations for the servants and apprentices. Out in the woods in the midst of little clearings and along the poorer ridges there were always the cabins of the freemen who had finished their terms or of men who paid their own fares across the sea and set up for themselves, poor lands for poor men. These turned their hogs and cows "upon the common" as they had wished to do in England; they produced corn for their own needs; and managed once a year to drag a hogshead of tobacco to a greater farm-

[17] A. O. Craven, *Soil Exhaustion*, already cited, gives conclusive evidence, ably stated, on this subject.

THE TOBACCO PLANTATIONS 51

er's shed whence all went into the warehouse. Few of the sand ridgers ever became wealthy; but all were freer and more hopeful than their equals in England.

Still it was a more regulated society than that which later came to be known as the American frontier. Indentured servants were many and well-nigh helpless. They worked hard and labored long hours, although not without some relief after crops were "laid by" and at Christmas time. On the larger places Saturday afternoons were holidays.[18] Their terms were on the average five years. They were not permitted to move freely even on holidays; no indentured servants might marry till the end of their apprenticeships; and half of them died of climatic and other troubles during their first five years' residence. Yet they received instruction in the arts of the new agriculture; they were permitted to hunt in the forests on occasion and at the end they were, as I have shown, set up as tenants in cabins, with a few animals, and some of the simpler farm implements. At twenty-five or thirty years of age the surviving indentured immigrant really started in life, and if he were provident he might go a considerable way before old age (50 years) overtook him.[19]

Great effects sometimes follow small causes. In August 1619 a Dutch war vessel, on the initiative of Samuel Argall and Robert Rich, second earl of Warwick, sea rovers of piratical inclinations, brought twenty Negroes into Virginia and sold them for terms of service, like white servants, the busy farmers quite willing to take a chance with the strange black folk. Axes and mattocks were put into their hands and in time they came to be regarded as valuable workers. They were slower than English peasants; but they were of tougher fibre for warm climates. Five years later, when hundreds of the English settlers had died of the "plague", every one of the blacks was alive

[18] Peter Force. *Tracts and Other Papers*, III, *Leah and Rachel*, 12.
[19] Bruce, *Economic History*, I, 572 and following pages.

and contented. They were already acclimated; and white men came to think that a Negro loved to bask in the hottest summer sun and was not subject to "swamp fevers." If they suffered in winter there is no record of the fact. Their new masters gave them the simplest and cheapest food, and they were not shocked to have them work about their houses stark naked. Living in little sheds or special cabins, the Negroes began to work their ways silently into the sad economy of plantation slavery.[20] Other blacks were occasionally brought from Africa or from the West Indies, men and women; and as the years passed they multiplied at the same rate as the white people, their color in the earlier decades hardly stamping them hopelessly inferior. They worshipped in the churches with their masters and when they obtained their freedom some of them acquired property and were actually accorded the status of citizenship.

[20] Bruce, *Economic History*, II, 59, 106.

4
Virginia vs. Maryland

"On the 28th of April 1635, Sir John Harvey was thrust out of his government and captain John West acts as Governor till the king's pleasure known."—Hening, I, 223.

I

WHILE THE PRICE OF TOBACCO REMAINED HIGH IN London newcomers put foot upon Virginia shores every time a ship dropped anchor in the James River. In spite of the heavy toll of life, due to mysterious diseases, to disasters at sea and to Indian scalpings, there were in the year 1628 almost five thousand hopeful people settled about Jamestown, up and down the James River, or roving the virgin wilderness in search of eligible sites for future homes. Tobacco was then selling at three shillings a pound in London, a slight decline in price which warned only the wise that worse times might be coming. That year the King offered the Virginians three and a half shillings a pound and a monopoly of the British market if they would submit to regulation and consign all their crops to the royal agent.[1] Anyone might see that such an offer from Majesty itself, even at a reduced price, meant prosperity; and some years thereafter as many as two thousand immigrants hastened to the office of the secretary of the colony to secure their grants or take up their lodgings with their masters in the hope of the better life promised at the expiration of their terms of service. Land

[1] Hening, I, 134.

was easy to obtain, but to produce the first tobacco crop required a considerable outlay of capital: to cross the Atlantic still cost six pounds; to build a log house, clear a few acres of ground, and to supply the needful tools more than doubled the debt already incurred. A freeman could hardly begin operations with obligations less than the value of his first year's crop.

However, the Virginians declined in part the King's offer; they declined through the agency of the House of Burgesses, growing every year to be a more effective voice of the Virginians. It is a little difficult to understand why the Virginia authorities failed to accept such a proposition. The burgesses were, however, becoming more conscious of their powers. Its members came up in 1629 from the hundreds and plantations as chosen spokesmen of their neighbors, every freeman casting a vote; and the poorest servant might be a freeman in due time.[2] The hundreds and plantations were themselves organized somewhat like the counties of England with commissioners and sheriffs who decided controversies and held courts bi-monthly. Of like area was the parish, the unit around the little church fronting a river or creek to which men and women came on foot or on their canoes and with arms slung over their shoulders, there to offer prayers and listen to sermons, more or less heartening, and to elect their own vestrymen who in turn soon learned to choose their pastors and to regulate the elementary matters of the parish. It was self government and all so far away from the great sources of power in London that both political and religious freedom quickly became the normal, if not the legal, fruit of their prayers in England and their new environment. The utmost wish of Sir Edwin Sandys was thus realized. With parishes, hundreds and a House of

[2] Hening, I, 225; 333-334; Alexander Brown, *English Politics in Early Virginia*, 235.

Burgesses, all duly connected, popular self expression was easy.[3] There were, however, other institutions.

The governor, the liberal Sir Francis Wyatt or the arbitrary Sir John Harvey, lived on a plantation near Jamestown, as the little capital on the great river was called after 1630. He was a planter like the rest. He held great tracts of lands for the expected rise in value, and his agents traded far and near with the Indians and not without considerable increase of his income; his tobacco went with the rest once a year across the ocean. He represented the unpopular King at Whitehall, held a commission duly signed by the royal hand, and he gathered about him as many of the six or eight councillors as chose to attend meetings, all approved by the same unloved monarch and all the owners of great tracts of land, improved or wild, their servants clearing new areas in winter and tending tobacco fields in the summer. These ambitious and enterprising representatives of royalty early developed into a little House of Lords and as such passed upon the bills which came up to them from the burgesses. They were a check upon the people but the wilderness was no place for the niceties of balanced government. The Council, if a little more dignified and careful, was not unlike the burgesses, holding sessions in the church at Jamestown. The governor was an important official on ordinary occasions and all deferred to him as men deferred to the monarch in England; but when important matters were under discussion in the burgesses, he was unable or unwilling to maintain a stiff attitude. He was, to be sure, head of the little state and he was likewise in the early decades of Virginia history head of the church; but there was not the odor of sanctity about his person that Englishmen associated with the name of the high official.

There was thus a considerable mixture of powers and

[3] Hening, I, 134.

offices, of plain business interest and official routine in the same persons and in the same institutions. The governor was a great planter; his salary was paid in tobacco, sometimes omitted; he was also president of the Council which gradually became the court of last resort—the first American supreme court; and he supervised the collection of duties on imports and exports which passed through Jamestown and the warehouses up and down the river. This system was the expression of the purposes of the liberal spirits of the defunct London Company, of the opponents of a dictatorship in England and of the exigencies of a little British community on a far frontier. It might emerge into a democracy. The leaders and the struggles between 1628 and 1642 reveal much to anyone who would like to know what has happened in the *Old South*. Perhaps a brief summary of the unwritten biographies of the most eminent Virginians of that day may help one to understand the difficulties of the time.

II

William Claiborne, of an aristocratic family in Westmorland county, England, came to Virginia in 1621 where at the age of thirty-five he became surveyor general of the colony. A year or two later he was made secretary to the council and as the prospects of a great fortune seized his imagination, he began to bring over indentured servants and acquire great tracts of land. In 1626 he joined his friend Samuel Mathews, an ex-indentured servant who had acquired lands and a reputable status, and they offered to build, at a cost of £500, a great palisade from the navigable waters of the James River to those of the York, six miles distant. They asked in compensation a stretch of land along the eastern side of the wall about a half mile wide. Their object was to build cabins near the palisade and put tenants in them; and these newcomers were to watch and report Indian movements. They would thus secure undisturbed tobacco planting and stock raising all over the peninsula between the two great rivers, some 300,00 acres of land.[4] It was the first great private venture of the colony and it would have made half the settlers fairly secure against another massacre. The plan was approved by the burgesses and Council and finally by the King himself. In 1631 the palisade was built, though the price of tobacco had fallen to a level which took all profits from Claiborne and Mathews, two of the ablest followers of Sir Edwin Sandys, half-defeated. But Claiborne next procured a great grant of land where Hampton now stands, brought over servants and slaves, and engaged Indian traders as helpers; his place was called *Kecoughton,* a great centre of Indian trade. About the same time he was granted the ownership of the famous Isle of Kent, near the mouth of the Susquehanna River. He put more boats upon the Chesapeake Bay and sent Indian traders all the way to the Iroquois country of the New Amsterdam region, where he hoped to acquire an Indian trade worth £5,000 a year. He would thus compete with the Dutch and perhaps become the richest man in North America.[5] He was then forty-five years old and as important as the Governor himself. His friend Mathews procured about the same time a great tract of land on the north side of the James River, halfway between Jamestown and *Kecoughton* where he slowly gathered servants, slaves and tenants about him and, after some years, built a convenient, if modest, home which he called *Denbigh.* He was wise enough to raise great quantities of grain, to keep scores of cattle and droves of hogs in his swamps and thus be able to supply British and Dutch ships with food as they came into the great river

[4] Bruce, *Economic History,* I, 300, 312.
[5] Fiske, John, *Old Virginia,* I, 269-74.

and, when the people of New England were threatened with starvation, to sell his surplus crops at a good profit. From 1630 to 1635, he was, like Claiborne, a leading member of the Virginia Council and was authorized to build Fort Comfort as soon as the palisade was finished. A traveller who visited Mathew's place about 1648 wrote:[6]

> he hath a fine house and all things answerable to it; he sowes yearly stores of hemp, and causes it to be spun; he keeps weavers and hath a tan house, causes leather to be dressed and he hath forty negro servants; he kills scores of beeves and sells them to the ships; he is married to the daughter of Sir Thomas Hinton, and he lives bravely and is worthy of much honor.

Perhaps the most interesting of the liberal, if not democratic, leaders of this early Virginia was John West, younger brother of Lord De La Warr, who invested so much of his fortune in the Westover property on the James River and other Virginia ventures that, after his death in 1628, Charles I felt compelled to grant his helpless widow a pension of £500 a year. John West inherited the Westover estate which later became the property of Richard Bland I and was still later the home of the famous Byrd family. He became a member of the Virginia council in 1630 and in the next few years bought a tract of land near the present-day Yorktown, and a little later became the master of a great estate where West Point was to be built.[7] He was a friend of Claiborne and Mathews and so popular that he was exempted, by legislative decree, from the payment of taxes. Claiborne, Mathews and West were committed to the philosophy of Sir Edwin Sandys and too powerful to be ignored by the ablest of governors. There was perhaps a score of other enterprising "planters" like Adam Thoroughgood, a

[6] Force, Peter, *Tracts and Other Papers*, II, 15.
[7] Brown, *Genesis*, II, 104-48; Mathew P. West, *Virginia, the Old Dominion*, Ch. VIII.

former indentured servant, who owned a growing estate in southern Accomac county, Henry Woodhouse of Lower Norfolk and Abraham Wood, also brought over as a servant, of upper Charles City county. All these men, keenly alive to the drift of things in England, were determined to maintain religious freedom—under cover of the established church—manhood suffrage and parliamentary (burgess) control of Virginia affairs.

When the Virginians were still contending in 1629 with His Majesty about their right to all the area that had been included in the Company charter of 1609 and Governor Sir John Harvey was seeking to put into effect the first tobacco control scheme, the leaders of British liberalism Sir John Eliot, John Hampden, John Pym and a score of others compelled Charles I, in the famous Petition of Right of June 7, 1628, to abandon arbitrary court procedure, unlawful imprisonment of opponents and leave to the House of Commons the right to grant or not grant taxes. It was the beginning of the most prolonged struggle for personal rights and self-government in modern Europe. There were bonfires all over London, and the county leaders everywhere rejoiced. Virginia was equally resolute against an absolutist governor and staunchly opposed to Catholic immigration, the more at the moment because Queen Henrietta Maria, sister of the ardent Catholic king of France, had set up a Catholic chapel in London and was encouraging Capuchin and Jesuit priests and teachers to slip into England, contrary to law, and apply the propaganda methods which had done so much to bring on the Thirty Years' war in Germany.

One of the closest, if secret, co-operators with the Queen in this activity was George Calvert, who had been secretary of state to James I, had been made Lord Baltimore in 1625 and allowed to receive £6,000 when, on account of violent opposition, he resigned his position. His lordship owned great estates in York county and in

Ireland; but he and his family went promptly to Newfoundland, which had been granted him as a proprietary colony, where he had some fifty farmers and servants. Quickly realizing that the settlement was sure to be one of the least profitable in North America, he and his family and several servants took ship for the Chesapeake Bay, where tobacco was thought to be the source of even greater wealth than the hoped-for gold mines.[8]

On October 1, 1629, when religious and political freedom were the subjects of intense feeling in English and Virginia minds, Baltimore arrived at Jamestown—giving up as hopeless his expensive Newfoundland adventure. The acting Governor, Dr. John Pott, supported by the Council, recalled the Catholic activities of his lordship and at once demanded of him the oath of supremacy which no loyal Catholic could give. Claiborne and all the Virginia Council pressed the demand upon him. Calvert had come expecting to bring his half a hundred settlers from his Newfoundland colony. Refusing to take the Virginia oath, and after some offensive treatment, his lordship sailed for London where he meant to insist upon a large grant of land in the Carolina region. Suspecting that Charles I would give Baltimore a great stretch of Virginia land, the Governor and Council hurried Claiborne off to London to defeat the scheme. There was much delay, but Claiborne returned and, as we know, with approval of his own grant of the Isle of Kent from the King himself. However, in 1632, Lord Baltimore was proclaimed absolute master of the Virginia lands on both sides of the upper Chesapeake Bay as far north as the site of Philadelphia, and instructed to check the moves of Dutch settlers on the Delaware River. It was designed to be a Catholic realm in the new world to match the rising Puritanism of Massachusetts and counter-balance the Dutch Protestants of New Amsterdam and the Virginia

[8] Andrews, Matthew P., *The Founding of Maryland*, Ch. II.

settlers of the Sandys model. The settlement was to bear the name of the unwelcome Queen Henrietta Maria: Maryland. Lord Baltimore was authorized to exercise all the powers of the mediaeval bishops of Durham: ownership of all the land in the colony, the right to decide upon men's religious faith, to grant or refuse a representative assembly, to appoint or dismiss officials and even to take men's lives.[9] He might, after all, become a wealthy proprietor.

III

But Lord Baltimore died, in 1632, before the grant received final approval, and more than two years passed before his son, the second Lord Baltimore, could find a considerable number of emigrants who were willing to undertake the venture, the price of Virginia tobacco having declined from two shillings the pound in 1629 to two pennies the pound in 1631! However, late in November, 1633, Leonard Calvert, second son of the deceased lord, sailed from the Isle of Wight with two ships: the *Arke,* 300 tons burden, and the *Dove,* 50 tons. There were 300 prospective settlers aboard with their belongings, crude beds rolled up in bundles, tools for the clearing of forests and some guns and ammunition for probable wars with the natives. There were more Protestants than Catholics on the little ships, and consequently the dream of a Catholic colony was postponed. Religious liberty had actually been promised in order to get poor folk to go with them. But the ships were hardly out of the channel before a terrible storm made the emigrants think their time had come:

> This amazed the stoutest hearts and all the Catholics fell to praier, confessions and vows . . . We were in fear of imminent

[9] Brown, William H., *George and Cecilius Calvert, Barons of Baltimore.*

death all this night, never lookeing to see day again in this world, till it pleased God to send some ease. This deliverie assured us of God's mercy.[10]

In spite of the peril of so many scoffing Puritans on board, the faithful and the unfaithful alike continued their journey, the hope of a better price for tobacco and ample lands in a wondrous world outweighing their fears. In March, 1634, the *Arke* and the *Dove* anchored safely in the little bay on the northern side of the Potomac, which Leonard Calvert promptly called Saint Mary's in honor of the Queen, Henrietta Maria. Happily the Indians who then occupied that peninsula of the grant were already harassed by more powerful tribes to the northward, and for a song they gladly sold their cleared patches of ground and gave the settlers opportunity to grow corn and plant tobacco as soon as the season allowed. Calvert granted manors of a thousand acres each to a few of the emigrants, gave farms of one hundred acres to freemen, and set the indentured servants to work after the manner of the Virginians, with the promise of a freeman's status at the end of five or six years, everyone to pay a quit rent of two shillings, or one pound of tobacco, per year for each hundred acres—on the assumption that tobacco prices would rise. There was thus an overlord of all in England, the second Lord Baltimore; there was Leonard Calvert, the Governor in Maryland, much like the governors of Virginia; there was a Council selected by Calvert from prospective masters of manors, mostly Catholic; and there might be an assembly of all the freemen, Catholic and Protestant, when the exigencies of the new situation required it to be called. Another miniature of the English system, including the unwelcome representative as-

---

[10] Clayton C. Hall, *Narratives of Early Maryland*, 31: Father White's *Briefe Relation*.

sembly. The weakness here as in Virginia was the method of raising money. The Governor might get his salary from quit rents; but the planters in Virginia did not pay quit rents regularly. They might not pay in Maryland. There would surely be an Indian attack, and they were living on lands formerly granted to Virginia. To meet these difficulties the freemen would be called into session; and then the quarrel over rights, privileges and quit rents would come.

The Marylanders, after some resistance, bought the first season's supplies from their distrusted southern neighbors, the most surly Virginians hardly able to decline profitable sales. They planted little patches of corn and bigger patches of tobacco. They cleared new ground and built a crude church, the priests arguing with their more numerous and stiff-necked Protestant fellows to accept the true faith.

Whether the Virginia farmers sent workers across the Potomac to teach their unwelcome competitors how to plant, cultivate and cure tobacco at a price, the records do not tell us; but one has to presume this generous conduct, since the Marylanders were quickly offering their tobacco, properly grown, cured and packed, all after the Virginia manner, to the ship captains who soon found their way to a new warehouse on Saint Mary's Bay. It must have been distressing to find that, after perilous experiences at sea and toilsome digging of roots and stumps, the price of tobacco showed little sign of ever rising again, even to the level of six pence per pound. But here as in Virginia there were ample stretches of wild lands where hogs might roam at large and cattle graze freely, all increasing in numbers without much cost to the owners. The colonists need not starve, although Indian corn bread and hominy were hardly welcome to English palates. The Virginia forest clearing, farming and cattle raising were re-applied. Besides the ample food one might obtain, there was an occasional purchase of pork, beef and staves by ship captains who entered Saint Mary's harbor.[11]

And there was always the Indian trade. Henry Fleete, the Virginia Daniel Boone of that day, piloted the Marylanders into the deep woods where the Indians exchanged valuable beaver and other skins for cheap trinkets. Here, however, the Marylanders ran at once into conflict with the Indian traders of the redoubtable William Claiborne who reported to the red men that the Marylanders were Spaniards and proper people to scalp; and there were other reasons for trouble to come. Leonard Calvert was ambitious to found a great and profitable Catholic proprietary; Claiborne was a powerful rival with an earlier charter. Calvert was angry and insisted upon the rights of his later charter: it gave him all the unoccupied lands northeastward to the Delaware River. But Claiborne occupied the Isle of Kent in the upper Chesapeake Bay and so might control the eastern shore of the bay and the entrance to the Susquehanna, and hence the best approaches to the Iroquois fur trade. The problem was carried in the summer of 1634 to Lord Baltimore, who was asked to over-rule Claiborne, the best known man in Virginia and leader of the majority of the people represented by Mathews, West and other opponents of the Stuart methods of government.[12]

IV

There was thus a sharp issue between Maryland and Virginia in 1634-35, and Governor Harvey, who had begun his service in 1629, was in a difficult position. He was an admirer of Charles I; and the King had more than

[11] Hall, *Original Narratives*, Maryland, 82-83; Edward D. Neill, *Founders of Maryland*, 9-37.

[12] Tyler, Lyon G., *Cyclopedia of Virginia*, gives some of the facts and ideas involved.

once encouraged him to over-rule council and burgess majorities. He occasionally issued decrees to local county authorities that were regarded as invalid, and now and then he granted lands to favorites that already belonged to others. In matters of trade and the collection of fees he was an offensive grafter even in those days, and his treatment of colonial dignitaries and burgesses had been so arbitrary and offensive that he had no popular support. When, therefore, in the winter of 1634–35 the news came to Jamestown that Claiborne's Isle of Kent, duly represented in the House of Burgesses, was to be seized by the Maryland militia and Claiborne himself was to be captured, there was an unprecedented uproar in Virginia. The Governor was allied to Leonard Calvert, and the controversy seems to have been welcome as a means of overcoming his opponents.

And Richard Kemp, of whom little is recorded in Virginia history, seems to have been recommended as Claiborne's successor at that moment by no less persons than the earls of Montgomery and Pembroke, the King himself approving. Kemp had already brought indentured servants to Virginia and in 1635 was the master of more than two thousand acres of land on the banks of the James and Appomattox rivers. Within ten years he dwelt in the handsomest brick house in Jamestown and owned more than twelve thousand acres on the Powhatan and other branches of the James River. He was considered a friend and follower of the famous Archbishop William Laud,[13] who was to be executed as a traitor on Tower Hill, London, eight years later. Kemp was more than ready to assist Leonard Calvert in his campaign to drive Claiborne and other Virginians out of Maryland. Harvey and Kemp were assisted at this time by Henry Fleete, the clever trader who lived on the east side of the Chesapeake Bay, opposite Saint Mary's. He seems to have been a mas-

[13] Neill, *Virginia Carolorum*, 143.

ter of Indian languages, and was connected with English fur traders in London who had commissioned him in 1631 to make large deals with the natives all the way from New England to Virginia. Although Governor Harvey forbade his expected return to London in 1633 and deprived his employers in London of their profits,[14] Fleete seems not to have been offended, and undertook to defeat Claiborne's trade activities with Susquehanna and upper Hudson River Indians. He continued to give assistance to the Marylanders in their efforts to drive Secretary Claiborne away from his Isle of Kent settlement and trade headquarters. He was an enterprising commercialist who during the next fifteen years brought 118 indentured servants to the colony and became the owner of 6,400 acres of land on the north side of the Rappahannock, and was later the Virginia diplomat to the restless natives of the Potomac region. Harvey, Kemp and Fleete were thus active supporters of the Marylanders and opponents of the real leaders of Virginia.

Although an official committee of Marylanders and Virginians had decided in the summer of 1634 that the Isle of Kent was a Virginia possession and recognized it as a new county, Leonard Calvert, with the support of his Jesuit friends and Catholic advisers, was uneasy about the prospects of his settlement, and urged Lord Baltimore to decide what should be done; and his lordship promptly authorized the seizure of the Isle of Kent in case its settlers were not willing to become Marylanders. At the same time, Cloberry and Company of London, Claiborne's partners, carried the case to Charles I, who ordered Sir John Harvey to recognize the Virginia claims. Here was the beginning of a controversy that merged later into actual warfare. When the news reached Jamestown that the Marylanders were about to capture the Virginia traders on the Isle of Kent, Sir John Harvey compelled Clai-

[14] *State Papers, Colonial*, I, 184.

borne to resign the secretaryship of the colony and promptly installed Richard Kemp in his place.[15] This angered Mathews, West and the great majority of the population almost to the point of revolt. A little later came the report that the Marylanders had captured one of Claiborne's ships and imprisoned its crew. There was then a petition of many voters for the assembling of the burgesses in special session on May 7. They would compel the Governor to proclaim again the rights of Virginians to own lands anywhere within the borders prescribed by Charles I when he confirmed in 1625 the charter of 1609. Although Harvey had already received instructions from the King to maintain Claiborne's rights, he promptly took the side of the Marylanders for whom Fleete was still active.

Sometime before the burgesses and the councillors met in Jamestown, an indignation meeting was held in York county, where the sheriff, William English, representative for the Isle of Wight, Nicholas Mastian, representative for the Isle of Kent and Francis Pott, brother of the former acting Governor, and Dr. John Pott, made angry protests against Sir John, Richard Kemp and their support of Lord Baltimore's claims. The next day, April 28, the angry Governor arrested all three of these men and carried them to Jamestown, where he called the Council together. Sir John demanded at once that his prisoners be instantly put to death. George Menefie, a new member of the Council, announced that he too was ready to express an opposing view of what had been done. The Governor struck Menefie violently, and announced: "I arrest you on suspicion of treason." Whereupon Samuel Mathews seized Sir John, forced him to take his seat, and a signal was given which caused the office to be surrounded by scores of armed men. Mathews then told the Governor he must go to London and answer the charges of Vir-

[15] *State Papers, Colonial*, I, 207.

ginia against him. The Council, under the leadership of Mathews, prepared the indictment that was to be sent to the King and proclaimed the popular John West as acting Governor.[16] When the burgesses met on May 7, they approved all that had been done, and ordered Sir John Harvey to take ship for Plymouth, his quondam prisoner, Francis Pott, to be his custodian across the Atlantic. The Virginians had put their arbitrary-minded Governor out of office and sent him under indictment to London. John West and the assembly were now the governors of Virginia, and Claiborne, collecting what followers he needed, sailed toward the upper end of Chesapeake Bay and engaged in a naval battle with the Marylanders under the command of Captain Thomas Cornwallis, a Puritan supporter of Leonard Calvert. The outcome was not decisive, but Claiborne was left in possession of his coveted island.

V

When Sir John Harvey reached Plymouth, on July 14, he was able to thrust his guard, Francis Pott, into prison, where he remained more than a year, in spite of the protests of his Virginia and English friends. The state of things in England was such that the complaints of the Virginians against Harvey, and their demand for democratic self-government could hardly be entertained. The King had not allowed the re-assembling of parliament since 1629, and he was violating the solemn promises of the Petition of Right every day: trying to collect taxes without the consent of the Commons, thrusting people into prison on the slightest pretexts and re-establishing the hated Star Chamber court. Nor were these all the serious difficulties. As the Netherlands approached the end of their eighty-years' war against Spain, their trading

[16] *State Papers, Colonial,* I, 212-214. Fiske, *Old Virginia,* I, 278-79.

ships were to be seen in every harbor in the known world. Their independence was secure; free trade everywhere was their slogan, and freedom of religious beliefs was their practice at home. They were the leaders of what has since been called modern civilization. This little country of two million inhabitants had captured more than half of the British trade,[17] and its ships frequently appeared in West Indian and Chesapeake Bay harbors. They sold industrial goods at half the prices English settlers had been paying to their mother country, and they took thousands of Negroes as slaves from Africa to the Spanish-Portuguese settlements in Latin America. Commercial England was actually on the decline.

And Charles I thought to remake his country by suppressing what free speech and freedom of religion had been won during the Reformation period. He appointed the semi-Catholic William Laud Archbishop of Canterbury with the purpose of subordinating all church people to his will, and Henrietta Maria was receiving gifts from the popes to support her Capuchin and Jesuit propagandists and their fellow-priests at home as well as in Maryland. Lord Baltimore was in close relations with the Queen's earnest endeavor to make England Romanist again. Sir John Harvey, though not a Catholic, belonged to the same group and conferred sympathetically with Laud about the latter's plan to bring all colonial priests and churches into the strictest subordination;[18] and Secretary Kemp was, as we know, a close co-worker. Sir John had not been long in London before the King, the Queen and the Archbishop of Canterbury journeyed to Oxford to give instructions there that all teachers and students must conform to the new religious dictatorship.

While John West and his co-workers, Mathews, George Menefie and Thomas Willoughby were endeavor-

[17] Trevelyan, G.M., *England under the Stuarts*, 182.
[18] *State Papers, Colonial*, I, 259.

ing to restore friendly relations between Virginia and Maryland, Harvey was urging the King through the Lords of Plantations to confiscate all the property of Claiborne, Mathews, Menefie and others, and restore him to his governorship with more powers than he had exercised in 1635. But before any decisions were actually made, the Cloberry Company sent George Evelin to the Isle of Kent in the hope of making Claiborne's 1632 trade adventure more profitable. He made certain secret promises to Leonard Calvert, and managed so to offend Claiborne that he journeyed early in 1637 to London. Evelin then turned to Governor West, showed powers of attorney from the Cloberry Company, sold a shipload of supplies sent to Claiborne, and in the next few months forced the unwilling Kent islanders to acknowledge themselves subjects of Lord Baltimore and, before the end of the year, Leonard Calvert made Evelin lord of a great manor on the western shore of Maryland, on the pretense that he had brought the settlers of the Isle of Kent to the colony.[19] Claiborne labored in London, procured one more order from the King to Baltimore to leave him alone; but at the same time Lord Baltimore pressed the Lords of Plantations for the union of Maryland and Virginia and his own appointment as Governor of both colonies. He asked an annual salary of £2,000, and promised to regulate tobacco planting so as to yield the crown eight thousand pounds a year! This would bring all the Chesapeake Bay settlements under one authority and connect them more sympathetically with the Queen and her religious associates. Charles I did not make the appointment, but he did appoint his friend, George Lord Goring, head of a commission to regulate tobacco trade and planting in such a way as to protect His Majesty against Dutch competition and also limit production to a little more than a million pounds a

[19] Andrews, Matthew P., *The Founding of Maryland*, 107-09.

year.[20] The Virginians protested against Goring's rulings and sold tobacco occasionally to Dutch shipmasters, but agreed to limit their crops and ordered farmers once more to produce necessary foodstuffs. Their hope was to raise prices at least to twopence a pound and escape if possible from the depression which had begun in 1630.

However, the King sent Sir John back to his post, and the unwelcome Governor appeared again in Jamestown early in 1637 while Claiborne was on his way to England, and Calvert was helping George Evelin secure for him the possession of the Isle of Kent. When West was ordered to return to his estate on the York River, the restored Governor confiscated the property and servants of his popular predecessor. The estates of Mathews, Peirce, Utie and others of the Council were likewise seized and these men were hurried off for trial in London. The bitter conflict was thus renewed—the old English habit; however, the King was in too much trouble to approve these drastic measures. He ordered the release of the Virginia prisoners and the restoration of their properties. Harvey refused to obey orders for more than a year, and the Lords of Plantations in London then urged his removal and the re-appointment of Sir Francis Wyatt to the governorship of Virginia. Lord Baltimore and his brother Leonard had failed to unite the two tobacco colonies under their control; and the acts and attitudes of the Maryland assembly in 1638 showed the strong, popular purpose of the Puritan majority to be self-governing, contrary to the real purposes of their Governor and the Lord Proprietor.

[20] *State Papers, Colonial*, I, 273.

5

The Dutch Republic and Early Chesapeake Bay Settlers

> "That the people of Virginia have free trade as the people of England do enjoy to all places and peoples."—Hening, I, 364.

I

WHILE CLAIBORNE, MATHEWS AND WEST HAD clamored for their rights in London, Charles I and the famous Thomas Wentworth, soon to be the Earl of Strafford, endeavored to organize an army in the north of England, where Catholics were most numerous, and then march into Scotland, 1639. They would compel the Scots to abandon their John Knox faith, accept the 1637 Church decrees of William Laud and then lend aid to the monarch in his plan to break the power of the ancient House of Commons. John Hampden, John Pym and their resolute supporters were ready to risk a civil war rather than submit to the autocracy for which the Stuarts were still contending. The first campaign against Scotland failed. Many officers and privates of the royal army deserted the King and championed the cause of Puritanism and self-government. The tense struggle in the mother country stirred the farmers of Virginia and Maryland almost as deeply as it did the pious settlers of Massachusetts; nor were the people of the British West Indies of a different mind.

While the English monarch was waging this first war for a royal dictatorship, if not his wife's Catholicism, the

Spanish and the Portuguese renewed their struggle against the Netherlanders who had been fighting, as we know, seventy years for religious freedom at home and free trade over the four corners of the earth. The Dutch naval commander, Martin Tromp, fell upon the Spanish fleet off the Belgian coast about the time Charles lost his first campaign against Scotland. When another and more powerful Spanish-Portuguese armada, with twenty thousand soldiers on board, appeared in the North Sea, near the mouth of the Thames, Charles I agreed to give the enemies of Holland a great loan if the Spanish King would later lend him money to equip an army for the suppression of British liberty. But in September, 1640, Admiral Tromp drove boldly into the mouth of the Thames, destroyed the large fleet and killed or captured the twenty thousand helpless soldiers. This great battle was a warning to British extremists, as it was the definite guarantee of success to the Hollanders. Portuguese colonial harbors in the Far East, on the coast of Africa and in all Latin America were now to be guaranteed them.[1] The merchants of Amsterdam and Rotterdam were now free to send their trading ships into the West Indies, the Virginia rivers and Massachusetts bays.

The King was thus in a most dangerous position in 1640 when the famous earls of Essex, Northampton and Warwick announced their hostility to the Stuart-Laud policy. Even Henry Rich, who had negotiated the marriage of Charles I to the ardent Henrietta Maria, abandoned the Queen's cause; and Lucius Cary, Viscount of Falkland, whose brother-in-law, Richard Moryson, was an eminent Virginia leader, declared in parliament in April, 1640, that he would never abandon the rights of Englishmen in favor of any claims of the monarch.[2] The King now made Thomas Wentworth Earl of Strafford

[1] Gardiner, S. R., *History of England,* IX, 60-69.
[2] Gardiner, *Dictionary of National Biography.*

and what would today be called Prime Minister of the Kingdom. Archbishop Laud still considered himself the religious master of the realm and all the colonies, regardless of former promises to men who had emigrated. These three men even thought to make England a complete political and religious dictatorship. Parliament was called into session in April, 1640, and given orders to impeach Hampden and Pym and promptly grant the King all needful supplies. A compulsory standing army was to be created, Scotland was to be conquered, both Puritans and established church people were to be made half-Catholic by Laud, and the universities were to be subordinated to the archbishop's control.

But English townsfolk and country squires had practised freedom too long and their representatives were unsubmissive. When the House of Commons met, its leaders locked their heavy doors against the King's messengers, refused all grants to the Crown and talked of the impeachment of Laud and the Earl of Strafford. Parliament was promptly dismissed, and Strafford then tried to arm the English people against their wills and even authorized the Catholic Irish to march upon the Scottish counties in the north. In spite of desertions and the revolts of his "press-gang" army, the great earl moved toward Scotland. Both moves failed, and the King was compelled once more to grant the Scots all their political and religious claims—promising a liberal payment in gold if the Scotchmen would return to their homes. There was nothing else to do but call parliament together again. They met on November 11, 1640, and in spite of all His Majesty and the Earl of Strafford could do, both Commons and Lords agreed to order Laud and Strafford into the tower of London there to await their trials for treason. The King was now helpless, and parliament refused to adjourn.[3]

[3] Trevelyan, George M., *England under the Stuarts*, 186-194.

THE DUTCH REPUBLIC 75

While parliament had thus been reassuming its supreme power, Claiborne, Mathews, John West and others had been in London but were in 1640–41 back in Virginia contending for Virginia's rights: religious freedom, and the right of the burgesses to reassemble in spite of Sir John Harvey's opposition. Under their pressure, Sir Francis Wyatt, of the old Sir George Sandys group, was returned to the governorship in 1639 for a brief time. It was an intense struggle of English middle and even upper class people everywhere. Curiously enough, just before Strafford's head was cut off upon the decree of the House of Lords, Charles I arranged for the marriage of his Catholic ten-year old daughter, Mary, to William of Orange, son of Frederic Henry, grandson of the famous Orange of 1572. The King seemed to forget that he had allied himself eighteen months before to the King of Spain and lent all the aid he could to the great Spanish-Portuguese fleet that was to have broken the power of the heroic Netherlanders. Virginians could hardly have ignored these events, and especially the demand of Lord Baltimore to annex Virginia to Maryland.

But a month after the bloody work on Tower Hill, June, 1641, Charles I appointed the young Sir William Berkeley of the famous Gloucester family and author of a popular play called *The Lost Lady*, Governor of Virginia.[4] And when the new Governor arrived in 1642 to take the place of the popular Sir Francis Wyatt, he brought with him a confirmed list of new councillors. Sir William was a royalist and friendly to the church methods of Archbishop Laud; but he seems to have been really interested in colonial welfare. He and the King had made out the list of new councillors whose members were not free of the partisanship of the preceding decade of hard times. Richard Kemp was the new secretary, or chief, of the Council; William Brocas, speculator in lands above

[4] Hazlitt, W. C., *Collection of Old English Plays*, 543.

the York River; Robert Peters, owner of a handsome estate some miles east of Jamestown; Henry Browne, of "Four Mile Tree" in Surrey county, all outward royalists, were expected to be the dominating group of the new régime. But John West, of the famous De La Warr family, acting Governor when Sir John Harvey was sent to England to be tried, and George Ludlow, an ex-indentured servant from Massachusetts and leader of the Puritan people south of the James River, were also appointed members of the new Council. Thomas Harrison, a Virginia clergyman of some fame, was made chaplain of the new Governor.[5] While Charles I was now about to begin his doubtful civil war in England, the victorious Netherlanders proclaimed their famous free trade policy with all Latin America, expanded their trade upon every sea and developed their New Netherlands settlements as far north as Albany, and laid claim to all the coast from middle Connecticut to northern Delaware of today. The fur trade of the Hudson River region yielded them £10,000 a year, something like £100,000 of present-day money. Dutch competition in the Maryland-Virginia rivers and the failure of English control raised the price of tobacco from a penny, even halfpenny, a pound to two and threepence.[6] A new prosperity had thus spread over the Chesapeake country before Sir William arrived, and several Dutch trading ships were in the James River loading tobacco for European markets.

II

When the promising Sir William Berkeley arrived in Virginia, the Council and the Burgesses, elected by all the

[5] Hening, I, 238: Stanard, William G., *The Colonial Virginia Register,* 35.
[6] Bruce: *Economic History of Virginia,* I, 348.

freemen of the colony, assembled promptly. The Governor allowed the displaced Claiborne, whose Isle of Kent was still in the possession of Maryland, to become treasurer of Virginia and collector of customs at Point Comfort. Laws regulating the settlement of lands were enacted; explorations in the Roanoke River region were approved; legal processes against English debtors who had fled to Virginia were suspended. Planters were ordered to build neat brick houses in Jamestown, where they were expected to indulge in liberal hospitality during sessions of the assembly, as aristocratic people had done in London from time immemorial. Towns were ordered to be built at strategic points on rivers, and tobacco warehouses were enlarged or new ones built in expanding settlements. Tobacco continued to sell at fair prices, European goods were delivered at lower prices by Dutch traders, and immigrants were increasing in numbers. It was the beginning of the second era of prosperity for both Maryland and Virginia.

But the Governor assumed the rôle of a bishop over the self-governing churches, improved the status of ministers and coaxed the vestries everywhere to lay heavier church taxes and provide better houses and glebes for preachers. Children must be baptized promptly, taught the British catechism and brought up as members of the established church.

One of his more positive orders from the Crown was: "You are to forbid all trade and trucking for any merchandise whatsoever with the Dutch."[7] The Council and Burgesses agreed to most of the new instructions, but refused outright to cease trade with the Hollanders, and Berkeley himself failed to order Dutch ships to leave the James and York rivers. Sir William, although a royalist and orthodox churchman, endeavored to be a cooperative Governor in economic matters from 1642 to 1648. He

[7] *Virginia Magazine of History and Biography*, II, 281-88.

brought with him many indentured servants, and accordingly was promptly granted the Greenspring estate of a thousand acres and other lands in proportion to the number of his servants. His salary was fixed at a thousand pounds a year, not less than $10,000 a year of present-day currency. He resumed former governors' rights to trade with the Indians, which must have greatly increased his income; the Greenspring house was duly enlarged, though he was not a man of family; he persuaded the assembly to widen and improve the road from Jamestown to his house, four miles away, and traveled in a handsome carriage with four outriders, front and rear, to enhance his dignity—entertainments of gentlefolk; many and elaborate. Thus the author of *The Lost Lady* and representative of one of the foremost families of England showed Virginia how a gentleman ought to live. Nor did Richard Kemp, the Secretary, or Samuel Mathews, the Puritan plantation master, fail to live in similar style. The Virginians were beginning to feel themselves important, almost a free people.

Although the ministers and members of nearly all the twenty churches along the river banks were quite willing to cooperate with Sir William in the improvement of religious affairs and in a general way count themselves Church of England regulars, there were many people everywhere who were later called "low-church" folk. But the most popular leaders in the then prosperous colony, Claiborne, Mathews, West and the young Richard Bennet, a successful plantation master on the Nansemond River, were Puritans. The first assembly of Berkeley's governorship had hardly adjourned before reports came from England that parliament had appointed the Earl of Warwick admiral of the British navy and governor-general of all the colonies. It was the same shrewd Robert Rich who had sometimes been called the "Puritan pope" and who had lent a hand to the New England settlers ten

From a miniature owned by Morris Keene Barroll.
Photo courtesy Frick Art Reference Library

SIR WILLIAM BERKELEY

ST. LUKE'S CHURCH, ISLE OF WIGHT COUNTY, VIRGINIA

From "Old Historic Churches of America,"
by Edward F. Rines, The Macmillan Co.

years before.[8] It was at this time that Philip Bennet, brother of Richard, went to Boston where he persuaded John Winthrop to assist three missionaries to go to southern Virginia to preach the "true gospel." After heroic and "miraculous" experiences at sea, the new preachers began their work south of the James River; nor would they have been unwelcome north of the river. While the missionaries were preaching in churches and private houses, further news came from England: Charles I had abandoned London and was trying to raise another army in the Yorkshire region. The dangers to the royalist cause at home were such that Leonard Calvert asked his Catholic neighbor, Giles Brent, to accept the governorship of Maryland. While he labored with his brother, Lord Baltimore, in England to save their colony, even His Majesty's cause was rapidly declining. In spite of all these dangers, Sir William persuaded the next assembly to denounce the New England preachers and declare: "All ministers whatsoever which shall reside in the collony are to be conformable to the orders of the Church of England."[9] The Governor ordered the Puritan ministers to leave the colony, and there followed a migration of hundreds of settlers to the Annapolis area of Maryland, even the wealthy Richard Bennet abandoned his plantation and accompanied his fellow-emigrants.

The high price of tobacco, expanding European market and the increasing population stirred the Indians southwest of the Appomattox and especially north of the York River to a renewed hostility. To avoid another massacre like that of 1622, Sir William had agreed with the natives not to allow more of their lands to be taken. However, the lands of many farmers were "wearing out" and there was an increasing number of speculators who had brought

[8] Crane, W. F., *Life of Robert Rich*, Cornell Dissertation.
[9] Hening, I, 277; also John H. Latané, *Early Relations between Virginia and Maryland,* Johns Hopkins Studies, XIII, 162-64.

over scores of indentured servants. This had caused many farmers to move west and north and burn their little houses in order to take their nails with them. They encroached every year upon Indian lands, and the greater planters seized large tracts of land for speculation or the opening of new plantations. In the spring of 1644 the Indians, under the leadership of the aged Opechancanough, who had massacred so many Virginians in 1622, made ready to destroy all the settlers. On the April day when Sir William had asked all Virginians to fast and pray for his endangered Majesty at home, the savages fell suddenly upon the exposed settlements west and north and killed from three to five hundred men, women and children.[10] It was the 18th of April. Unwarned and unarmed, a terrific panic seized the people. The Governor collected as many county militiamen as he could and, with the help of Claiborne, Edward Hill and John West, he drove the Indians far into the wilderness. The aged Opechancanough was captured and held a prisoner in Jamestown till he was murdered by one of his guards. The Virginians were then free to migrate north, west and south for decades to come, and Berkeley hurried off to England, leaving Richard Kemp, the unpopular secretary of the Council, as Governor-in-Charge. Thus Giles Brent, a liberal Catholic and Richard Kemp, who had been a supporter of the reactionary Laud colonial policy, were in charge of the two rival tobacco colonies at the time Charles I lost the great battles of Marston Moor and Naseby.

At this critical moment Richard Ingle, representing the Earl of Warwick and the merchants of Boston, appeared in Saint Mary's Bay, challenged the authority of Brent, sold arms and ammunition to the recent Virginian Puritan settlers and collected tobacco for European markets and foodstuffs for the West Indian settlers—prosperous sugar growers. When Brent managed to capture Ingle, Clai-

[10] Tyler, *The English in America*, 107-108.

borne carried other ships into Maryland harbors, plundered St. Mary's and was about to enable the hopeful Puritans to take control of the colony, the redoubtable Claiborne once more in possession of his Isle of Kent. Calvert returned almost hopeless to his governorship in the autumn of 1644 and Sir William was again in Virginia in the autumn of 1645. He found that Thomas Harrison, the distinguished chaplain, had abandoned the established church and become the popular leader of the southside Virginia dissenters who had not been expelled to Maryland with Richard Bennet in 1643. Thus the "low church" Virginians and the dissenter majority in Maryland seemed about to come into control of the two colonies. But Sir William held his leadership, offered Leonard Calvert asylum in Virginia and persuaded the assembly to send Edward Hill and Thomas Willoughby, kinsman of the famous Lord Willoughby of England and the West Indies, with troops to Maryland. They were to compel Claiborne and his Virginia Puritans to give up their possessions. But Hill made himself Governor of Maryland, allowed Claiborne and Ingle to escape and thus gave Berkeley and Kemp serious doubts as to what was to be done. Calvert did get back to his governorship late in 1646 as a result of a certain understanding between Oliver Cromwell, the rising master of England, and Lord Baltimore. But the situation was still so critical, both in England and Maryland, that Governor Calvert, before his death in 1647, ordered that Thomas Greene, a Catholic leader, be his successor with the promise to observe the 1634 religious freedom.

However, the shrewd Lord Baltimore disapproved of Greene and appointed William Stone, Puritan sheriff of Northampton county, Virginia, Governor in 1648. Before Charles I was beheaded, it seemed quite evident that both religious and political freedom, at least for the Puritans in Maryland and low church folk in Virginia, were

82   THE OLD SOUTH

to be granted. Before Charles I was executed, January 30, 1649, the whole Chesapeake Bay region, more prosperous than ever before, was about to become the political and religious democracy which Sir Edwin Sandys had planned in 1619.[11] It was a time for rapid growth.

III

During the two or three doubtful years in which Cromwell grew to be master of England, Sir William Berkeley held his own in Virginia, and William Stone succeeded fairly well as Governor of Maryland. The majority was in control, and there was every reason to think that the Catholic asylum would become a Puritan stronghold. But the prosperity of 1642 hardly abated anywhere, and the secular interests of men took precedence over religious and dynastic considerations. After the bloody reprisals against the Indians, wide stretches of land were opened as far as the site of Mount Vernon on the Potomac, west along the banks of the James River somewhat beyond the present site of Richmond and south into the dense wilderness between the Nansemond settlements and the Roanoke River. And there came out of England now a little group, now a shipload of broken royalists with four or five times their number of indentured servants to attend their wants in prospective new homes or to clear tracts of land for tobacco. Sometimes they brought capital saved out of the wreck in England; more often they left accumulating debts behind them which the Burgesses obligingly forbade English creditors to collect; but rich or poor, all were welcome in busy Virginia. The newcomers, now as ever, quickly learned the art of growing and curing tobacco, and as fast as possible they put stock to pasture in the wilderness. A new and better Virginia

[11] Mereness, Newton D. *Maryland as a Proprietary Province,* 20-25.

was widely advertised in Puritan England; and the number of immigrants, whether cavalier or roundhead, men of property or wards of English parishes, increased from year to year. The law still allowed a hundred acres of land for each settler who paid his own way into the country, fifty acres for transporting a servant, and convenient additions for each and every dependent of one's family. But a freed servant, now as earlier, received an outfit of clothes, tools and stock, and the chance to cultivate tobacco on fifty to a hundred acres of land. However, every informed servant knew that upon the date of his emancipation or of a successful run-away he might take his chances as a squatter upon the Indian lands without money or outfit and make his own way fishing, hunting and trapping. The development was like that of many another region in the rising United States during the next two centuries. It was a loose and a lawless system, but the need for labor was so urgent that officers of England and the colonies of the highest standing winked at its abuses. A free worker received twice as much in Virginia or Maryland as in England; and a tenant was never so low there as a peasant at home. The position of the larger planters was such that food, better clothing and easier hours was the rule on all the greater places than had ever been known in Europe. Only the appalling dangers and plagues of the dirty ocean-going ships stood between the poor of England and the wide spaces of the Chesapeake Bay. But these did not deter many thousands. The population of Virginia increased from five thousand in 1640 to fourteen thousand in 1652 and to forty thousand in 1666.[12] This rapid growth in Virginia was hardly matched in Maryland, although there, too, new frontiers were set up and tobacco growing spread on both sides of the bay from St. Mary's to the south side of the Susquehanna. With the rapid spread of settle-

[12] Tyler, *England in America*, 114; Bruce, *Economic History*, I, 391, 397.

ments further and further up the banks of the rivers over an area which stretched from the site of Baltimore of today to the Roanoke River in North Carolina, there came also steady improvements in the arts of agriculture. As the deadened trees fell in the fields and the stumps and roots were pulled out of the soil, one saw here and there a yoke of oxen slowly drawing a crude English plow between rows of tobacco or hills of corn. There were perhaps a hundred and fifty such improved implements of agriculture in Virginia and Maryland about the middle of the 17th century.[13] Scores of Virginians now rode horses about their large farms, and some had carriages.

And as the lure of Virginia and the West Indies to distressed royalists and their less fortunate parish wards increased, inventions and widening markets hastened colonial development. Sir James Drax, an enterprising planter of Barbados, off the mouth of the Orinoco River, visited Brazil about 1643, then under Dutch control, and learned that sugar-cane stalks, if laid lengthwise in rows, produced better and hardier plants; he also learned, what was of more importance, a new method of extracting sugar from the cane stalks. He brought his knowledge back to his own country, and in five years the small farmer islanders abandoned the planting of cotton and tobacco, turned to the new methods of sugar culture and made their little country of a hundred and sixty square miles one of the richest spots in the world. Dutch bankers loaned money for the hasty development of the plantations; Dutch shipmasters brought some thousands of slaves from Africa, and carried thousands of hogsheads of the new sugar to the European markets. The Barbados farmer of 1642 with a hundred acres of land, a servant to help him and a few cows on the common, was in 1648 a planter with five thousand acres, a hundred

[13] Bruce, *Economic History*, I, 338.

slaves, a great factory and an annual output worth two thousand pounds of the best money in the world. A tract of land in Barbados which sold in 1640 for a hundred pounds sterling, sold in 1648 for seven thousand pounds; and the total sugar crop of the island in 1650 sold for three million sterling. There had not been so rich a development since the Spaniards first carried their loads of gold and silver from Mexican mines to the courts of Madrid. It was at this time that Lord Willoughby emigrated to the sugar plantations, and rich merchants abandoned their London trade and their delightful country houses for the new Eldorado.[14] What happened on the island of Barbados happened likewise, if to less degree, in St. Christopher's and other British possessions in the West Indies. Here were new markets for Virginia and Massachusetts products.

As the British islands abandoned the tobacco business, Virginia and Maryland became the sole producers for England and the continent. The economic and social system of the Chesapeake Bay communities gradually stabilized. With the passing years the habit of smoking, snuffing and chewing spread downward to the lower social levels in every European country, and the need of drastic tobacco legislation like that of 1640 was no longer thought necessary. Through all the changes of Stuart and parliamentary politics to 1649, the London merchants held sufficient control of the English tobacco trade as granted to them by James I; they disposed of their imports from Virginia at a profit to manufacturers who in turn put their manufactured tobacco upon the domestic as well as the continental markets, and the Government collected regularly a duty of four pence a pound. It was not an unprofitable business as the shipments mounted into the millions of pounds per year, the Dutch keeping the price high by their active and unhindered tobacco

[14] Vincent T. Harlow, *A History of Barbados,* Ch. II.

and sugar trade on the continent. In turn the same or allied London merchants paid for their imports of tobacco in cheap cloths, coarse shoes and rough hardware for farm and plantation consumption; and with the increasing migration to the Virginia tobacco fields this trade became a source of steady and fixed income for all engaged. Fitting thus neatly but not yet slavishly into the British economic system, the Virginia authorities now regulated leisurely the manner of their operations. They laid an export duty of two shillings a hogshead on every shipment of tobacco; every planter must bring his crop to the nearest warehouse carefully packed in hogsheads which contained about three hundred and fifty pounds, and these must be so constructed that the public inspectors, appointed by the Governor and Council, might easily open them and put their approval or disapproval upon the contents.[15]

The assembly sought periodically to regulate the planting and harvesting in the hope of limiting the output and securing the best possible quality of tobacco. In years of overproduction this oversight was not without effect, but the planters of Maryland, aware of the Virginia attempts at reduction of output, usually planted a larger crop when their southern neighbor planted a smaller, causing endless crimination and recrimination between the rival colonies. Moreover, the lawmakers of Virginia regularly prescribed that every planter or farmer must continue to cultivate two acres of corn or English wheat for every servant on his place. While this was not strictly enforced, it had the effect of producing a fairly steady surplus of foodstuffs which found a ready sale in the West Indies at prices considerably above the prices of foodstuffs in England.[16] There was plenty on the Vir-

---

[15] Hening, I, 435, 456; the two-shilling tax (Hening, I, 491) was a subject of controversy for many years.
[16] Harlow, *Barbados*, Ch. II.

ginia farms. A great planter shipped fifty to a hundred hogsheads of tobacco a year and received a credit on the books of his London merchant or factor of a hundred and fifty to three or four hundred pounds sterling. The smaller farmer or tenant brought a few hogsheads to the public warehouse at the wharf of his greater neighbor and there submitted to the inspector's instructions and scoldings about his pack.[17] When the tobacco was duly inspected and stamped the planter or farmer received a slip of paper indicating the amount and condition of his deposit in the warehouse. This was deposited at a neighboring store in payment of last year's debts or given to a shipmaster who brought out consignments of goods. It was not always the tobacco that circulated throughout Virginia and Maryland, as so many have believed, but the certificates of deposit from the public warehouses and credits on merchants' books. If there was a margin after the payment of debts or the purchase of goods, a credit was left at the stores of Jamestown, Saint Mary's or with merchants at other shipping points. There was then a credit system as between the greater planters who made consignments direct to London merchants and another credit system as between the little-known farmers and tenants who dealt with local merchants or the larger planters, never quite approved by the simple folk; and it became a subject of unceasing complaint [18] later when the price of tobacco stood at low levels and the price of manufactured goods continued quite fifty percent higher than in London. A day's wage was reckoned in tobacco; a horse sold for two or three hundred pounds of tobacco, and a servant was auctioned off at the wharf at five or six hundred pounds. The system worked fairly well with the exchange of very little metallic money; and it continued with little change till the outbreak of the

[17] Hening, I, 488.
[18] Force, *Leah and Rachel*, 19.

seven years war—when nearly every tobacco farmer or planter was in debt beyond the possibility of payment.

But there was a considerable prosperity during the great disturbances in England. The Dutch brought gold and silver from the continent or the Spanish possessions in Central and South America. They offered sound money for tobacco, or they paid in goods at prices which ranged from twenty to fifty percent lower than those of English traders. Moreover, the Virginians learned to rive endless numbers of staves from their cypress and oak forests; they sawed considerable quantities of lumber by hand on the banks of their rivers, and they dressed shiploads of pork and beef. The staves were sold to the West Indian sugar planters for the making of hogsheads for the precious sugar; the lumber went into plantation mansions for the new sugar lords, and the beef and pork supplied West Indian tables. Barbados was thus in 1650 one of the richest markets in the world, and their system of money economy was much like that of modern America or Europe. In return for these shipments, the Virginians received gold and silver, and there was for a time a steady if inadequate flow of the precious metals into the needy tobacco region. A traveler's report of the operations of one of the greater planters illustrates the system from which net returns were received:[19]

an old planter above thirty years' standing and a most deserving commonwealth's man sowes yeerly store of hemp and flax, hath eight shoemakers, forty Negro servants, sowes abundance of wheat which he selleth at four shillings the bushel, kills stores of beeves and sells them to victuall the ships when they come hither; hath abundance of kine, swine in great store.

[19] Force, II, *A Perfect Description,* 14-15, condensed.

6

A Coherent Social Order

> "Hardly can any travaile two miles together, but they will find a Justice which hath power of himself to hear and determine mean differences." Force's *Tracts*, III, *Leah and Rachel*, 15.

I

WITH THEIR ECONOMIC ORDER FAIRLY SECURE, THE settlers on the shores of the Chesapeake Bay and its many tributaries, during the decades before and after 1650, set the patterns of their religious, legal and social life for a hundred years to come, and thus created models for the Southern structure down to 1860. The Church of England, if not then powerful at home, was accepted as the legal religious mentor and guardian of the people but without conscious desire on the part of the masses to persecute or even molest the large number of actual or potential Puritans and Quakers.[1] In this as in most other things the Virginians were spiritual descendants of Sir Edwin Sandys. There were about twenty-five churches in the older communities, located on the banks of the rivers and creeks, and a few chapels of ease convenient to the newer settlements which always sprang up where there were good lands and reasonable facilities for the marketing of tobacco.[2] Some of the churches were built of brick or lumber toilsomely sawed out of the forests, supplied with high pulpits and elaborate pews designed for

[1] The welcome presence in the council of John West, religious liberal, Samuel Mathews and Richard Bennet, Puritan leaders, as well as the repeated failure to enforce the laws against dissenters, shows this.
[2] Force, III, *Virginia's Cure*, 4.

and even installed by the more substantial members.[3] In these screened spaces, with protecting doors, there were straight-backed, cushioned seats and neat little benches on which one knelt to drone through the rubrics of the Book of Common Prayer, or to peek furtively at the fine clothes of one's wealthy neighbor. People who lived in a lonely clearing of the great wilderness or along the shores of a mysterious river, whose sources they knew not, were apt to feel the need of the consolations of religion as well as the satisfactions of social gatherings. A close reminder of the habits of old England and a means of social intercourse, the church was during the seventeenth and far into the eighteenth century the greatest institution in Virginia. There was a tax of ten pounds of tobacco per capita for the payment of the minister, and there were frequent special assessments of corn or tobacco for the purpose of building new or repairing old churches or chapels. On Sundays the masters of estates, the freedmen, released from their bonds, and the indentured servants, with now and then a black man from Africa or the islands, met on the yard or in the grove about the church an hour or more before the services to discuss the state of the tobacco crop, the "wicked" conduct of the Indians or the last great flood in the James River. While there were differences of rank known and acknowledged everywhere, all classes were brought into close and welcome contact with each other, the vestrymen and the squires; and the preacher was more of a leader here than in England, and not without political power. In rare cases some planter vestryman and member of the Governor's Council enjoyed the prestige of having the congregation await with deference the appearance of his carriage before anyone entered the church; and now and then a fine lady showed her pride of station and ugly temper in arbitrary conduct on the sacred lawn. But on the whole it was a

[3] Bruce, *Institutional History*, I, 108.

wholesome if not a democratic-minded atmosphere which prevailed in the churches as in the gossipy gatherings round-about.

The Virginia minister of the seventeenth century was apt to be a recent immigrant, a young man from Oxford or Cambridge with none too much education and little wealth. He was nominally the appointee of the Bishop of London or of the Governor who tried to take a lively interest in the church, if not in religion. His sermons were not too long and they rarely included serious rebukes to leading vestrymen. A preacher in Virginia must please his communicants, not a great landlord from whom he received his living and a bed in the garret.[4] The vestrymen won almost at the beginning of Virginia history the right to regulate all the affairs of their church and many of the interests of the parish. In elections, which were conducted in all form once in three years, twelve leading farmers were chosen vestrymen. These in turn selected two or more wardens whose business it was to observe, report and correct the morals and the ill manners of the membership. The vestrymen assessed the amounts of extra taxes when there was a new church to build or repairs to be made, and they recommended the amount and kind of the general levy for the clergy, fixed from time to time by the assembly. They instructed the wardens to visit every man's house, like tax gatherers in England, and compel each to pay his assessment into the church treasury for the preacher, tobacco which must be properly cured and neatly packed, ready to be put into hogsheads for the market. Nobody had quite so firm a hold on the different communities of Virginia as the vestrymen and wardens. Nor was it a matter of tax gathering and upkeep of the churches alone. The vestrymen asserted early

---

[4] T. B. Macaulay, *History of England*, I, 319-321, Tauchnitz edition. Macaulay's picture is a little severe but is supported in W. E. H. Lecky's *England in the Eighteenth Century*.

the right to choose and dismiss the preacher, the Governor and the Bishop of London powerless to enforce their wills or the law of the Church across the wide Atlantic.[5]

An expectant clergyman, recommended, to be sure, by the Governor, visited the leading vestrymen of a vacant parish. The salary was fifty to a hundred pounds sterling, that is, tobacco equivalent to sums ranging between those figures—an income considerably above that of a country vicar in England. There was a parsonage of decent, even pretentious appointments; and there was a glebe of a hundred to three hundred acres of land, some cleared, some covered with trees and brambles. There were barns for tobacco, cribs for corn and sheds for a cow and a horse, sometimes servants, later slaves, attached to the church itself for working the glebe lands and assisting the pastor or the pastor's wife.[6] If the newcomer pleased the vestrymen and the wardens, he was duly accepted and conducted to his house. But his appointment was for a year. If he made himself a part of the community, he was reasonably sure of his tenure. If he talked of the old country and expected to return as soon as a living could be found there, his tenure was uncertain, his services discounted and his stipend sometimes left unpaid. He was not expected to set his own tobacco plants or gather the fodder for his horse and cow; but if he did both his parishioners liked him the better, and the wardens collected the minister's tobacco the more easily. When the parsonage required repairs, the vestrymen issued the proper order; when the preacher's lands wore out and ceased to produce fair tobacco, they were sold or abandoned and better lands provided.[7] Whatever was made on the glebe was the property of the minister and his family; and some ministers knew how to become thrifty planters. But

[5] Bruce, *Institutional History*, I, chs. on the parish, the vestry and the clergy.
[6] *Ibid.*, 167.
[7] Bruce, *Institutional History*, I, 164-66.

if the preacher was young and unmarried, as was often the case, he leased his glebe, rented the premises and took a room in some planter's house where he taught the three R's to the young of the neighborhood—lease money and rentals added to his stipend.

It was not a bad position for an Oxford student who had struggled through his examinations, if he could accustom his ears to the roar of the forests and learn to appreciate the honest if uncouth manners of the farmers, freedmen and servants who composed the great body of his parishioners. He might not drink and carouse in an "ordinary" as freely as he might have done at home, but he was a welcome visitor at horse races, and if he won a wager and tippled reasonably there was no complaint; and he might pick his wife from a leading family. He baptised the children betimes and he catechised them without rigor; he married every young couple and sometimes received as much as a guinea for his blessing; he laid away the dead and had his fee for the funeral sermon; he rode a horse when he visited the distant membership or had oarsmen to row his boat up and down the rivers; and when his youngfolk came to maturity, they married into good if not first families. He went once a week to his church in case it were one of the larger ones, or once a month if it were a smaller. If the weather was rough or the rivers overflowed their banks, he remained quietly at his desk or dozed by his fireside without pangs of conscience. On Sunday afternoons he sometimes travelled twenty miles to repeat his morning sermon to faithful communicants who patiently awaited his appearance. If this was not always a light task, it improved his health and enabled him to visit isolated farmers, learn the state of their crops and inform them of the news of the latest ship from London or Bristol.[8] As the years

---

[8] Wertenbaker, *First Americans*, Ch. V, for an excellent account of the Virginia church.

passed, the best of them acquired the authority that churchmen have always coveted: they might gently upbraid their greater parishioners, even vestrymen, for ignoring the laws of trade, for seizing without right or reason great tracts of Indian lands and for ignoring the payment of quit rents due to the most unpopular of kings. These quiet reminders did not offend because they were not to be heeded and they did not embarrass the preacher when he presided at the next session of the vestry, where he took a lively and positive hand in the punishment of women who talked too freely of their "betters" or in the discipline of servant people who broke the terms of their bondage.[9]

From all the evidence one sees in the laws of the time, there was a great and distressing amount of illegitimacy in a community where three-fourths of the people were young and a third of them at any one time were bound not to marry except upon approval of masters whose interest it was to hold every servant strictly to his single estate. It was peculiarly the business of the church to cure the evil, and hence sinners were required to appear in church wrapped in white sheets, a wand in hand, a tell-tale cap on their heads, and kneel on a little platform, young man and young woman, at the beginning of the services, make open and audible confession, beg forgiveness from the Son of the "immaculate" Virgin, promise never to sin again and then stand mute for a time before the solemn congregation.[10] If this did not render them immune to the temptations of the wicked one, the pastor and the wardens might report what all knew to the commissioner of the peace, apt to be one of the vestrymen who had witnessed the confession; or the owner of one or both of the sinners, who held a civil trial, kept a record

[9] Perry, W. S., *Historical Collections Relating to the American Colonial Episcopal Church*, I, 335.
[10] Arthur P. Scott, *Criminal Law in Colonial Virginia*, 317, an excellent account of the legal institutions and procedure in colonial Virginia.

A COHERENT SOCIAL ORDER 95

and added one or two years to the term or terms of service of the culprits. In the worst of cases the commissioner remanded the parties to the county court for more strenuous discipline.[11] Thus the ministry, the wardens and the vestrymen worked together to steady the morals of the new state and to save men's souls against the blandishments of one "who roamed the earth seeking whom he might devour"; and this social tutelage and discipline, at a time of great laxity, was quite as important as the more public work of the justices of the peace when they sat, their law books at their sides, every second month upon the county bench.

II

From vestryman and church warden to commissioner of the shire, the latter generally chosen from the former, was but a short step. The commissioners of the company whose business it had been to settle men's disputes about landmarks and boundaries or about servants and the sales of goods in the various neighborhoods grew slowly under the early governors to be called commissioners of the shires, then of the shire courts, and finally, about 1640, justices of the peace. Such an official in England was apt to be an important character, a landowner of high standing, a vestryman and sometimes a member of the House of Commons. In Virginia he soon came to be a similar dignitary. He spoke in the accents of Elizabeth and Shakespeare, he read plain English with some difficulty, though he could puzzle painfully through a little Latin; on occasion he read the service at the church and his wife must have been proud of his dignity. The better trained or well-to-do had a little office in the corner of the yard or he commanded the better part of the best

[11] Hening, I, 585; Bruce, *Institutional History*, I, Chs. IV and V.

room in the farm house, and there were a few books on his two-foot shelf: Dalton's *Justice of the Peace,* dog-eared and dirty from the thumbing of his predecessor; a copy of the *Virginia Statutes* and sometimes *Justinian, Third and Fourth Parts.* And there was the family Bible, old and shabby, if not thumbed, the *Whole Duty of Man, Saint's Everlasting Rest* and the *Practice of Piety.*[12] That was a body of learning and wisdom to astonish visitors who painfully spelled out the titles while the justice drew on his coat and made ready to hear the petitions and remonstrances of contentious neighbors. To him the constable, the coroner and the church wardens reported suspected or open lawbreakers and unruly members of the congregation already noted. In the superior atmosphere which surrounded the magistrate, appointed by the Governor and approved by the King, both the criminal and the sinner were apt to yield and make amends to injured parties, the sterner penalties of the county court threatening on the next court day. If quarrels about cattle ranges, brands or earmarks, cases of drunkenness and the pulling down of great men's fences could not be righted by the justice, the parties were remanded to the county court which met in early times every two months, later every month, in some gentleman's private house or in a rude court house set up at the most convenient place. The spirit of the law was ferocious, though less so than the spirit of English law of the same period. If one stole a pig, the punishment was severe; if the offense was repeated a third time the offender might be hanged. If any servant struck his master or mistress his term of service was increased two years; if a slave were killed in the process of punishment by his master, the deed was not a high crime; any person of low or high degree who committed the offense of swearing, drunkenness, fornication or adultery might be deprived of the right to appear as a witness or

[12] Bruce, *Institutional History,* I, 585.

debarred from holding any public office;[13] to steal a horse or participate in an organized effort to resist the government was punished with death. Leaders of insurrections were hanged, quartered and parts of the body nailed upon mileposts or fixed upon the tops of chimneys where all might observe and profit from the observation.[14] But withal there were many offenses and there was a spirit of resistance in all the counties which no punishments seemed to check. If a local justice assumed too much importance or transcended the public sense of right, a young frontiersman, a country lout or even a most respectable freeholder like William Hatcher of Henrico swaggered into the court room, called the doubtful decision into question and insulted the justice with epithets like "hog-trough maker" till the offender was ordered to be bound over to the county court for punishment; and here again public opinion was self-assertive, and officious judges were subject to ridicule and attack. There was clearly a tendency, in spite of the high esteem in which justices were held, for men to assert more of their sense of equality than one witnessed in England the next hundred years.[15]

But the county court was the most important institution in Virginia, after the Established Church. It was composed of eight or ten or even more men of substance and family. They were loyal justices, familiar with the affairs of their neighborhoods, and vestrymen, as already indicated, accustomed to sit in the best of pews and to the deference of their neighbors. At the appointed time they turned the heads of their horses or the prows of their boats toward the county court house, all the litigants and many of their neighbors taking the same course about the same time. The justices took their seats behind

[13] Hening, I, 433; Isabel Ferguson, *County Court in Virginia*, in *N. C. Hist. Review* 1931, gives an excellent account on early pages.
[14] Scott, *Criminal Law*, 191.
[15] *Ibid.*, 201-203.

a high desk at one end of the court room. "His Honor," the member of the Governor's Council for the country or region, was apt to be present and to preside over the court in important cases or when there was public excitement. Ordinarily the senior justice was president of the court. He called the first case on the docket, the sheriff summoned the witnesses, waiting about the room or on the courtyard outside, and the clerk of the court read the indictment. If there were no lawyers, and there were often none, rulings and decisions came fast and prompt. If the evidence in a case failed, the defendant was set free; if it were a doubtful and a complicated issue, the parties were bound over to appear at the general court, the solemn body at Jamestown composed of the Governor and three or four members of his Council. While the county court proceeded with its work, the sheriff called the grand jury, a body of twenty-four men taken from all the neighborhoods, fifteen a quorum.[16] These were church wardens, vestrymen or simply respectable farmers familiar with the affairs, the feuds and the quarrels of their neighborhoods. They met in the vicinity of the court and studied the wrongs and tentative evidences of crime that had come to their knowledge, handed in "true bills" and then adjourned. A new grand jury composed of the same men or others from the different neighborhoods was then appointed on the approval of the court and they returned to their homes, objects of a certain anxious concern even to innocent parishioners.

The petit jury drawn from lists made up by the clerk of the court before the assembling of the justices, and summoned by the sheriff, was composed of twelve men familiar with the habits and the doings of the parties to a suit. They heard the evidence, listened to the arguments and the instructions of the presiding judge and went out

[16] Hening, II, 69-70, gives first elaborate act establishing and regulating the county court and its procedure.

for a decision.¹⁷ The verdict was as apt to represent what jurymen thought of the defendant as what the evidence proved. But the county court might not inflict penalties which involved life or limb, and hence the jury had to do mainly with cases involving property to the value of a thousand pounds of tobacco, awards of damages in smaller amounts, the whipping of run-away servants, the clipping of men's ears or putting them in stocks, the first and second trials of men charged with petit larceny and the enforcement sometimes of unpaid bets on horse races. Now and then there was a case of witchcraft and more often a suit for slander, breach of promise or the execution of a contract between landlord and tenant. The returns of the jury were ready and prompt and the court pronounced sentence; and since the jails were inadequate or non-existent, punishments were administered summarily on the court yard and in the presence of great numbers of people. A whipping of thirty-nine lashes on the bare back "well laid on" was the penalty for most of the offenses and it was thought the spectacle had a wholesome effect upon potential criminals.¹⁸ There was some sentiment, however, in the courts. A woman received less than thirty-nine lashes for talking too much, and a "witch" might have her ducking at the tail of a boat postponed from the cold of winter to a more moderate season. If a defendant lost his suit, he paid the penalty and the cost; if his case were referred to a higher tribunal, the clerk of the court received a fee for preparing the proper papers. The sheriff had his four pounds of tobacco each for summoning witnesses, and the jurors presented their attendance to the sheriff and received a small per diem, eight or ten pounds of tobacco.

The county justices served, however, like the vestrymen of the churches, in many capacities. The day before

[17] Scott, *Criminal Law.*
[18] Bruce, *Institutional History*, I, Chs. XIV and XV.

the court assembled in regular session, they met for other purposes: as an orphans' court to apprentice fatherless or bastard children, appoint guardians for, and to hear the reports of those who administered the estates of minors; as trustees to receive bequests to the church or the cause of education in the form of lands and cows and servants, and set up commissions to administer them, one of their own number acting as chairman of the commission. There were always new roads to open or old ones to repair, ferrymen to license and bridges to build.[19] Every county court was a place of record where deeds, marriage licenses and wills were verified, recorded or probated. The clerk of the court, who had a permanent office in the court house or in a four-square cabin on the court yard, received fees for his services. He was a registrar of local land grants, and in the counties near the border his returns for this work were large. The clerk's opportunity in all the counties to act upon advanced knowledge and accumulate an "honest" fortune was great. But the "high sheriff" was the great man of the county, after the member of the Governor's Council. He was recommended to the Governor by the court to serve year after year; the recommendation was tantamount to appointment, and once a sheriff, long a sheriff, unless accumulating riches led to higher office in the commonwealth. In concert with the court he named the constables who acted as his assistants in the parishes, likewise the coroners. These minor officers were, like justices of the peace, apt to be vestrymen or wardens; they received minor fees and the costs of their journeys; but the sheriff was their chief and he received the larger share of the emoluments of administration in the Virginia counties. He collected the taxes; he paid the bills of the county; and he made returns annually to the treasurer

[19] Bruce, *Institutional History*, I, 308, 337, 543.

of the colony, who was a member of the Governor's Council. He brought malefactors into the court; he saw that the jail was in order if there was one, if not, he had personal custody of prisoners. And there was always the small fee. Like the clerk of the court and county, he received advanced information about bankruptcies, lands about to escheat or removal of Indians to distant regions. It often happened that a sheriff was escheat officer, clerk of the court and surveyor of public lands; and thus he became an object of bitter complaint while he amassed a fortune, the greater the longer he held his office.[20]

The justice of the court, however, taken throughout the years, commanded the esteem of society. He was responsible for the public tone. He was thought to be a model of good behavior, and he sacrificed time and means for the public welfare. He kept an open if a modest house, spent as many as twenty or thirty days of each year on the bench, rode his own horse in all weathers and at his own cost to the sessions of the court, and he settled more cases through friendly advice out of court than he ever heard in public capacity. The small fees of earlier times were later denied him by law.[21] On rare occasions the judges, after long and weary labors, presented bills for their horse feed. The sheriff allowed them, but so many were the complaints and so sensitive was public opinion that the justices made many excuses and apologies. The sheriff and the clerk had their fees and made their fortunes; the preacher, if a good one, had his ten thousand pounds of tobacco a year. But the justice of the county court served without compensation, save as men touched their hats to him when he passed, or as they gave him the first chance to serve in the House of Burgesses which, however, paid only a small per diem before

[20] Hening, I, 257, 264, 271 and on many other pages.
[21] Hening, II, 244.

1660, or the long chance of competing with the sheriff in winning late in life the great office of councillor to the Governor.

III

In the Governor's Council one studies the combination of legislative, executive and judicial functions so important in early Southern history, so deeply dreaded in the later history of the United States. A justice or a sheriff of a county court, advanced to the Council, sat with the Governor as a court of last resort in Virginia, unless we note an occasional appeal to the assembly, composed of both the Council and the House of Burgesses. The Council of ten or twelve members ruled that the Governor and four or their number might compose the court, the Governor presiding. In case the latter travelled about the colony or visited England, the secretary of the colony presided. This body sat three times a year at Jamestown and heard all appeals in cases involving property worth more than a thousand pounds of tobacco. It tried afresh the murder cases and felonies beyond the jurisdiction of the counties. Most of the lawyers of the colony were apt to be present, watchful of chances to earn fees or ready to fight the causes of clients who had come on from the county jurisdictions. There was the King's attorney-general, Richard Lee, trained at one of the inns of court in London, one time a member of the Privy Council of Charles I, then secretary to Governor Berkeley; or, later, Peter Jennings of Gloucester county, devotee of the Stuart kings, his wife the daughter of Sir Thomas Lunsford; and there were the assistant attorneys-general from the different sections of the colony, familiar with the doings of the county courts and with the problems of law enforcement. There were also the frontier leaders in deerskin breeches and coonskin caps with their endless

A COHERENT SOCIAL ORDER 103

grievances against the Indians; and there were even representative braves, stolid, sullen and bitterly resentful, everlastingly asking the palefaces to remain on their side of established borders.[22] It was the greatest gathering in the commonwealth except when the burgesses joined the Council once or twice a year for legislative purposes. The Governor, members of the court and the lawyers came and went in their finery, doublets of broadcloth bordered with lace collars, sleeves with slits in them to display fine linen, fluffy white cuffs and velvet knee pants, pretty shoes and polished gold or silver buckles, sometimes a sword dangling at one's side. It was enough to impress the farmer-vestryman who had risen to the county bench and had come on to see how appeals were decided [23] and how great men thought great men must behave.

In addition to exercising a close oversight of the judicial procedure and trying cases involving the jeopardy of life or limb, the Council, sitting as a supreme court, heard complaints and petitions about land grants and the failure of the sheriffs to make prompt returns; it determined what should be done with abandoned estates, due to constant shifting of the area of tobacco culture; its individual members were expected to make investigation of threatened commotions in the regions of their personal acquaintance; and in case of servant or slave insurrection, the court appointed a commission, composed of one of its members and two justices of the peace most nearly concerned to act as a court of *oyer et terminer* and guarantee speedy justice. Its members were also the official collectors of customs for the different districts, the James River landings, the York River settlements, the eastern shore and the wild Rappahannock country; and their recommendations for the appointment of the inspectors of tobacco were almost certain to be accepted. And, as if

[22] Hening, I, 323-325.
[23] Bruce, *Institutional History,* I, Ch. XVII.

that were not enough, the members of the Council were muster generals of districts whose business it was to give direction to the colonels of the county militia and especially to watch the movements of the Indians of the northern, the western and the southern borders. Thus the county justice, without salary or fees, might become sheriff and quickly amass a small estate; he might be made clerk of the county and improve his fortune in the same way; he might be chosen to the House of Burgesses and finally, in cases of distinguished success in previous positions or distinguished wealth, have his name sent to the officers of the Crown in London for promotion to the Governor's council whence he might succeed even to the governorship itself and be the founder of a "first family."

IV

Between the county court and the Governor's Council there was a unique militia system, not unimportant at a time when men could not forget 1622 and 1643. The sense of danger, due to the constant encroachment of speculators and freedmen upon the Indian lands, required the local governments to give sharp attention to military affairs. Every man in the colony between the ages of sixteen and sixty, not physically unfit, was required to serve in the militia, some as cavalrymen after the appearance of horses in the community, some as footmen. There was a compensation of a shilling sixpence for horsemen and a shilling per day for footmen when engaged in actual frontier service. Over these soldiers there was a captain of the county who always appeared on horseback and received a hundred pounds of tobacco per day, ten shillings, when engaged in actual service; his lieutenant received sixty pounds.[24] These officers tended to become

[24] Bruce, *Institutional History*, II, 13, taken from Colonial Entry Book, 1682-95, 252, 350.

A COHERENT SOCIAL ORDER 105

lieutenant-colonels and colonels as the counties increased in size and the number of militiamen increased from a small company to a regiment; and the colonel of the county, often a member of the county court, was as much a part of the Virginia system as the sheriff himself. Three times a year these officers assembled the men of their county, Easter, Whitsuntide and Christmas, for drill in the use of firearms and the methods of company movements. These drills continued sometimes for two or three days; and under the continued sense of danger, the average militiaman was a fairly efficient soldier, subject to rigid discipline, if the published law meant anything. Prompt obedience was supposed to be enforced; if anyone resisted an officer the punishment was severe; if one raised his hand against a superior, the hand was to be cut off; to strike an officer was punishable with death at the hands of a firing squad.[25] Each man was required by law to keep a gun, two pounds of powder and eight pounds of shot in his house;[26] and the officers of each county made regular inspection to see that the law was obeyed. Above the colonels of the county regiments, there were generals of the musters, members of the Governor's Council, who gave close attention to the defense of their districts composed of two or three counties, sent spies into the Indian villages to ferret out plots or schemes of attack and maintained the frontier fort in their districts, Appomattox, the falls of the James, the upper Chickahominy, the upper York and lower Rappahannock settlements, in each of which there was a commandant somewhat of the character of a mediaeval count of the marches. The chief of all these was the muster master, Colonel John West during Berkeley's first régime and Colonel Mainwaring Hammond, of the Cromwellian

[25] These drastic punishments could hardly have been strictly applied in Virginia at any time.
[26] Hening, I, 525.

epoch, an officer appointed by the assembly and independent of the Governor and who received a salary of ten thousand pounds of tobacco a year.[27] The commander-in-chief, however, of all the forces was the Governor himself, who traveled about the colony, reviewed troops and inspected arms and ammunition stores at the court houses, thus bringing the department of defense, like that of the church and the judiciary, into close touch with the executive. Nor was all this mere make-believe. Companies were quickly gathered, equipped and marched on short notice a hundred miles into the wilderness, under conditions of great hardship and considerable danger, to overawe the Indians and accustom officers and men to the nature of their work. Such movements, sometimes converted into exploring companies like that of Colonel Abraham Wood in 1650, were undertaken after 1644, now on one part of the frontier, now on another.[28]

V

But the Governor played such a directing influence in this evolution that one needs to make a better acquaintance with that much abused colonial official; and of all these Sir William Berkeley, devoted through all vicissitudes to his King, worshipful of England and contemptuous of all who thought or dreamed of popular institutions or popular control of the great affairs of life, was the most important. He was in the midst of a life growing more democratic each year, with a House of Burgesses dependent upon manhood suffrage and with all salaries, including his own and those of the clergy, dependent upon

---

[27] Bruce, *Institutional History*, II, Chs. II and III for full discussion.
[28] Hening, I, gives scattered statutes. Bruce, *Institutional History*, II, Chs. I to V.

the popular will. Yet he managed to maintain his position fairly well through his earlier career and to set an example of moderate aristocratic behavior. Sir William entered Virginia a bachelor, but in 1670 he married the charming Frances Stephens (nee Culpeper), widow of Governor Samuel Stephens of North Carolina, who made his expanding mansion in the midst of a three thousand acre estate a shining model for the admiration and imitation of all.[29] Greenspring house became a model for the wealthier planters, and there was a dungeon and a gallows as became an English manor. There was a chaplain in the household to pray away the sins of an easy-going gentleman, a secretary to keep his accounts and write his letters; and his house was open to distressed cavaliers who escaped from the hard "tyrannies" of that "enemy of mankind," Oliver Cromwell. Richard Lee, founder of the Lee clan of years to come, Henry Norwood of the perilous voyage of 1649, Gawin Corbin, and the suave Thomas Ludwell, secretary of the colony after 1660, were his intimates; and any of them might have a horse and hounds for a hunt at any time or a letter to the unhappy Charles II at Breda. He raised scores of hogsheads of tobacco each year which he sent home in the joyous belief that Spanish tobacco would never again invade the London market; and he delighted in the shipment of beaver and otter skins, brought to his door by rugged traders, white and red, from the great woods, shipments which must have rejoiced the hearts of court ladies who were thus emancipating themselves from Amsterdam and Leipzig merchants. Such a man and Governor warmed the hearts of Virginians when they saw him at the head of their general court as well as when he entered their House of Burgesses where the county representatives assembled each year to make the laws of the colony, ignore the laws

[29] Force, III, *A Voyage to Virginia*, 495.

of England and issue orders to legalize the illegal Dutch trade in tobacco, beef and pork. For the Governor knew how to evade statutes as well as to impose upon the imaginations of his subjects. He might not preside over the deliberations of the House of Burgesses—the traditions of the colony were too strong for that—but he did present his elegantly dressed person now and then for admiration, and he made gestures which reminded one of Charles I.

The Governor and the Council were thus a second and an upper chamber as well as a court, its members rich and well-served as members of upper chambers were supposed to be—a group which read the bills of the burgesses, suggested changes or amendments in cautious language, debated them seriously and sometimes disallowed them, although this in the sixteen-forties or fifties was a little too dangerous for frequent practice, governors in Virginia not daring to treat plebeian legislators half so roughly as the Stuart Kings treated aristocratic members of the House of Commons. The councillors, in spite of all Berkeley's favors, were more Virginian than royalist; and they were and knew themselves to be the envied of every aspiring planter family from Norfolk to the upper reaches of the Rappahannock River. They and their sons and daughters to the fourth and fifth generations were the first or of the first families, and as such entitled to precedence in every church or court or dance hall in their flourishing little world. It was worth five hundred pounds a year in good English coin to be a member of this charmed and highest circle:[30] a little court with undisputed authority, a legislative body like the House of Lords, and finally an executive group which approved the lists of county justices, issued grants of land, ordered and controlled tobacco inspections, supervised military affairs, gave visés to the ships that came into port, and, through the Governor and

[30] Bruce, *Institutional History*, I, ch. XV.

A COHERENT SOCIAL ORDER 109

secretary, had direct communication with the Court of Saint James.

But the burgesses, elected by the free votes of all the freemen, including every year large accessions from the servants whose indentures had expired, were, after all, the supreme power in the community. They were, as already indicated, vestrymen in their churches, justices of the peace, colonels of the militia, and resolutely committed to the policy of independent self-government in their localities, men loved and respected by rich and poor and morally more powerful than governors and councillors. Snobbish as they might be, fond of their private pews and the covers of their little prayerbooks, they adhered stubbornly to the idea of universal manhood suffrage and to equal and direct representation for every county. They voted themselves a modest per diem and insisted upon freedom from arrest while engaged in their duties. They had no thought of allowing governors to lay taxes, appoint clergymen or issue decrees in lieu of statutes which they knew so well how to wrangle over and work into law. If the House of Commons dethroned the King and cut off the royal head and the Governor was beside himself with wrath and anger, they knew how to keep silent or allow the offer of meaningless overtures to their "beloved" prince, now called Charles II. They did not vote gifts or send legislative commissions, even if they did wink at Berkeley's officious relationship. If the Governor wished to see the record of the burgesses in secret session, he might do so unofficially; but if he demanded the record or undertook to say who should be speaker, there was a controversy the echoes of which reached London,[31] and members of the burgesses would adjourn and go home without enacting the most urgent legislation. The burgesses were building a structure and laying foundations

[31] This was well understood since 1635, when Sir John Harvey was thrust out of office.

in the popular will and tradition that would one day withstand the storms of a war with England and prove equal to the creation of a new empire.

Berkeley and his immediate atmosphere are fairly known. The larger set about Jamestown and the little groups in the counties who reflected the tastes and the attitudes of their superiors require some notice. Ralph Wormeley of Rosegill on the Rappahannock, who belonged to the lower English gentry, Richard Moryson, brother-in-law to Viscount Falkland who fell at Newbury, 1642, fighting for the King, Sir Thomas Lunsford, Thomas Ludwell, Robert Throgmorton, descended from the famous Throgmortons of Elizabethan times, and a score of others represented royalist ideals, owned property in England and readily acquired respectable if not great estates on the lower James or York rivers or in the wild Indian lands between the York and the Rappahannock. Their incomes were not great, though they maintained good houses and substantial tables. They brought with them as many servants as they might, and of necessity set up little villages about them.[32] They put more acres in tobacco than the law allowed, and, following the example of the country, bred as many cattle and raised as many hogs on the public domain as possible, receiving on the average as much as ten shillings for a hog and three pounds for a steer or cow from English, West Indian or Dutch traders. Their houses were constructed of logs or sawed timber and contained three to six rooms; sometimes there were brick or stone residences of fair proportions. Furniture was not plentiful or varied, and horses and carriages were few. Some men owned plows and rode from plantation to plantation,[33] and women were not abashed to go to church in jolting oxcarts. There were in the better houses silver spoons and steel table

[32] Harrison, Fairfax, *Memoirs of a Huguenot Refugee,* Ch. VI.
[33] Bruce, *Economic History,* I, 338.

A COHERENT SOCIAL ORDER 111

knives, forks hardly known;[34] even the cavalier in the new environment fell into farmer habits and learned to walk between plow handles and to strip his own tobacco leaves. The tendency of Virginia planters to work in their fields and share the hardships of a frontier life accorded with the drift of social life in England where there was for a time the beginning of a slow movement against aristocratic privilege. In spite of the general drift a rich man sometimes gave costly communion services; and the church membership generally paid the deference which men always pay to success or high distinction. At the races it was understood that a plebeian might not bet on a horse, but plebeians did so bet and the courts compelled payment. On the court yards, gentlemen enjoyed a prestige which gave them precedence on the juries and finally positions on the bench. But gentlemen, with certain exceptions, were plain persons. When the burgesses, the Council and the Governor were all in session in Jamestown and making the laws which were so often disobeyed, and the wives and the daughters of the county families joined the county justices as the latter labored with legislation and quarrelled with the Governor, there was something of a genteel and cohesive colony life. There were no great halls to match those at Westminster, but the hall of the assembly and the room of the general court, not to mention the large houses of Edward Hill, the speaker, and Richard Kemp, the secretary, offered space for weekly if not daily dinners. And there one might have madeira and sherry, port and claret, and drink oneself under the table quite as happily as in London.[35] There elderly ladies brought their daughters, dressed in last year's London fashion, to meet the favored sons of other county families; and there was love-making and proper matching of young folk and wide acres, just as in England. Only in

[34] Bruce, *Economic History*, I, 339.
[35] *Ibid.*, II, 215.

Virginia the family was more isolated and less wealthy. The church was dear to gentlefolk, but its canons were not law. People stayed at home or roamed the woods on Sundays. They played cards and even tested their horses for the races on Sabbath days; it was hard not to exercise their dogs in their wide fields and extensive forests; and there were wagers of ten shillings, even a guinea, upon the meagerest excuse, and the county courts hardly knew how to suppress the habit. The home in all its isolation and loneliness became the dearest spot on earth. There the women planted and watered their crepe myrtle, their lilacs, their thyme and marjoram; they imitated distantly, as their exports increased in value, the formal gardens of Hampden Court and Windsor Castle; and there was an elaborate vegetable garden, with walls and shrubs and winding paths.[36] But here, unlike England, there was the family graveyard and sometimes a vault or wide slab on which the age, the virtues and even the humors of the deceased were duly carved. The preachers and even the Bishop of London protested against this neglect of the hallowed churchyards. It mattered not. Virginians thought themselves as near Heaven on their lonely "God's acre" as in the most exclusive corner of the parish cemetery.[37]

VI

Of these "better people", in whose veins there flowed somewhat of the best blood of England, sons and daughters of knights, kinsmen and connections of merchants and explorers, there were probably one or two thousand of the total fifteen thousand inhabitants of Virginia, about the middle of the seventeenth century. There can be no question of their importance, although their mildly pre-

---

[36] Bruce, *Economic History*, II, 160-61.
[37] Bruce, *Institutional History*, I, 113.

A COHERENT SOCIAL ORDER 113

tentious habits were already before the hard necessities of a new and exacting frontier life. It was difficult to maintain an exclusive social status in a community so new and unstable; and there were no manorial estates after the forced style of Maryland.

Of more interest is the great mass of freemen and indentured servants who composed the working majority. Every ship that sailed into the Chesapeake Bay carried as many servants as possible, young people guilty of minor, sometimes major, offenses and crimes, debtors without hope of recovery, and simply the poor unemployed.[38] Sold for terms of three to five years immediately upon landing at some tobacco wharf, these ignorant if hopeful and ambitious young people went about their work expecting freedom and a future farmer's estate. As the terms of servitude expired they found their places as tenants or small proprietors on the lands that were available and became freemen with the right to vote and hold office, a status few of them had ever dreamed of in England. With hundreds arriving each year at the period around 1640,[39] there were probably more than a thousand arriving ten years later. This gave the Virginia population the moving, changing character all American society continued to show for two centuries. A planter saw a fifth or a fourth of his servants leave every year, and he welcomed that many or more newcomers. Since hardly a tenth of the whole population could be counted as of the planting and gentle, directional class, it follows that more than two-thirds of Virginia and Maryland were throughout their early history composed of indentured servants or freedmen one or two removes from that low estate. These are the people who cleared the fields, planted the tobacco and paid in their toil the taxes on which governors and councillors and preachers throve.

[38] Brown, *First Republic*, 423.
[39] Bruce, *Economic History*, I, 620-23.

More than half of all the women who signed legal papers now available showed in their signatures that they were unacquainted with the rudimentary art of writing; nearly half of the men signed in the same telltale marks,[40] which means that three-fourths of the Virginians of the seventeenth century were unable to read and write. And what applies to Virginia in that era applies with equal force to Maryland. The majority still lived in log cabins with chimneys built of sticks and dirt and lined with clay.[41] But the single-room cabin was now giving way to the double log house with the chimney between and sometimes built of homeburnt brick. A shed in the rear provided space for kitchen and dining room. When the family advanced in status and pride, the kitchen stood apart to keep flies and lingering dogs from the house. In the outside chimney corner there was a dog kennel where two or three lean, long-eared hounds slept or howled through the night. At the entrance to the front door there was always a shelf for the water bucket and a gourd hanging upon the wall. Inside the house there was a puncheon bench on four legs which was drawn to the front of the log fire at night;[42] and there was in some simple houses a sturdy chair of state, in which the master sat and dozed through the short hour before the family retired. There was little ceremony at table, dinner or other time. Some light, clean-scoured and hollowed pieces of board served as plates. A small and a large pot stood at the kitchen fireplace from which meats and soups and hominy were ladled with large wooden or pewter spoons; and there were in most houses squeaking cranes on which heavy pots and kettles were swung on and off the fire. There was a "spider" for the baking of bread, though the womenfolk were more accustomed to knead their corn meal into

[40] Bruce, *Institutional History*, I, 450-59.
[41] Force, *Tracts*, III, Leah and Rachel, 18; Hening, II, 76.
[42] There is a difference of opinion about early Virginia houses, but the evidence cited above leads me to the conclusion of the text.

THE ADAM THOROUGHGOOD HOUSE
Erected in 1636, Princess Anne County, Virginia.

Photo by Frances Benjamin Johnston

Courtesy Enoch Pratt Free Library

CLOCKER'S FANCY

A seventeenth century house built by Daniel Clocker near St. Mary's City, St. Mary's County, Maryland.

coarse pones of dough, rake off the larger coals from the fire and place them in the hot embers. In a few minutes they were pulled out and put upon the table for hungry children and servants, all sitting together. There were juniper or cypress tubs and "noggins" in the corners of the shed or sunning on the south wall of the house. If people went to church on Sunday there was a great ado washing and dressing by the kitchen fire in winter or outdoors in warm weather. Sheets or bed covers, suspended from the low beams just above one's head, divided the main room into apartments to save the modesty of men and women or guests, who were as welcome here as in the houses of the planters. There was a mean shed for the family cow and calf and a tightly built coop for chickens.[43] A "worm fence" surrounded the premises to prevent cows and pigs from hanging about the doors.

The occupants of such houses were not unindustrious or unambitious. The master was out before the first ray of sunshine in the morning, his wife made haste to have bacon, bread and milk for breakfast when the first light of the sun could be seen through the crevices between the logs; and before the day was a half-hour old, all were on their way to the forest or fields with hoes or axes on their shoulders. They returned to their houses at noon, drank deep draughts of hard cider or nips of apple brandy, waited a few minutes and then fell ravenously upon their venison, killed in the forest, their cured pork from the smokehouse, their "pones" of corn bread and clean white hominy soaked in lye, beaten and husked with a mortar and pestle and boiled with fat pork. In an hour all were again at their tasks, women and children joining the men in the fields during the busy seasons. And thus again in the evening, the cows were turned upon the meadow to graze; the children were slipped into their little trundles drawn from under the larger family beds; and the servants

[43] Force's *Tracts*, III, *Virginia's Cure*, 18.

climbed to their lofts above the main rooms or occupied crude log cabins on the premises.

The heads of such establishments were far from ignorant, even if reading remained a mystery. They earned their ways into the vestries of the different parishes, even became justices of the peace and members of the House of Burgesses. During the early Berkeley régime it was said a majority of that body was composed of men who had crossed the ocean as servants.[44] The mass of them still bore the humble mien they had borne in England, although in dress and appearance there was noticeable improvement. The men wore light jackets and canvas breeches; the women cotton or kersey petticoats; the children, lightly clad and barefooted, were counted more vigorous and more comely than the children of England.[45] Although law and custom required plain people to keep their place and get off the highway when gentlemen passed,[46] there were constant and increasing violations of both law and custom. Servants were eager to become freemen and there was an endless procession of runaways seeking the open frontier and tracts of land on which to assert themselves.[47] Of crime there was enough, as already suggested. The lawbooks are filled with rules and penalties for men who violated the seventh commandment; and the churches, as we have seen, frequently punished young women who committed the unpardonable sin. There were numerous offenses and frequent trials, though not many hangings.[48] Plain people burned their own houses when they abandoned worn-out lands; but that was in the hope of saving the nails for new ones. Gambling and fishing on the Sabbath day were common sins; and on

---

[44] Peter Force, III, *Virginia's Cure*, 16; this statement may be exaggerated.
[45] *Ibid.*, 6.
[46] Devereaux Jarrat, *Memoir*, 14.
[47] Bruce, *Economic History*, II, 10-29.
[48] Scott gives a complete and admirable account of crime and its punishment in Virginia.

court and election days there were fist fights and gougings, with now and then duels with prescribed weapons: a gentleman then as later refusing to shoot or stab a plebeian. But with all the wandering from place to place, the idleness on Sundays, there was a sense of security shown everywhere in open or unlocked doors or barns and dwellings, wherever the Indian menace had ceased. If great men fenced around the holdings of smaller ones, the latter retaliated by pulling down fences and putting their stock upon the common, as they had done in England. Thus the new social order, spreading further and further from the rivers, based on manhood suffrage and working out an effective social system, made steady advance over the best that had obtained in Europe since the days of the early Roman republic; and it gave promise of the great republic that was to be. It was this expanding democratic community over which Sir William Berkeley presided from 1642 to 1652 and which he looked upon with envy from his Greenspring mansion from the advent to power of Richard Bennet and William Claiborne till the restoration of Charles II.

7

The Dream of Sir Edwin Sandys

> "The inhabitants began to look with delight on their increasing stocks, to take pride in their tables, to grow not onely civil but to stand upon their reputations."—Force's Tracts, III, *Leah and Rachel*, 9.

I

THE INCREASING SOLEMNITY OF THE NEWS FROM ENGland during the year 1647 and 1648 added greatly to the prestige of the parliamentary party in Virginia under the leadership of Samuel Mathews, William Claiborne and John West, former adherents of the Established Church and prominent planters on the northern side of the James River. They now declared their adherence to the Puritan party; Richard Bennet, still in Maryland, and Thomas Harrison were of great influence on the south side of the river. Due to the attitudes of these men and their supporters in the burgesses and the council, Governor Berkeley had been unable to complete the expulsion of the dissenters under the law of 1643 or to discipline his renegade chaplain who stirred Virginians with religious oratory which later attracted great audiences in London under Cromwell.[1] But the Governor was resolute in his policy, as one sees from his jamming through the burgesses in November, 1647, a law which released all church members from the payment of any part of the salaries of ministers who declined to use the prayer book in their services,[2] and in ordering Harrison to leave the colony

---

[1] John H. Latané, *Johns Hopkins University Studies*, XIII, 162-164.
[2] Hening, I, 341.

at latest on the third ship that sailed. Harrison went to Boston, where his wife's kinsman was none other than John Winthrop himself; but he did not long remain in Massachusetts. Bennet and the well-known William Durant, a leading layman among the Puritans of southern Virginia, were active in Maryland, where William Stone, a Virginia dissenter from Northampton county, was supposed to offer a ready welcome. James Cox, another of the Virginia Puritans, was for the moment speaker of the Maryland assembly, and there was thus an immediate prospect of uniting the Puritans of both colonies. Berkeley was hardly pleased with the outlook; if he expelled his unruly Puritans, they would rule Maryland; if he left them at home they might control the assembly. It was increasingly difficult for him to hold even his followers in proper subordination, as may be seen from his pressure for a better military guard to accompany him on his travels, to linger about his office in Jamestown and to protect his home at Greenspring.[3]

Struggling thus among a forward people, Berkeley received the news in the early spring of 1649 that Charles I had been tried by a solemn court, named by none other than Cromwell himself, convicted of treason and sentenced to death. The King, who had never before showed either great wisdom or high courage, surprised his guardsmen, armed with weapons to prevent his escape and ropes to fasten his unruly limbs, and gently laid his head upon the block. In a moment the royal blood flowed upon the boards of the platform projected from a window in front of Whitehall.[4] The stodgy gentry and dull peasants of the English countryside, the traders and porters of London, assembled in a vast throng on the streets about the place and groaned as they saw the "sacred" head of a king fall into the executioner's basket. Such an

[3] Hening, I, 354.
[4] J. G. Muddiman, *Trial of King Charles the First*, 160-62.

event had never before occurred in western Europe! The heroic act of the condemned monarch atoned in the eyes of vast numbers of Englishmen for the sins and the disasters of a decade of civil war, and stirred in Sir William Berkeley and his doubtful majority of Virginians a loyalty which led the assembly on the tenth of October, 1649, to denounce the work of Cromwell and all the "wicked and impious" of England who had suffered so noble a monarch to die upon a shameful scaffold. The twenty-year-old son of Charles, two years an exile in Paris, was declared to be the rightful sovereign of Virginia, and any proposal to deal with or accept the commonwealth was denounced as treason. Men were forbidden even to speak ill of:

the late sainted king, or accept the aforesaid cursed and destructive principles, or go about by irreverent, or scandalous words or language to blast the memory and honor of the late most pious king; and whatever persons soever shall by words endeavor to insinuate any doubt concerning the undoubted right of his Majesty that now is to the colony of Virginia, such words and speeches shall be adjudged treason.[5]

These were loyal words, and Berkeley made haste to have them pronounced and accented in the ears of the gay young "Charles II" then under the protection of the French Government, and seeking all over Europe to secure support for regaining the throne of his ancestors. But the assembly of tobacco planters in their little capital on the banks of the James River, growing more prosperous and more independent every year and led by such resolute political or religious Puritans as West, Mathews, Claiborne and Hill, everyone with a grievance against the deceased "sacred Majesty" and even against Berkeley himself, was not apt to lend aid to the hanging and quartering of men who merely spoke ill of the dethroned

[5] Abbreviated from Hening, I, 330.

prince. Hence the penalty for violating the law, or committing the crime of treason as defined, was only "such censure as shall be thought fit by the Governor and Council." Bennet, Claiborne and Harrison pursued their historic programme of making still more converts in Virginia and of restoring Maryland, now more Puritan than Romanist, to Virginia. Before the assembly adjourned, Harrison procured from Cromwell himself a message to the Governor of Virginia which must have foreshadowed the defeat of that resolute champion of the banished Stuarts:[6]

We know that you can not be ignorant that the use of the common prayer book is prohibited by the parliament of England, and therefore you are hereby required to permit the same Mr. Harrison to return to his said congregation and to the exercise of his ministry.

As the year 1650 dragged on, the disturbed affairs of England became more regular, and Oliver Cromwell, with a vision that swept the horizon of Europe and America, thought of breaking the power of the declining Spanish monarchy, weak as it was at this time, and driving the exiled Stuarts, Charles II and his brother James, Duke of York, from Paris and their later asylum in the Netherlands. As a means to this end the parliament of England ordered that the products of the colonies must be shipped to England in English vessels, manned by English sailors, a scheme which would have ruined both the tobacco trade of Virginia and the rich sugar business of the West Indies.[7] The Dutch were too strong for Cromwell, though he sent what ships he could spare to Barbados and in 1651 sent a commission to Virginia to settle the affairs of the Chesapeake Bay and bring the recalcitrant Berkeley

[6] Latané, *Johns Hopkins Studies,* XIII, 167.
[7] George L. Beer, *The Old Colonial System,* I, 12-13.

and his little group of royalists to terms. Two of his commissioners were lost at sea. The third member, Edmund Curtis, a London merchant of large colonial interests, after defeats in Barbados, reached Virginia early in 1652, Berkeley still holding the reins of authority and endeavoring to arm the colony against the new and "despicable" power in England. It was a vain endeavor. Curtis informed Bennet, who was again the master of his Nansemond plantation, and Claiborne that they were empowered, with himself, to accept the submission of the two tobacco colonies. Berkeley, like the royalist party in Barbados, made an agreement with the Dutch, whose merchantmen, then in the James River, watched with interest the application of a policy that would half ruin the planters. In Virginia as in the sugar islands free trade with the Dutch was more important in the eyes of the so-called royalists than the fortunes of the exiled Stuarts.

The Commonwealth fleet proved too great for safe resistance, and on March 12, 1652, Berkeley surrendered. The Virginians would submit to parliament, but they were to "enjoy such freedoms and privileges as belong to the freeborn people of England" and their assembly, as theretofore, should convene and transact the affairs of the people, not contrary to the Commonwealth of England. Boundaries, patents to land and the right of newcomers not to pay quit rents for seven years, as agreed to by Charles I, were guaranteed by the commissioners. To make surety doubly sure, it was stipulated that "free trade as the people of England do enjoy" should not be abridged, a condition which the presence of the Dutch in the river doubtless tended to secure. Nor would the assembly agree to pay any part of the cost of this expensive demonstration of power which Berkeley had occasioned, though the dullest member of the House of Burgesses must have understood that it had been Berkeley's show of resistance and dickering with the Dutch that saved them from submission to Cromwell's Navigation act. Here was rather clever economic statecraft.[8]

There were other matters, personal, economic and religious, which occupied the backwoods diplomats. Governor Berkeley might have a year to sell his goods and depart for England or seek out his gracious master on the continent; the devoted and sincere members of the Established Church might use the prayer book and send up undisturbed petitions for the unhappy Stuarts for a full twelve-month; and all the violent speeches of the Governor and his friends should be generously overlooked, even by those emigrés whom he had sought to drive from their homes. The assembly, the Governor and the commissioners all agreed to the surrender.[9] Although the authorities of England never quite accepted the supremacy of the Virginia "grand assembly" or publicly acquiesced in the annulment of the Navigation act of 1651, Richard Bennet became Governor in the place of his irreconcilable enemy, and William Claiborne again became secretary of the colony—both of them commissioners of parliament for the general oversight of Maryland.[10] The government at St. Mary's deferred to the commissioners, and the authority and absolute ownership of Lord Baltimore were for a time in serious question—a result of the recognition on the part of the Commonwealth of the ancient boundaries of Virginia mentioned above.

Events would work out the salvation of both settlements. The burgesses in Virginia exacted from Bennet the recognition of their supremacy in more definite terms than their fathers had claimed in 1619. And in harmony with this theory the new governor conducted the affairs of the tobacco communities the next three years—chief executive of Virginia and parliamentary commissioner, with

[8] Hening, I, 363-368.
[9] *Ibid.*, 368.
[10] Thomas J. Wertenbaker, *Virginia Under the Stuarts*, 102-105.

Claiborne, of Maryland. Other members of the former Council and leaders in public affairs, Sir Henry Chicheley, Richard Lee, Thomas Lunsford and Ralph Wormeley, rarely appeared now even in the house of burgesses. The leaders, however, of what may be called the party of the dispossessed company, the low churchmen and the Puritans, were always in evidence. Leading members of the new Council were Nathaniel Littleton, Samuel Mathews, Thomas Peters, John West and Argul Yeardley; the last-named was the son of the former governor and nephew of West, a wealthy planter and tradesman who had not been active in public affairs for many years; the others were well-known representatives of democratic groups, Thomas Dew of Nansemond, the new speaker of the burgesses in 1652, was a land speculator and frontier explorer of southern Virginia; Samuel Mathews, father and son, were either on the council or in the burgesses throughout the Cromwell period.[11] Speakers of the house of burgesses were generally of the Puritan party. It was a group of leaders whose ideas of government were not unlike those of Sir Henry Vane, a friend of Harrison, later beheaded by Charles II. The compact of 1652 was to them what the more famous compact between the convention parliament of England and William and Mary was to be in 1689. They would have for the settlers on the Chesapeake Bay all the rights of Englishmen, and these rights involved religious toleration, if not freedom of conscience; the right of all freemen to vote in elections and to be represented in government was re-asserted, and the privilege to sell their products freely in the markets of Europe was guaranteed.

Bennet and the assembly now sent Mathews to London to argue the validity of the Virginia title to Maryland before parliament, but parliament itself was dissolved on

---

[11] The membership of the Council and House of Burgesses is given from time to time in Hening.

THE DREAM OF SIR EDWIN SANDYS 125

April 20, 1653, and the issue went to the new Council of state which gave expert advice to the Protector. It was not merely a question of charter right or even religious toleration; it was the old problem of uniting all the tobacco farmers under one economic roof and undoubtedly the natural desire of Claiborne to renew his commercial activity on the Isle of Kent and to capture the Iroquois fur trade so vital to the Dutch settlements on the Hudson. Cromwell, hitherto supposed to favor the Virginia contention, delayed answer and warned Bennet against positive action.[12] A special commission to study the problems was now appointed and Claiborne himself joined Mathews in London.

There was no decision. Early in 1655 Edward Digges, first "experiment farmer" in America, son of Sir Edward Digges, master of the rolls under the "sainted" Charles, then living on the plantation John West had first laid out on the south side of the York River, was elected Governor of Virginia by the assembly, and Bennet also went to London to fight for the re-annexation of Maryland. After three years of hesitation, Cromwell decided the conflict in favor of the astute Baltimore and the Catholics. A formal agreement between the Virginians and Lord Baltimore was now published, and the isolated communities of the St. Mary's and the Severn made peace.[13] There were to be two rival tobacco communities on the Chesapeake Bay, a fact of supreme importance on two great occasions in later American history.

II

Mathews returned to Virginia, an old man before his time, to succeed Sir Edward Digges in March, 1658,

[12] *Maryland Historical Magazine*, IV, 248-9.
[13] Latané, *Johns Hopkins Studies*, XIII, 180-82.

where he hesitated a little to accept the governor's office as a gift, pure and simple, of the "grand and supreme" assembly of the colony. But his own followers in the assembly, hardened by two decades of experience, were not to be cajoled into the abandonment of the teachings of their friendly chief because he had accepted too much of autocratic methods in London. Mathews yielded, accepted the leadership of a people as "free as the English are—much freer"—and in 1659 had his term extended two years; William Claiborne was still secretary and next in authority, Edward Hill of the same party speaker of the House of Burgesses.[14] It was the party of planters, farmers and traders which had put their doctrines into practice—practical men with none too much of religion and with no strong sense of loyalty to the Stuarts.

From the weakening of Berkeley's power in 1650 till the end of the Commonwealth, the burgesses enacted no measures of repression nor did the governors endeavor to enforce the older laws on the statute books. At the end of the first year of probation, Governor Berkeley and his friends were unmolested, as were also the Puritans whom he had harassed. Even the incoming Quakers, who not only refused to pay tithes to the liberal Church but who declined to bear arms, were left to their own devices. While Cromwell forbade the prayer book and the sacred vestments in the English churches and the fathers of New England pursued both churchmen and Baptists as enemies of mankind, the governors and lawmakers on the James River all but proclaimed religious freedom. A less liberal, if understandable, attitude of the party of Bennet and Mathews appeared in the persistent policy of the burgesses toward lawyers. In the early forties lawyers were forbidden to appear in the courts. Later the law was modified so that the governor and council might license attorneys to perform their accustomed legal functions.

[14] Hening, I, 506-13; Wertenbaker, *Virginia Under the Stuarts*, 109-10.

THE DREAM OF SIR EDWIN SANDYS 127

This practice continued only a year or two. In 1650 the sense of the people was strongly registered in the act which declared:

> Noe person or persons either lawyers or any other shall plead in any court of judicature within this collony or give councill in any cause or controversie whatsoever upon the penalty of five thousand pounds of tobacco upon every breach thereof.[15]

In this frontier attitude, representing also the deep resentment of the "underdogs" of English society, there was something of the idealism which resisted all external control of the churches and which would render no obedience to bishop or governor in the appointment or discipline of clergymen. The courts authorized the better educated laymen to give information or defend simple folk unable to argue their own cases before the bench, and thus leave judicial procedure simple and effective. Toward the end of the period Mathews endeavored in vain to modify this set purpose of his own party to ban all lawyers. It was the instinct of the trader who sold furs and hides and tobacco, and made contracts which were sometimes ignored or violated; but the most popular of governors was unable to do more than raise the question of constitutional rights of attorneys under *Magna Charta*. The resolute burgesses replied that they too had studied the famous document and found that their several statutes were as good law as the proposed vetoes of the governor and council. They repeated their argument that attorneys and lawyers only clog the dockets, increase litigation and delay justice. Their society was simple; they would keep it so. Was not Virginia an asylum for the poor and a thriving, expanding farmer community?[16]

And when one reads the figures there is no denial. The

[15] Abbreviated from Hening, I, 482-83.
[16] Hening, I, 495.

surplus grain and meat and staves of the colony continued to find ready market in the sugar islands; Virginia tobacco continued to be carried to the markets of Europe whence ample supplies of Dutch goods and French wines were obtained at low prices. The annual output had increased from a thousand hogsheads in 1640 to forty thousand hogsheads toward the end of the Commonwealth era; the value of this immense export to the farmers rose almost to the unprecedented sum of a hundred and fifty thousand sterling a year—upon which the British customs laid a duty of a hundred thousand pounds a year. In comparison with the annual income of little Barbados island this was small; but contrasted with the returns to Virginia farmers in the early forties this meant social stability and a steady pressure upon the great woods to the west and south. Hence the population increased from fifteen to forty thousand in the short term of 1650 to 1666, as already noted. Instead of stringent laws to banish dissenters and limit encroachments upon the Indians' preserves, there were now permits to Abraham Wood on the Appomattox and Thomas Dew on the Elizabeth rivers, to explore the regions south and west and extend their trade in skins and furs. The old treaties with the Indians were less restraining than ever to freed men and speculators who stole across the border; and new treaties and new laws which increased the area under cultivation were negotiated or enacted. There were as many as eighty ships of English and Irish build in the Virginia waters in a single year; and light, swift New England vessels plied in and out the Chesapeake Bay, harbingers of a great illicit trade of years to come. The planter class began to maintain good family tables and take pride in their reputations.

III

It was the time when Mrs. Elizabeth Digges maintained with pride her house in York county which boasted a yellow and a red room with a hall parlor between them, her silverware the envy of her neighbors. Richard Lee, of Lancaster county, braved the "tyranny" of Cromwell in London in order to make sure the quarterings of his coat of arms;[17] and Nathaniel Bacon, first cousin of Francis Bacon, the philosopher, having made the grand tour of the continent, now laid the foundations of the handsome estate on the southern banks of the York River, so much envied in the stormy years that were later to break upon the tobacco country. Sir William Berkeley, unwilling to risk his presence in England and hardly justified in joining his pushing brother, John, in the entourage of the exiled Stuarts, remained on the plantation which Virginia had granted him, sold one of his brick houses in Jamestown to accommodate Governor Bennet and continued in delightful, if carping, relations with disgruntled royalists like Thomas Ludwell, Ralph Wormeley and John Carter. Where men's fortunes increased rapidly, and "foolish" official leadership left great men alone, there was comfort and a lively hope of better times to come; but Cromwell could not live forever.

And indeed in the late autumn of 1658, when Mathews had hardly served the half of his first year, the ships in the bay reported that early the preceding September, in the midst of a terrible storm which swept and devastated England, the Protector had ceased to "plague" his country.[18] The rumor, so widely believed in England, that the Devil himself had been seen about the couch of the dying statesman was probably believed by some people in Virginia. When Mathews reported that Richard Cromwell

[17] Bruce, *Social Life of Virginia in the Seventeenth Century*, 160-63.
[18] Hening, I, 509.

had been appointed Protector of England, Ireland and the plantations, the burgesses assented readily, but, as we have seen, they yielded no particle of the power and independence claimed and exercised since 1652. In a year the master of Denbigh house on the James, champion of so many causes in London, was dead. A little later Charles II at Breda, in Brabant, was busy making ready his possible return to his puzzled country, and George Monck, the shrewd silent commander of the Puritan army, sent mysterious messengers hither and yon in the expectation of placing the young monarch upon the throne, not without profit to himself. The repeated rumors from Breda gave Berkeley and his eager royalist followers the promise of an early release from their constructive exile.[19]

The thirty-year-old Charles landed at Dover on May 26, 1660, where Monck greeted him as cordially as if he had not had a share in the bloody deed of 1649. The prince wondered why he had stayed away so long. The dour James, Duke of York, was of the joyous party; and George Berkeley, a cousin of Sir William, shouted and sang with the rest. Another and a less agile courtier, Edward Hyde, made the fourth distinguished member of the group. He had lost much and suffered long since that dread day in 1642 when he had abandoned parliament and hastened to the camp of Charles I. The five easygoing men of still easier morals with troupes of lackeys and on-hangers made their way to London and found both the city and the country ready and waiting to ask a thousand pardons for the wrongs of the past, and beg the maltreated prince to mount the vacant throne. It was the 29th of May. A jubilant parliament granted the restored King a million and a quarter sterling a year the rest of his life; the King quickly gave Monck seven thousand a year, made him Knight of the Garter and second Duke

[19] Wertenbaker, *Virginia Under the Stuarts*, 110.

of Albemarle. Hyde was made Earl of Clarendon, granted £20,000 and given the position of chancellor of the restored monarchy. The Duke of York became the Lord High Admiral of the navy with an income of £100,000 a year. It would have been difficult to say in the summer of that year 1660 which of the Stuart brothers was the more dissolute or the more contemptuous of the decencies of life, even for the 17th century. Charles surrounded himself with mistresses of personal charm and political prejudices; James with women as coarse and ruthless as brawlers of the street.[20] In a few months the clever Henry Bennet, kinsman of the Virginia Bennets, returned from his successful mission to the Spanish Court where he had negotiated a favorable treaty for his master. There was also John Berkeley, a fellow-exile with the King, brother of the Governor of Virginia, close and powerful associate of the Duke of York. Here was a group of statesmen, adventurers and procurers as far in spirit and practical life from the rude builders of a greater England on the Chesapeake Bay as the vast spaces which separated Europe from North America suggested. At the moment when the Virginians could hardly be induced to persecute Quakers, worst of all the sects, the King's friends in London were about to set up a régime of social depravity and religious intolerance rarely matched in the history of the great "little island." [21] The England from which most Virginians had emigrated was thus replaced with a new and a different England.

IV

Scenting the change which was creeping over English public opinion, Sir William Berkeley, unmolested and prosperous on his plantation these eight years, made

---
[20] Trevelyan, George M., *England Under the Stuarts*, 351.
[21] Macaulay, Ch. II.

ready at the death of Samuel Mathews in January, 1660, to reassume the position he had vacated in 1652. Without change of personnel in the burgesses and with a Council which, including new liberals like Thomas Dew, Thomas Swann and Augustine Warner, was even less royalist than it had been in 1653, the assembly reaffirmed the independence and supremacy of the two houses, ordered that all writs should issue in their name and asked Berkeley to appear before them and answer whether he would become governor again on the same terms as his immediate predecessors. Aware of the drift toward the Restoration in which his brother, his cousins and all the exiled prince's friends were active, the master of Greenspring replied with caution:

> My intelligence is not enough to tell me what mixt or individual power there is in England. But you have, Mr. Speaker, taken care the authoritie you entrust me with, for which I gave you my humble thanks; this wisdome of yours hath animated my caution of assumeing this burden.[22]

The restored governor was sensitive to the new position and its obligations, as he wrote Peter Stuyvesant of New Netherlands a little later, "I am but a servant of the assembly's but they do not arrogate to themselves any power further than the miserable distractions of England force them to." This was not quite the fact as to the pretensions of the Virginians, although one sees evidence in some of the laws and in the appointments that were made or sustained in 1660. The assembly retained in the secretaryship the redoubtable William Claiborne; they exempted their favorite John West from taxation the rest of his life; but they also allowed the appointment of Mainwaring Hammond, the militant royalist, muster general of all the militia, and paid his expenses as special

[22] The *Southern Literary Messenger*, XI, pp. 1-5 (1845) gives Berkeley's speeches and letters bearing on his restoration.

THE DREAM OF SIR EDWIN SANDYS 133

agent of the colony to beg pardon at the foot of the restored throne for all the sins of Virginians. The Governor's salary was fixed at £700 a year, besides the perquisites of a far-flung Indian trade and the collection, under supervision of the sheriffs, of large arrears of rents due from squatters on his lands in Lancaster, Rappahannock and Northumberland counties.[23]

While these measures, designed to pave the way for better understanding in London and ease the relations of burgesses and the new Governor, were being passed, one might have seen definite earnest of a different time to come in the enactment of the most drastic statute against the Quakers that Virginians had ever known:

> Who contrary to law do dayly gather in unlawful assemblies teaching and publishing lies, miracles, false visions and attempting thereby to destroy religion and all bonds of civil societie.[24]

No ship captain might bring a Quaker into the colony under penalty of one hundred pounds sterling, no person should entertain a Quaker under like penalty; and any member of the outlawed sect who returned a third time to the community should be put to death. But the drastic punishment of men who sat in church with their hats on and waited for the divine inspiration to prompt their services did not improve the price of tobacco, nor was the law ever taken very seriously. The very year of the Restoration, the demand for the great Virginia staple declined on the markets of Europe by half. And at the moment the markets showed this astounding weakness, the parliament which restored Charles II undertook to restore the obsolete statute of Cromwell designed to compel all colonials to sell their produce in English towns and buy all their goods from English merchants. Thus the

[23] Hening, I, 543-51.
[24] Abbreviated from Hening, I, 532.

Navigation act of 1651 was now amended so that tobacco and sugar must be carried to English markets in English ships manned by sailors three-fourths of whom were to be English subjects. Here was a proposed policy which late in 1660 gave every Virginian cause to regret the events at which so many of them had for a moment rejoiced.[25]

In the spring of 1661, with a new and obsequious House of Burgesses about him, Sir William Berkeley prepared his real programme. He would remove William Claiborne, the fighting secretary of the colony, the most important leader of the liberal if not Puritan régime, and replace him with Thomas Ludwell, the grandnephew of Philip Lord Cottington of Somersetshire, a royalist and a kinsman of Berkeley as well. At the same time Berkeley turned his attention to Major John Bond, a member of the burgesses and a justice of the peace of the Isle of Wight county, and compelled his expulsion as a dangerous schismatic. The unsubmissive representative of the dissenter region of Virginia was then declared forever incapable of holding any office of trust. With this loud warning, the governor turned to Henry Soane, the acceptable speaker of the house, and caused the assembly to vote him a hearty endorsement and a gift of six thousand pounds of tobacco for his insignificant service to the new régime. It was the beginning of personal favoritisms which later gave so much trouble. The burgesses then appointed a committee of correspondence whose business it should be to keep the governor informed during his proposed sojourn in London and also to persuade the burgesses to adopt recommendations which should be duly sent them from England. Henry Soane was made chairman of this first American committee of correspondence and with him was associated the elder Nathaniel Bacon, Miles Cary and other well-known cavaliers of known and

[25] Beer, *The Old Colonial System*, II, 1-10.

THE DREAM OF SIR EDWIN SANDYS   135

dependable opinions. Richard Moryson, who had fought valiantly for Charles I on the battlefields of England, became acting governor; and the proposed new members of the Council were of the same political complexion. To make the task of social guidance the more easy, all Virginians were compelled by law to meet in their churches on each January 30 and do solemn penance for "the bloody massacre of the late King Charles I of blessed memory" and on May 29 to "thank God for the birth and restoration of Charles II to his late distracted kingdoms." Baptists and Quakers must take part in these demonstrations upon heavy penalties for failure to do so, while every justice of the peace and every church warden was doubly charged to report and prosecute every infraction of the law of 1660 against dissenters.[26] Moryson and the members of the Council were instructed to renew the former custom of riding the judicial circuits and of presiding over the sessions of the self-governing county courts. There was henceforth to be order up and down the banks of the Virginia rivers. These precautions duly taken, Berkeley procured from the assembly a grant of three hundred thousand pounds of tobacco, to be packed and stored on the York River, three times as much as had been granted the year before to Mainwaring Hammond for his mission of apology to the King; and Sir William set out for England where he would protest against the enlarged and sharpened commercial policy of Cromwell, already known as the Navigation acts.[27]

[26] Hening, II, 24-25, 33-39.
[27] *Ibid.*, 17.

8
The Asylum for Troubled Consciences

> "Permit no clause to pass prejudicial to the immunities and privileges of that church which is the only true guide to eternal happiness."—Thomas Cornwaleys to Cecilius Lord Baltimore, 1638.

I

WHILE THE VIRGINIANS WORKED THEIR WAY PAINfully toward the "liberties of Englishmen" and the unimagined prosperity of the Commonwealth, the second Lord Baltimore struggled along an even more tortuous way toward the riches and the power which a gracious king had promised in the Maryland palatinate. Leonard Calvert, governor and lieutenant-general of Saint Mary's, managed his affairs with a degree of success the first two years, 1634–36. But his lordship's plans were difficult of application. If there were soon to be five or ten thousand industrious hunters, fishermen and tobacco growers, all paying annual tribute, there must be master managers and hordes of tenants and servants to do their bidding in the great American wilderness. To this end a score of leaders like Thomas Cornwaleys, John Lewger, Giles Brent and Jerome Hawley, members of the governor's council, were granted peninsulas of lands that could easily be fenced off from the natives and quickly turned into productive estates which were to be endowed with full mediaeval privileges, and called manors.[1] Each master of a manor must pay his overlord in England twenty shillings quit-rent a

[1] Abbreviated from William Hande Brown, *George Calvert and Cecilius Calvert*, 108.

year per thousand acres and set twenty immigrants to work. As the urge to enter the new paradise increased, these peninsula holdings might expand to many thousands of acres and be increased in number—a palatine aristocracy in alliance with the proprietor. The manor house when erected should be on a strong position and in due time defended by at least fifteen trained militiamen who were to serve the colony in time of danger. A hundred acres were always to be reserved as a glebe for an orthodox priest who should have the care of both Catholic and Protestant souls and direct the services in the manorial chapel. There was to be an approach to the mansion with servants' quarters to right and left. Either in the great house or in a courtyard in the rear there were to be accommodations for baronial and leet courts. In these the quarrels and the sins of both freemen and servants were to be settled or punished after the manner of mediaeval England. No marriage was to be valid except when performed in the chapel by the priest; children were to be baptized in conventional style; the lord of the manor and the priest were to receive the accustomed fees and the members of the gentle family were to be buried under the aisles of the chapel, while freemen and servants were to be laid away in a cemetery at a convenient and respectful distance. And as the seventeenth century advanced all these conditions and privileges of life were widely applied.[2]

The prospect was enticing and not a few loyal kinsmen and ambitious friends of the Baltimores carried considerable sums of good English money and many hopeful freemen and servants to the promontories of the upper Chesapeake Bay. The lords of manors were Catholics, while their dependents were generally Protestants, fit subjects for the propaganda of the Holy Church. It was,

[2] John Johnson, *Old Maryland Manors,* Johns Hopkins University Studies, VII.

however, a trying time in England for Catholics. The elder Baltimore, himself a proselyte during the days of James I, lived much under cover and came into close association with Richard Blount, one of the strange products of his intolerant era. Blount surrendered a fellowship and turned Catholic while a student at Oxford, worked his way through Douay and the college at Rome to priesthood and thence through curious experiences in Spain where he became a Jesuit. In 1591 he returned to England in violation of law and later became the secret head of the Jesuit order there numbering a hundred and nine devoted priests, working mainly at night and under the screened patronage of Queen Henrietta Maria. As the Puritans gained control of parliament, Blount, in imminent danger of his life, moved from his Sussex hiding place to London and dwelt in some obscure quarters known only to the little clique of saints and the pious Queen in whose chapel his remains were buried in 1638. This devoted and heroic chief of the Jesuits came into touch with the Baltimores, and it was upon his initiative that Andrew White, Thomas Copley and other Jesuit fathers were given control of the religious interests of the Maryland palatinate. It was for English Catholics one of the rare opportunities of the time: the chapels and the churches of Mother Church would be the only recourse of the freemen and servants who cleared the forests and worked the fields of the new country. Moreover, these ardent missionaries of the true faith at Saint Mary's would counteract the influence of the easy-going Virginia clergy and, like their French brethren on the Saint Lawrence or the Spanish Jesuits in South America, save the souls of poor Indians and take their lands in compensation. There has rarely been a better opportunity for earnest religious leaders.

But the chief of the Jesuits was not the pious Father White of the *Arke*. He was the ambitious Thomas Copley, who, like his master Blount, was born of Protestant parents and partially trained in Madrid during the last decade of Elizabeth's reign. The family found its way back to England in 1603 and the boy went to Louvain in 1611 and became a Jesuit priest five years later. Working as best one might under the supervision of Richard Blount, Copley learned the arts of intrigue, opposition to the dominant Church of England and complete loyalty to the papal authority in Rome. In 1637 he was sent to Saint Mary's to lead the missionaries of the palatinate.[3] He at once assumed a status of equality, if not superiority, to the governor and lieutenant-general; and the lieutenant-general, less wise or less avaricious than his lordship in London, yielded his will to the more persistent clerical chief. A manor was asked and granted. Servants and freemen were engaged, but no true churchman could either pay quit-rents to a worldly chief for his lands or maintain fifteen militiamen for the common defense. Nor was this all. Copley and his fellows made overtures to the Indian chiefs of the wilderness and obtained vast grants within the realm of Lord Baltimore. These were to be held forever without taxation and for the advancement of Mother Church; the Saint Mary's priests were always in close touch with the papal propaganda. The old principle of mortmain was thus reasserted in the Baltimore palatinate and at the same time both prospective princes of the church and the regular priests, who labored under their instructions, were to be exempt from the laws of the land and the decrees of the civil courts. The temporary priestly lord of the new manor with his monastery upon "the Hill" would soon be succeeded by a bishop with vast lands to the westward, a thousand Indian subjects and scores of dutiful tenants and servants entirely without the range of the proprietor's authority. Leonard Calvert approved the scheme; and the curious cabinet with which he surrounded himself, Jerome Hawley, ex-member of the discredited

[3] *Dictionary of American Biography.*

Harvey faction in Virginia, John Lewger, a "renegade" Catholic priest, and Thomas Cornwaleys, Jesuit counsellor and governmental adviser at the same time, lent its influence to the Copley party.[4]

But the assembly of 1635 as well as that of 1637, with duly recognized lay members from the seven districts, called hundreds, although Catholic in sentiment, resisted the elaborate plan of the Jesuits. If new settlers were to be expected from England, there must be freedom of religion, so frequently proclaimed by his lordship in London; moreover, the Jesuits, of all the great orders of the Mother Church, were the most hated and feared in Virginia with a population five times as great as that of Saint Mary's as late as 1640. It was too great a risk. After prescribing the privileges and rules of succession for the manors and defining the powers of baronial and leet courts, the leaders of the Council joined the freemen of the assembly and undertook to apply the statutes of England to Saint Mary's. Since every true Englishman of that age imagined that *Magna Charta* was an everlasting guarantee of popular liberties, they debated the great document and showed how completely it denied the claims of the Jesuits. Copley and his fellow-priests refused to sit in such an assembly and wrote long letters of protest to Lord Baltimore, with Leonard Calvert still supporting their cause.

His lordship took the other view and prevailed upon Richard Blount the last year of his life to warn Copley and his supporters of the dangers of making the Maryland palatinate a Jesuit domain. Copley hurried to England, there to argue his case while Governor Calvert and his little colony reasserted their claims to Kent Island. Meanwhile William Claiborne labored in London, as we have seen, for the restoration of his prior rights in the

[4] *State Papers*, I, at many points, and V, 218, give scattered information; *Dictionary of National Biography*.

upper Chesapeake, especially the prospect of capturing the Susquehanna-Iroquois Indian trade which the French and Dutch then controlled. John Lewger was made acting governor. Leonard Calvert and Thomas Cornwaleys hurried off in the winter of 1638 with a sufficient force to the coveted island and there negotiated with Claiborne's brother-in-law, John Boteler, and at the same time captured Thomas Smith and others of the more resolute Virginia traders. Before Claiborne returned from London his property was a second time in the possession of the Saint Mary's authorities. Smith was indicted in the assembly, convicted of piracy and ordered to be hanged. He asked the benefit of clergy. The request was refused by the Catholic majority and the prisoner went to the gallows, his property at Kent Island confiscated. Claiborne was attainted and the Kent Island fort was added to the grant of Giles Brent, already master of the promontory east of the island and lord of the manor that later developed into the county of Kent. These successes, highly endorsed by official Virginia—then hostile to Claiborne—stirred the low church and Puritan party there led by West, Mathews and young Richard Bennet. Calvert, Lewger and Cornwaleys had broken the power of the Virginians and there was every reason to think their palatinate would become a Catholic stronghold. It was at this time that the Calverts asked that Virginia and Maryland be united under the Baltimore family.[5]

But success is sometimes worse than defeat. Lord Baltimore, always concerned for the profits of his venture and uneasy lest the growing power of the parliamentary party in England should lead to the cancellation of his charter, accepted the assembly's acts of 1639 which gave the little colony something of a freeman status. It provided that no subject of His Majesty's kingdom or any other foreign prince should hold land in the palatinate

[5] Chapter IV.

except upon specific approval of the proprietor. That closed the issue with the Jesuits. And to thwart the Virginia fur traders at the mouth of the Susquehanna, the assembly agreed that a commission should have the power to "seize and search all ships engaged in the illicit Indian trade." This was to be done in the name of the proprietor and it served notice to William Claiborne and his fellows that Lord Baltimore was henceforth to be master of the bay above the mouth of the Potomac. It was further stipulated that both the Holy Church of Rome and the less holy church of England might enjoy freedom of worship and that no person might be persecuted for his religious views: [6]

all inhabitants of this province, being Christians, shall enjoy all such liberties, immunities and free customs as any natural born subject of England.

There were regulations as to the granting of lands, the status of indentured servants and the succession to manors. Definite procedure was fixed for the general and local courts; and the task of applying statutes and precedents was definitely set. Not even in Massachusetts was there so much emphasis upon *Magna Charta* and its many guarantees and immunities. The proprietor, more of a student than his brother, the governor and lieutenant-general, was ready and willing to concede much in order that religious freedom might prevail. However, the Saint Mary's settlement was content in the early years with less of the liberties of Englishmen than the Virginians of the same date, who had thrust a royal governor out of office and sent him home for trial before His Majesty's privy council. But the Marylanders did insist upon the right of all freemen to vote for representatives in a general assembly; and this assembly, like that of Virginia,

[6] *Archives of Maryland*, I, 41.

ASYLUM FOR TROUBLED CONSCIENCES 143

was accorded the right to lay and collect taxes, to levy troops and to prescribe the penalties and the rules under which society should develop. And above all the new community enjoyed freedom of conscience within the limits prescribed by the regulations of the two churches named above, although one needs to remember that the Church of England had no priests in the settlement the first fifteen years of its existence, numerous as were the common folk who preferred the promises of that or the Puritan creed.

The liege lords of the manors, the servants of the greater farms and the increasing number of freemen continued the prosaic and toilsome work of making themselves homes in the wilderness which lay to the north and west of the Potomac, a peninsula of land more fertile than the tracts between the James and the York, and one which stretched westward past the present site of Washington toward the great and most luxuriant region which lies between Harper's Ferry and Gettysburg of today. Nor were the Indians really hostile during the first twenty years of Maryland history. This meant a more profitable fur trade and richer returns to the hunters of venison and wild turkeys. The conditions of life, though easier than in early Virginia, were hard enough. The log cabins of Catholic saints were scattered about the woods and by the side of natural springs just as were those of the less pious farmers on the southern shores of the bay. The swine, the cows and even the horses roamed the forests and multiplied till they became so numerous at times that they were simply abandoned by their owners or ordered by law to be killed and put out of the way. At other times the terrific cold of winter destroyed so many that serious consequences were threatened. Thus with animals as with men it was a rough and an exposed existence, contrary to the roseate pictures of his lordship's propaganda in England.

II

Lord Baltimore's assumption of complete mastery of the trade of the upper Chesapeake Bay, on the eve of the civil war in England, was a challenge to Virginia almost as great as the previous effort of the Jesuits to become overlords of the native tribes in the region from the Potomac to the Susquehanna. When Claiborne returned to his estate and Indian trading headquarters near Point Comfort, outlawed by the Saint Mary's authorities and forbidden to enter the upper bay, there was certain to be trouble. The Bennet-Mathews-West influence was so great in 1642 that Berkeley was persuaded to install Claiborne in the office of treasurer of Virginia for life and at the same time allow him to resume frontier trade operations with the natives in the wild Potomac country. The prosperity of Virginia was so marked and the activities of the dissenters on the lower James River and in Saint Mary's were so serious that Leonard Calvert appointed Giles Brent acting governor and himself sailed in April, 1642, for England to take counsel with his "beloved brother," who pondered day and night how to maintain a perfect equilibrium between the King, his royal master, and the driving second Earl of Warwick, "Puritan pope" and lord high admiral in command of all the fleets of England. Warwick was the famous Robert Rich, the aristocratic pirate of 1618–20, with vast interests in the West Indian and Chesapeake Bay settlements. While the Calvert brothers made estimates of their properties in the palatinate, to be used in case the charter were invalidated, and calculated the delicate balance of power between the Protestants, the Catholics and Indians on the shores of the Chesapeake, Philip Bennet, of Virginia, brother of Richard Bennet, went to Massachusetts to procure ministers of the true faith for all the southside dissenters and to enlist the support of John Winthrop in case of difficulties with the intolerant Sir William Berkeley. At the moment Claiborne assumed the high office of treasurer of Virginia and Leonard Calvert set sail for England, Richard Ingle, a representative of the Earl of Warwick and a prosperous trader, if not a ruthless pirate, sailed into the harbor of Saint Mary's in command of the *Eleanor,* a semi-armed ship, with none other than the Catholic, Thomas Cornwaleys, attorney-general of the colony and counsel of the Jesuit order, on board! It was the same resolute colonel who had captured or killed Claiborne's employees at Kent Island four years before. In the delicate situation both in the bay and in England, Governor Brent hardly knew whether to welcome or arrest a "piratical" ship captain who paid three times as much for tobacco as had been the rule a year before; and the "pirate" sailed away while official eyes were averted. A year later Ingle reappeared in the bay. He now commanded a larger ship which bore the suggestive name *Reformation;* it was loaded with tobacco and was not without an ample supply of ammunition. He was thought to be an ally of Claiborne. Ingle was arrested for form's sake; Cornwaleys and the sheriff, with the connivance of Brent, arranged his escape. Would the "pirate" seize Kent Island for the Virginia Protestants?[7]

Growing more and more concerned about the ominous look of things in Virginia, Sir William Berkeley ordered the expulsion of the Boston preachers whom Philip Bennet had brought to the southside, and likewise made ready to sail for England. It was at that moment the Indians broke into the colony from the west and north. It was a coalition which included some Potomac tribes. For a day or two it seemed that Virginia would be wiped out of

[7] Andrews, *Founding of Maryland,* Ch. VIII.

existence. Were the angry Jesuits and uneasy Maryland Catholics aware of this tremendous drive upon their enemies to the south?

While Claiborne conducted a devastating campaign against the natives that summer and Ingle took possession of Kent Island in his own and Claiborne's interest, Leonard Calvert returned helpless to his post and found Brent dispossessed of his island fort and at loggerheads with John Lewger and Thomas Cornwaleys, members of the Saint Mary's council. For two years the upper bay and the whole Catholic colony were at the mercy of Ingle and subject to depredations almost as ruthless as those which the Virginians visited upon the Indians. However, if conditions were bad in Maryland, they were worse in England, and the distressed Lord Baltimore contemplated for a time permanent exile to his palatinate; but the palatinate itself seemed to be slipping from him. Then he decided to abandon the cause of Charles I, and paid judicious court to the parliamentary leaders: there was something to admire even in the Earl of Warwick! Meanwhile poor Leonard struggled in vain against Ingle and Claiborne; his friend, Giles Brent, gave up in disgust and became "lord of a manor" in upper Virginia. Margaret Brent, his sister, a lawyer and acting governor of Saint Mary's for a season, took up her residence near the brother's manor, which she called *Peace*. Leonard Calvert gave up his stormy career when his great brother in London invited the dissenters of Virginia to migrate to the northern end of the palatinate! The newcomers were to have all the liberties of Englishmen. For a time Philip Bennet and his followers were in doubt. But when his lordship showed how far he had drifted from the original understanding with the Jesuit chiefs of 1636 by the appointment of William Stone, Puritan leader of Northampton county, Virginia, as governor of all his colony, three hundred southside Virginians migrated to the Severn

ASYLUM FOR TROUBLED CONSCIENCES 147

Valley and the screened peninsula just north of the mouth of that river. It was a strategic position like that to which Leonard Calvert had appointed Giles Brent on the eastern shore in 1637. The Severn Valley community increased rapidly and, with the support of Puritan Virginia, it was almost certain to neutralize the influence of the Catholics at Saint Mary's and thereafter to give Maryland the sectional character so common to most embryo American states. It was the autumn of 1648, when the head of Charles I was soon to fall into the Cromwellian basket in front of Whitehall.

Learning nothing from the disasters at Naseby and Marston Moor, Sir William Berkeley continued his drastic actions against the southside Virginians. William Durant, Virginia kinsman of that famous John Durant, who the next year seized Canterbury cathedral and from the sacred throne of religious England issued his famous books: *Comfort and Counsell for Dejected Souls* and *Silence the Duty of Saints,* led more and more of the Virginia dissenters to the settlements about Kent Island. When the Saint Mary's assembly met in April 1649, it was a legislature of both sections of the palatinate, but dominated by a Puritan majority. They forthwith resolved that [8]

> Noe person or persons whatsoever within this province shall henceforth bee any waies troubled for or in respect to his or her religion ... professing to believe in Jesus Christ.

The other rights of Englishmen were reasserted, namely, that all freemen should enjoy the right of suffrage; that the assembly, duly elected, should exercise the sovereign powers of self-government; and that the powers of war and peace with their uncertain neighbors inhered in the legislature. But to repeat the assurance that the Jesuits

[8] *Archives of Maryland,* I, 246.

should not increase their power in the community, it was again decreed that no man or party of men should hold land except upon grant of his lordship, the proprietor. When it came to the troublesome question of free trade, so stoutly demanded and exercised in Virginia, little was said. Baltimore was the rightful lord of the Maryland trade; however, in the stormy years that witnessed the downfall of the Stuarts, the rivers and harbors of the upper Chesapeake Bay were as free to Dutch and West Indian traders as to Commonwealth ships. Laws penalizing runaway servants, compelling the cultivation of corn against possible famine and fixing the relations with the natives were passed. The new settlements about the Severn and on the former Giles Brent peninsula were duly admitted into the Saint Mary's colony and the palatinate was now divided into four counties: Saint Mary's and Charles counties in the south, Anne Arundell and Kent counties in the north. These larger districts were for the time subdivided into hundreds for representative purposes. Within these the dominant leaders were the "lords of manors" and other favorites of the proprietor, who held large tracts of land at strategic points along the Potomac and on both sides of the upper bay. The settlement might now be called the colony of Maryland.[9]

But Governor Stone and his uneasy dissenters were never certain as to their future, every ship from England bringing fresh information as to wars in Europe and piracies in the South Atlantic. After many stories from Jamestown as to the designs of the commissioners of the Commonwealth waiting there in 1652 to receive the surrender of Sir William Berkeley and his stalwart cavaliers had been told in Saint Mary's, Richard Bennet and William Claiborne appeared in the harbor of Saint Mary's

---

[9] Andrews, *Founding of Maryland,* Chs. XIII and XIV, gives an excellent account of religious and political struggles of the mid-seventeenth century.

ASYLUM FOR TROUBLED CONSCIENCES 149

on June 28, 1652, as the spokesmen of the new government of England and with instructions to set the Chesapeake Bay country into proper order. Few men would have been less welcome in southern Maryland. Certain, however, of their position, Bennet and Claiborne took no advantage of their Catholic opponents and accepted the cautious Stone, without assurance of his attitude, as a partner in the government of the new and greater commonwealth of Virginia. The proprietor was to be dispossessed of his political powers, if not his lands. On December 18, however, Stone proclaimed himself the loyal representative of Baltimore! Bennet and Claiborne were taken by surprise. A little later came the news of Cromwell's protectorship and of the renewal in London of all Baltimore's powers. At once the Protestants of the Severn Valley advised the Virginians to reassume control at Saint Mary's. Stone resisted and held his own for two years, Puritan head of a Catholic council and Protestant assembly. In June, 1654, a new assembly met and arranged one more "permanent settlement." Now both Romanists and Episcopalians were left without the religious liberty that had been guaranteed in 1633 and 1648. Lord Baltimore was still to be dispossessed and his Protestant governor deprived of authority. Maryland was to be a self-governing part of Virginia; there was to be no more papal influence, no prelates; no work should be done on the Sabbath day; no fishing, hunting nor fowling should be allowed to interfere with divine worship; no swearing, slander or licentious conduct anywhere; young men were to behave themselves, young women to be modest; and monopoly prices on imported goods, as well as the engrossing of lands, were forbidden. There must henceforth be triennial elections, without the call of the governor, in which all freemen were to participate: one of the unrecognized demands of 1640.[10]

[10] Clayton C. Hall, *Narratives of Early Maryland*, 93-94.

But in 1655 the Lord Protector wrote a stern rebuke to Bennet and Claiborne for turning autocrats like himself and "trespassing upon Cecil Lord Baltimore's lands and people";[11] and his lordship rebuked the helpless Stone even more severely for his yielding so much to the Puritan saints. The humbled Governor at once proceeded, in the names of the Protestant Cromwell and the Catholic Baltimore, to restore both "popery and prelacy" and to make war upon the settlers in the valley of the Severn. He would recover all lost ground. On March 25, 1655, however, the resolute Maryland-Virginia dissenters in "the glorious presence of the Lord of Hosts" defeated Stone in battle at Providence and compelled his men "to throw down their arms and beg for mercy." The Governor himself was a prisoner. Several former Catholic councillors and a considerable number of women were also held incomunicado. They were soon condemned to death. Four of the men were executed and their property confiscated, after the manner of the time. Leonard Strong, a leader of the victorious party, wrote and published an account of these events under the appealing title: *Babylon's Fall: A Fair Warning to Lord Baltimore*.[12]

With Governor Stone discredited and in prison and the people deeply concerned as to their foodstuffs and markets, there followed another year of semi-anarchy. In this dilemma, the proprietor, uncertain whether Cromwell would recognize the claims of Bennet and Mathews, then in London arguing again the Virginia case, authorized Josias Fendall, an emotional-minded member of the council who had rendered Governor Stone earnest assistance on the day of the battle of the Severn, to assume the vacant governorship. To make the offer more welcome, Fendall was granted two thousand acres of land in Charles county on the Potomac, increased the next

[11] Browne, 148.
[12] Hall, 235.

year to six thousand, and elevated to the status of lord of a manor. But a combination of Puritans and Catholics delayed recognition of the new governor and forced him into the supreme court of the palatinate on charges of sedition and conspiracy against the proprietor. Captain William Fuller, another assistant to Stone, therefore served as acting governor. Fendall was put under bond to keep the peace until the claims of Virginia were brought to a decision before Cromwell's committee on trade and plantations. But Fendall, acting under instructions from the proprietor, paid high compliments to Thomas Truman and George Thompson, Protestant members of the council, and granted them lands to match their official dignity. He likewise paid tribute to men who had fallen in battle fighting for his lordship and made reparations to the unhappy widows of the prisoners who had been executed for being Catholics. At the same time John Langford received a great tract of land for writing a vigorous reply to Leonard Strong's *Fall of Babylon*. While these vain efforts at compromise were advertised far and near, Philip Calvert, half-brother of the proprietor, appeared at Saint Mary's to assume the secretaryship of the colony, to validate the recent gifts of land and to moderate the doings of Fendall who was now called to London to meet and argue with Bennet and Mathews. In spite of Claiborne's resumption of control, for the fourth time, over Kent Island, and the urgent appeals of the Puritan leaders of Virginia, the decision of Cromwell fell at last to his lordship.[13] The Virginians returned defeated to little Jamestown at the end of the year 1657, and on February 26, 1658, Fendall again became governor of Maryland. Doubting the loyalty of Fendall, Baltimore appointed two confidential friends, Thomas Cornwaleys, whose curious career is too little known, and Richard Preston, members of the council.

[13] Claiborne, Ch. VIII.

Philip Calvert and the new council were the real executives. Fendall, offended and never very loyal to the proprietor, secretly joined the Puritan majority and assisted the lower house of assembly in 1660 to proclaim a new government with a house of burgesses "the lawful assembly without dependence upon any other power in the province." [14]

Here was another revolt of the majority against the distant and unwelcome control of the Calvert family. Fendall now surrendered his commission from Lord Baltimore and accepted one from the new assembly. He sought to play the rôle of a little Cromwell. But before the story of the new upturn in Saint Mary's was told in England, Charles II was on his way to London, and Baltimore hastened to greet his returning Majesty with becoming gestures. On June 24, 1660, Philip Calvert received a commission from his brother and in a few days he proclaimed the news of the happy return of his "glorious Majesty" to the throne of his murdered and "saintly" father. Maryland was no fit place for Fendall, and Virginia hardly dared receive the unhappy exile, although the Northern Neck, the home of the Brents, had been recognized as an asylum for unhappy Marylanders. To the surprise of all, the condemned ex-governor was soon pardoned by the supreme court at Saint Mary's and he was left to develop his huge manor on the Potomac where he calmly awaited the next troubled era in Maryland's life. While Charles II prepared to put the Duke of Argyle to death and laid legal snares to catch Sir Henry Vane, Calvert endeavored to conciliate all parties and to entice immigrants from all persecuted elements of the nascent British-American empire. Nor was the cautious half-brother of the wise proprietor unsuccessful in his diplomatic rôle. He kept the saints of Saint Mary's county

[14] Andrews, Matthew P., *History of Maryland*, 1929, pp. 132-35.

from active warfare against the Severn Valley and the upper Chesapeake Bay settlements.

III

When Philip Calvert had been two years in the colony, Charles Calvert, son and heir of the proprietor, appeared at Saint Mary's to take up the duties of governor and lieutenant-general of Maryland. It was to be a sort of apprenticeship to the greater responsibility which would come to him as the third Lord Baltimore. The uncle dutifully accepted the position of secretary and chief justice of the colony and contented himself to spend the remainder of his years in the pretty little Maryland capital of three hundred inhabitants. John Lewger had disappeared from the troubled scene; and Thomas Cornwaleys, stormy petrel of the war-torn palatinate, petitioned the Supreme Court for relief from scurrilous charges of wicked enemies, and made ready to return with his family and the remnant of his belongings to London. Giles Brent, as we know, now lived in quiet retirement at his manor in Stafford county, Virginia, where his redoubtable sister, Margaret, died in 1663. William Stone, released from prison sometime after the battle of the Severn, now lived in semi-exile at his "Avon" manor in Charles county. And the "wicked" Josias Fendall, "that perfidious and perjured fellow" whom his lordship had ordered to be hanged, quietly managed his ten-thousand-acre estate not far away.[15] The day of the founders had passed and the young heir to the growing palatinate surrounded himself with younger men.

Edward Lloyd, James Neale and Henry Sewall, founders of well-known Maryland families, were added

[15] *Dictionary of American Biography.*

to the council and served as members of the general or supreme court. Saint Mary's county was still the largest of the governmental units and it was represented by four burgesses, a disproportionate influence in the colony. But the masters of the early manors lived there; the older Catholic leaders could hardly content themselves with mere equality; and there was also the Jesuit manor and its wide stretches of land granted in 1637. There were, however, trading posts and hustling settlements on both sides of the bay. Calvert county was a new creation with Richard Preston and Thomas Truman for spokesmen in the burgesses—resolute men to be heard from in later crises. The spokesmen of the Severn region were always in evidence, if not always welcome; and fourteen miles up the deep Potomac Sound one saw the beginnings of the later city of Baltimore, a lively Indian trading post. The Isle of Kent and Kent county on the eastern side of the bay were at last free of Claiborne intrigues, while Talbot county filled out the loose connection between the upper bay and the Virginia settlements on the eastern shore. Charles county on the northern bank of the Potomac lay opposite the homes of the Fitzhughs, the Brents, and the wide-spreading acres of John Washington.

While the southern and northern communities had fought each other twenty years about religion and the rights of Claiborne, the "trembling" Quaker exiles from England and Massachusetts had been sent by the shipload into the unoccupied spaces of the palatinate. In Charles, Anne Arundell and Baltimore counties they were numerous and, when George Fox visited them in 1670, they were fairly supplied with little meeting houses, sad consequence of his lordship's vetoing the Jesuit policy of 1637! Catholics, Puritans and Quakers made a heterogeneous population; but Lord Baltimore now added Baptists and Jews. The more industrious farmers and busy Indian traders there were, the greater the two-

ASYLUM FOR TROUBLED CONSCIENCES 155

shillings export tobacco tax, one-half of which found its way into the proprietor's treasury. Nor were the unruly squatters, so common in Virginia, wanting on the frontiers of the Baltimore palatinate. Altogether the Marylanders numbered some twenty thousand, about half as many as their southern neighbors. They exported tobacco to British traders at low prices and received farm and household supplies from the self-same traders at high prices. Not even the "absolute and supreme" lord proprietor and his watchful kinsfolk at Saint Mary's were equal to the control of the tobacco trade. But to make law even more difficult to enforce, the Duke of York unceremoniously annexed New Netherland in 1664 and then authorized John Lord Berkeley and Sir George Carteret, perhaps the richest man in England, to appropriate the lands and become the overlords of the peaceful settlements of the Dutch and the Swedes on the Delaware River. In consequence, there was bitter war between the United Provinces and England, and thereafter Dutch privateers and war vessels steered into the bay and either loaded their ships with the produce of the region or captured British ships whenever that was possible. It was impossible for Lord Baltimore to protect the Chesapeake Bay. British customs officials estimated the losses on the Maryland tobacco trade alone at ten thousand sterling a year.

From the time when the new commercial policy, as revealed in the organization of the first Royal African Company and the Navigation Act of 1663, the Virginians, the Barbadians and the Marylanders endeavored, apparently, at first, with the approval of the British Government, so to regulate their plantings as not to "glut" the market. It was the so-called tobacco "stint" of 1663 and 1664; but to populations which had doubled the last fifteen years this was a most difficult thing to do. Lords of manors on the Potomac and the Patuxent and master planters on the York and James might have accepted the stern remedy. Not so with the small farmers and freemen whose new tracts of land gave the first prospect of prosperity they had ever known. They would not submit. However, with the depression growing worse e ery year, Charles Calvert and his council, in concert with Sir William Berkeley and his great planter neighbors, demanded of the Maryland burgesses in April, 1666, an absolute "cessation" of tobacco planting: [16]

> Upon a glutt of tobacco follows the ruin of the house-holder and master of servants, the tobacco they make being of so little worth that a servant's cargo (annual output) shall not cloath him, the consequence of which must be that the richest of us must beat his own bread for want of servants.

The leaders of the Maryland burgesses did not object to rich men making their own bread. They resented the idea of a complete abandonment of tobacco planting for a year, quarreled with their superiors the better part of a month, and finally refused to enact the required legislation. In a little while a message from the proprietor announced that his lordship had never approved the plan. The King and his customs officials absolutely forbade a cessation. The great people in London seemed to be on the popular side. Men must grow huge crops at a loss for the increase of the royal revenue. But as fortune would have it, heavy and destructive rains delayed the plantings of 1667 and in August there came a storm which washed away all the lowland crops, swept ten thousand Virginia houses into the rivers and left as good as no tobacco in Virginia and only half a crop in Maryland.[17]

> On the 27th of August followed the most dreadful hurricane that ever this country groaned under. . . . When the Morning

[16] Abbreviated from *Archives of Maryland*, II, 48.
[17] Abbreviated from Secretary Thomas Ludwell's account. Compare quotation in Chapter I.

ASYLUM FOR TROUBLED CONSCIENCES 157

(came) and the Sun (had) risen, it would have comforted us had it not lighted to the ruins of our Plantations, of which I think not one escaped. The nearest computation is at least 10,000 houses blown down; all the Indian grain laid flat upon the Ground; all the Tobacco in the fields torn to pieces.

There was at least a stint; and the price rose accordingly the next year; but huge plantings followed and the former distress continued.

There were other troubles. The last Dutch war, 1672–1674, increased the uncertainty of commerce in the bay and tempted the different religious groups into partisan attitudes; Maryland seemed to be the land of uneasy consciences. However, the diplomatic Calverts and their allies were able to maintain the equipoise as between the rival sections and, by stressing the necessity of mutual toleration, the Catholics and the Puritans learned to endure each other, although both resented the prayerful assertion of the Quakers that they "were to be governed by God's law and the light within them and not by man's law." It was another right of an Englishman; but it was a difficult thing in a new and strenuous life, where war was as much the rule of existence as peace, to excuse a growing and a prospering element from all militia and military duty, not to mention the "right" not to pay taxes toward the common defense.

At the moment when George Fox and his ardent coworker, William Edmundson,[18]

preached and spread abroad the truth to great folks, people of account, magistrates and officers who felt the power of the Lord,

on the Patuxent and the Coptank rivers, the Susquehannock Indians, who had been crowded southward to the falls of the Potomac, the Senecas of the Six Nations and the smaller tribes, that had been pushed up the banks of

[18] Norman Penney, *The Journal of George Fox,* 305-06.

the rivers and away from the coast by the hustling whites, were giving repeated evidence of concerted resistance and attack. Even the Doegs on the southern side of the Potomac were resenting the encroachments of the Virginians, led by George Mason and John Washington. Far away in New England a cloud of terrible war rose steadily above the horizon. Under this pressure the Maryland governor and assembly joined their southern neighbors and organized little companies of horsemen whose duty it was to ride the frontier from the site of the present Mount Vernon past the falls of the rivers to the mouth of the Susquehanna. John Allen of the burgesses and Thomas Truman of the council were the commanders. Would not the "sons of the inner light" assist in contributions to meet this expense—being excused from personal participation? Lord Baltimore left the answer to the Quakers. The assembly laid the tax, but at the same time laid John Allen and his horsemen under bond not to rob the Indians. It was the ranger system which prevailed all the way from Petersburg of our day to the site of the present Baltimore. Pious Christians of all denominations were in imminent danger of a coalition of the naïve sons of the wilderness to resist the most un-Christian conduct: persistent violation of treaties and unlawful seizure of lands.

The second Lord Baltimore was on his deathbed in London, November, 1675, when the first concerted Indian war had spent its force all along the frontier line from the Connecticut River to the falls of the unknown Roanoke, in Carolina; and the Marylanders were trying to hang their distinguished councillor, Thomas Truman, for concerting some months before with John Washington in the murder of Susquehannock bearers of a flag of truce, close to the site of the present Washington City. While the palatinate of Saint Mary's was in distress and the sixty-nine-year old lord was wholly disillusioned, the venture had not been so complete a failure that his Quaker rival, William Penn, was not ready to ask for another and a greater concession of Indian lands, at the head of Chesapeake Bay.

The three hundred Catholics and Puritans on the *Arke* and the *Dove* had multiplied to five or six thousand. The disciples of Richard Bennet and William Durant on the Severn and the Potapsco had increased in similar proportions. Nor had the gentle followers of George Fox failed of their contribution. It was an interesting complex, the outcome of the original asylum for English Catholics and hated Jesuits. The twenty thousand lords, freemen and servants produced fifty thousand hogsheads of tobacco at an average return of one and a half to two pounds sterling each a year. That was hardly sufficient to pay for men's modest clothing. An indentured servant (for a term of four or five years) sold at Saint Mary's, Providence or on the Severn at five or six pounds, yet a day's common labor was worth a shilling. It was a simple hard life from which none but the most energetic could hope to escape. Yet few men ever thought of returning to England where life was even worse for all but the privileged.

Nor had the generous proprietor who had thus found homes for "such as could not live with ease anywhere else" failed of compensation.[19] If he spent much in the early years, he received more in later times: five thousand pounds annually from the tobacco tax; port dues from every ship (save those of pirates) that entered a Maryland river; two shillings for every hundred acres of land granted; fees for title deeds and profits from escheats, not to mention grants and favors to a score of kinsmen and close friends. It all probably approached ten

[19] Browne, 98.

or twelve thousand pounds a year. Out of this came the salary of the governor, always a brother or a son, and the stipends of a few other officers. At least five thousand sterling a year went across the Atlantic, not counting the under-cover returns from New England ship captains and other unlawful intruders into his realm. Five thousand a year in 1670 was hardly less than fifty thousand pounds today. One need not wonder then at the eager generosity of William Penn to settle other unwelcome and penurious subjects of Charles II on Indian lands and treat Baltimore as Baltimore had treated Claiborne.

Nor had the king reason to complain. The royal revenues from Maryland tobacco were not less than fifty thousand pounds a year. And the profits from the Indian trade to British merchants were not small. Moreover, the simple and poverty-stricken emigrants, deeply concerned as to their souls' salvation, occupied the strategic spaces and promontories on the Chesapeake Bay and supported His Majesty's authority on the Delaware and the Hudson rivers, while their very existence strengthened the British power all the way south to the Saint Johns River. It was, therefore, more than a presumptuous claim of the Maryland assembly when on June 15, 1676, the bowing legislators unanimously voted a renewal of the two-shilling tax and other perquisites to the son and little grandson of the dead proprietor for their natural lives.[20] It was their vote of thanks and regretful good-bye, as well as a shrewd assertion of that complete popular sovereignty so dear to American hearts then and later. His departing lordship graciously declined the legislative gift; but were not the profits of the deceased father the rightful property of the eldest son? The Maryland aslyum for troubled souls had been the area of more warfare about religion than any other American colony; but

[20] *Archives of Maryland*, II, 514.

the rights promised in 1633 had not been lost, and even Quakers might have homes and meeting houses there if they were willing to cross the dangerous Atlantic on little sail boats.

9

Stuart Economic Nationalism

> "The men of Westminster might have strengthened us to beare those heavy chaines they are making for us, given us some assurance that we shall eat the bread which our oxen plow; but instead, we are made their worships' slaves, bought with their money, and, by consequence, we ought not to buy and sell."—Sir William Berkeley. Neill, *Virginia Carolorum*, 212-213.

I

WITH A HUGE GRANT OF TOBACCO TO MEET HIS EXpenses for a long sojourn in England, and representing a community of forty thousand people already committed to the ideals of free trade, near-freedom of conscience, manhood suffrage, equal representation in a sovereign parliament and free access to fresh lands, Sir William Berkeley appeared in London in the early summer of 1661.[1] It was not the England from which he had departed so sadly in 1645. Charles Stuart, escorted from Holland a year before by Sir William's exiled brother, John Lord Berkeley, Edward Hyde, now the great Earl of Clarendon, and a score of other enthusiastic royalists, sat proudly upon the throne. The thirty-one year old monarch, a clever manipulator of men and a libertine of unsurpassed effrontery, had shown one phase of his character on the preceding January 30 by taking the decaying remains of Oliver Cromwell, John Bradshaw and Henry Ireton from their tombs in Westminster and hanging them upon a great gallows at Tyburn, where thousands

[1] Hening, *Statutes*, II, 17.

of people were permitted to stare at them several days. He then ordered the Protector's head to be placed on the top of a pole on Parliament House for the delight or warning of wrangling members. A month before the Governor's arrival, George Monck, already Earl of Albemarle, published a private letter of his former friend, the Scotch Duke of Argyle, written while both were in the service of Cromwell; and the letter was at once used as sufficient evidence for the execution of the great Scotch nobleman at Tolbooth Place, Edinburgh, where the head was fastened to a tall stake for the satisfaction of professing royalists, and there it remained for three years. And to finish the revealing picture of the new régime, Sir Henry Vane, member of Parliament and one time Governor of Massachusetts, was led to the block on Tower Hill, London, June 14, about the time of Sir William's arrival. Assured by His Majesty of his safety and innocence of any crime the preceding year, the heroic victim tried to say a few words before the fall of the fatal axe. The King ordered drummers to raise a noisy racket all about the yard so that no one might hear what was said. The gentle victim laid his head upon the block, and the monarch's over-zealous followers shouted joyously.[2] It must have been an interesting season for the Virginia Governor who had been unable to keep the King's opponents out of the Virginia Council and had been compelled to recognize the power of the southside Virginia Puritans in the House of Burgesses as well as the Council.

Nor was the Stuart family less interesting. James, Duke of York, twenty-eight year old brother of His Majesty, of Catholic predilection and autocratic temper, was made Lord High Admiral of the Navy. Some time before Charles II made Barbara Villiers his chief mistress and gave her vast sums out of the public treasury, the Duke

[2] British *Dictionary of National Biography* is exceedingly good for sketches of the men of the Stuart era.

of York seduced Anne Hyde, the daughter of the Earl of Clarendon, and was compelled, on September 3, 1660, to marry the unhappy young woman who nevertheless failed to wean her husband from the embraces of Anne Carnegie, another shameless mistress of the new court circle. Charles I, with the unprecedented grant of £1,200,000 a year, and James, with £100,000,[3] each with mistresses always at command, suggested something new to the England which had so recently shown its temper and taste in the Puritan domination in all departments of life. But there were other remarkable personages in the Restoration group. Henrietta Maria, mother of Charles II and daughter of the great Henry IV and Maria de' Medici, then in her 52nd year, lived again in London and re-opened her Catholic-Jesuit chapel. She enjoyed £60,000 a year from the public treasury, and again subsidized Jesuit priests for their doubtful propaganda amongst the unruly English people. Nor was Henrietta, the King's seventeen-year old sister, of less influence in the marvellous social circle that was developing about the English court. She had journeyed in triumph from Paris to London in the autumn of 1660 where she received a gift of £10,000 from the submissive Cavalier parliament. A little before Sir William Berkeley arrived, she had agreed to marry the Duke of Orleans, having failed to capture her bridegroom's brother, Louis XIV, and she journeyed back to Versailles in the autumn of 1660, where she played a semi-diplomatic rôle for her lecherous brother and in due time sent him a new mistress to take the place of the fading Barbara Villiers, "Duchess of Cleveland"; Parliament assented to the elevation of the new mistress to the rank of "Duchess of Portsmouth" and voted her huge gifts from the public treasury. All this was not, as time was soon to reveal, a natural ex-

[3] A pound sterling of 1660 was equal to ten pounds of present day currency.

STUART ECONOMIC NATIONALISM 165

pression of English taste and morals. It was a curious imitation of the new French system which was soon to be reflected in every court of Europe.[4]

Moreover, Charles II maintained important contacts on the continent. He was the grandson of Henry IV, one of the greatest kings of France, and a kinsman, therefore, of Louis XIV, just twenty-three years old, already beginning to imagine himself the master of western Europe. And Charles' nephew, William of Orange, eleven years old, was dreaming of the day when he would become the King of the United Netherlands and succeed to the power and fame of the great House of Orange. And to complicate matters, the States General of the Netherlands had generously made Charles II a gift of 75,000 gulden when he had departed for England in May, 1660. While Jean de Witt, the greatest of all Dutch statesmen but one and master of the Netherlands parliament, opposed young William's claims to the crown, his mother, Mary Stuart, Charles' oldest sister, maneuvered day and night for the elevation of her only son to royal status. Although he had been a guest of the Netherlands for several years, against the protests of Oliver Cromwell, with Dutch money in his pockets at a critical moment and had been assisted by de Witt to regain the throne of England, Charles refused assistance to his ambitious sister and nephew.[5]

Louis XIV had not failed to give the Stuart family valuable support during those critical May days when they journeyed with Lord Berkeley and his fellow royalists to Dover. With the Netherlands favorable and the French lending aid on the promise of Charles to restore Dunkirk, which Cromwell had seized three years before,

[4] Burnet, Gilbert, Bishop of Salisbury, in his *History of his own Time*, Vol. I, gives excellent account of manners and morals of the Stuart epoch.
[5] Blok, P. J., *Geschichte der Niederlaende*, Vol. V, portrays admirably the economic and political life of the Netherlands during the second half of the seventeenth century.

the new King was in a strong position. And his shrewd, intriguing friend, Henry Bennet, had persuaded Philip IV of Spain to lend a helping hand to the Stuarts in return for the restoration of the strategic island of Jamaica, conquered by William Penn, father of the Quaker pacifist, in 1655. Louis XIV, married to the daughter of the King of Spain and expecting to annex the Spanish Netherlands as his wife's dowry, patronizingly advised Charles to marry the unattractive little nun, Catharine of Braganza, daughter of the important King of Portugal. The shrewd agents of the English King negotiated the proposed match in 1662; and Catharine abandoned her religious vows in order to become the wife of the British libertine, while the King of Portugal guaranteed his royal son-in-law £300,000 and England the right to trade in Portuguese harbors all over the world, the possession of Tangiers, naval base and stronghold which guarded the western entrance to the Mediterranean, and the unknown far eastern Bombay, which was destined to expand into the vast British Indian empire of the eighteenth century.[6] While Louis XIV counted on the absorption of the Spanish Netherlands, perhaps the annexation of Spain, the Portuguese nun conveyed to England the key possessions which enabled it to become the greatest commercial empire the world had ever seen—a curious, poverty-stricken semi-Catholic family was thus beginning an English policy which was to give their troubled Protestant subjects a marvellous hold on the four corners of the world!

II

Such was the high royal circle still claiming as late as 1661 the divine right of kings to govern according to

[6] Clark, G. N., *The Later Stuarts*, 56-59.

their sweet wills. The wisest man in the next circle, the Privy Council, which included some thirty members, was Edward Hyde, the fifty-two year old Earl of Clarendon, Chancellor of the Exchequer and author, day by day, of a diary which grew into the greatest history of his own time ever written—for whom two counties of the Old South were named. Clarendon had lost all his British property because he supported Charles I; he had lived with the young King during the painful exile; and he had played a delicate and sometimes treacherous game with George Monck to regain for his young master the coveted Stuart throne. But the great Earl had no patience at all with Charles' libertinism, and during the seven years of his prime ministry he refused to attend "cabal" or cabinet meetings called at the palaces of the King's mistresses; and he was terribly embarrassed when he learned from the monarch himself that his daughter, Anne, had played fast and loose with the Duke of York before their departure from Breda and was consequently due to give birth to a child in the autumn of 1660. The Earl was so exasperated that he promptly told the King that his daughter should be thrust into the Tower for her crime. Strange to say, the unruly daughter gave birth in the next few years to the two queens of England who did most to break forever the power of the Stuart dynasty: Mary, who married William of Orange, and Anne, who aided General John Churchill, later the Duke of Marlborough, to place William on the throne of her father in 1688. But Clarendon was never again quite happy, though he built himself a beautiful mansion which to the Puritan masses of the London people was such a monument to his profiteering that they threw stones through the windows and gave it the name of Dunkirk House—implying graft from the £400,000 which Louis XIV paid Charles for the surrender of Dunkirk. The daughter's behavior in 1660 and the vast mansion were pretexts if not causes of the Chancellor's fall and exile in 1667.[7]

A little less powerful in the Restoration government was George Monck, chief of all Cromwell's generals, who intrigued in marvellous style for Charles' return to the throne in the winter and spring of 1660. Although he had exacted from the returning monarch a promise to spare all but five of the surviving regicides, he quickly yielded, as we have seen, to the ruthlessness of the new régime, and received rich gifts from Parliament and the title of Duke of Albemarle—a name borne today by several counties in the Old South. He was also made Admiral of the Navy and a member of the famous "cabal" in which he played a rôle second only to that of Clarendon himself. Moreover, Albemarle's friends and kinsmen received important appointments and gifts both in England and the West Indies: two figures in the Stuart régime which played a great and decisive rôle in shaping the course of American history.[8]

Nor was Sir George Carteret, one-time pirate operating from the island of Jersey, of minor influence in London and North America. He had also intrigued for the Stuart restoration, and he was not without his reward in money and honors. A member of the Privy Council with Clarendon and Albemarle, he clamored always for war with the Netherlands, and in appreciation of his growing interest in British colonial expansion, the King made him, in 1663, one of the eight proprietors of the vast Spanish domain between Virginia and Florida—a domain which took the name of Carolina, in honor of the "marvellous" monarch himself. The next year the Duke of York, titular overlord of all the region of North America between present-day Pennsylvania and Nova Scotia, awarded him

[7] *Dictionary of National Biography* for Hyde's and his daughter's troubles.
[8] Guizot, François, has written best *Life* of Monck.

and John Lord Berkeley in 1664 the great peninsula between the Delaware and the Hudson rivers. When England was about to lose the Dutch war which Carteret had urged, he loaned the Government £280,000. Although the third most powerful member of the Privy Council, he was expelled from the House of Commons for corrupt practices in 1669. Nor did the early Carolinians fail to name counties and boys for the "richest man in England."

Of even more influence in the founding and rapid expansion of the plantation colonies of North America was the remarkable Berkeley group of courtiers of 1660–1670. The great Lord John, whom we already know, was absentee Governor of Connaught, Ireland, on a huge salary; he was an ally of the Catholic group, yet a member of the Privy Council from 1663, and partner of Carteret in the ownership of New Jersey after 1664. A bitter enemy of Clarendon, he was nevertheless an intimate of the King and able to procure for himself two other offices: Commissioner of Tangiers and master of ordnance at the beginning of the second Dutch war. All these offices poured enormous profits into his private purse, and consequently he built himself a palace in Piccadilly which rivalled in magnificence the Clarendon mansion, both approaching the grandeur of Whitehall itself, residence of the King. Nor was Berkeley omitted when Charles gave Carolina to a few of his favorites.

No colonial governor of North America ever returned to England at a more momentous time or contacted with so powerful a family clique at court. While his elder brother held five or six profitable appointments and figured conspicuously at the courts of the royal and ducal mistresses, his kinsman, George Lord Berkeley of Gloucester, was made superintendent of the palace and grounds of the "Duchess of Cleveland" in 1660. In 1661 he became a member of the Privy Council's Committee for Foreign Plantations, and in 1663 he was a heavy stockholder in the Royal African (slave) Company. Sir Charles Berkeley, another relative, was the treasurer of the King's household. While one of Sir Charles' sons was also a favorite of the Duke of York, another son, Sir William, was the Rear-Admiral of the Navy who later courted death in battle with the Dutch and consequently was buried with national honors in Westminster Abbey in 1666. No family in England ever held so many positions in the Government at the same time, or had quite so many intimate contacts in the royal circle.[9]

Of similar influence was the forty-year old Sir Anthony Ashley Cooper, later the great Earl of Shaftesbury, who, although a deist, parliamentarian and shrewd opponent of the Stuart restoration, was nevertheless made a member of the Privy Council in 1660. Two rivers in South Carolina bear his name. Equally crafty, if not so able, was the famous Henry Bennet, later Earl of Arlington, who shared with Sir Charles Berkeley the management of the King's mistresses, and maneuvered in 1663 the retirement from the cabinet of Sir Edward Nicholas, the most upright and self-sacrificing man in the whole régime. Henry Bennet, kinsman of Richard Bennet, Puritan leader of Virginia, was more of a deist than a Christian, a shrewd profiteer at the public expense, who managed to engineer himself into the cabinet and was quickly made Earl of Arlington, a name perpetuated in the name of a fashionable street in Boston and the famous national cemetery in the suburbs of Washington.[10]

These were the leading members of the King's official family from 1660 to 1667, some of them intimate personal friends. Most of them were very able men; two of them were honest public servants who deprecated the un-

---

[9] There is no adequate biography of any member of this most interesting and distinguished family.

[10] Barbour, Viola, *Henry Bennet, Earl of Arlington*—an excellent biography.

English morals of the new court; but all of them worked day and night to lay the foundations of a new England, a "national socialism" which taught all British subjects that their rulers were superior to all men everywhere, and ordered all their colonists of the West Indies and North America that they must fit themselves into a new economic system which would enrich English merchants and enable the British Government to build and maintain a navy big enough to conquer and control forever the "Seven Seas."

III

The Parliament which assembled in the spring of 1661 was exclusively royalist and Episcopalian in sentiment. Its members were ready to assent to the most drastic religious policy, and they were delighted to know that the King wished to have no more elections. For sixteen years the House of Commons adjourned and reassembled at the command of the restored monarch, new members elected only to fill vacancies. This was thought to guarantee a consistent royalist policy. It did not please the English people, amongst whom there were constant rumors of plots and uprisings, the Dutch always suspected of encouraging such movements. But there was a consistent programme. Scotland and Ireland were brought into complete subordination. The guarantee of the "freedom of tender consciences" promised at Breda in 1660 was ignored. All the chartered towns where dissenters were in control were compelled in 1661 to submit to the Church of England creed. The next year two thousand Puritan clergymen were deprived of their positions and salaries because they did not accept the Prayer Book; in 1664 everyone who persisted in attending dissenter religious services was transported to the American colonies, subject to death penalties if they returned; and in 1665 every unsubmissive clergyman or schoolmaster was forbidden to come within five miles of any city or corporate town. The famous John Bunyan lay in the Bedford jail twelve years and wrote the classical *Pilgrim's Progress,* more widely read in young America than any book whatever, with possible exception of the Bible. Thousands of other religious souls suffered a similar fate. It was to be a completely united England, and the decrees bore the name: Clarendon Code. With royal authority fully restored and all troublesome religious opposition in process of suppression,[11] the way was open for the formulation of a colonial solidarity that would yield large profits to the Crown and rich monopolies to British business men.

Since the days of Sir Francis Drake, English seamen had warred upon Spanish trade with the Americas and again and again demanded recognition of the principle of freedom of the seas. This had grown into a piratical warfare of the most ferocious kind. In 1642 the Dutch had won their seventy-five year struggle for independence and, since their victory came at a moment when England was engaged in a terrific civil war, they quickly became the foremost commercial state in the world. They procured access to all Spanish markets, established themselves upon the west coast of Africa and carried thousands of Negroes to Barbados and other English settlements, taking pay in enormous quantities of sugar and tobacco which they sold on the continent of Europe at great profit. Everybody learned the use of sugar, as they had fifty years before learned the use of tobacco. Dutch slave trade and Amsterdam bank loans gave Barbados the marvellous prosperity already described. This was a subject for English statesmen to study. Clarendon, Albemarle, George Downing, Sir George Carteret and the Duke of York cast their wits together in the hope of driving Spain off the coast of North America, seizing

[11] Trevelyan, *England under the Stuarts,* 340-44.

Spanish possessions in the Caribbean Sea and annexing the Dutch settlement at the mouth of the Hudson River, a key position of great importance. Such a masterful stroke for the little island kingdom of four million people, with perhaps a half a million unemployed, looked impossible.[12]

But Oliver Cromwell had made the beginning in 1655, when Admiral William Penn had captured Jamaica, a strategic position of the first importance in the Caribbean Sea, and which Charles had promised to restore to Spain if ever he came to the British throne. George Downing, the Machiavelli of English history, who having served Cromwell as Ambassador at the Hague for eight years, had no thought of allowing his new master to keep his promise. He hated and feared the Dutch with whom he had lived so long. Cromwell had also captured Nova Scotia, at the mouth of the Saint Lawrence, and Downing had no thought of yielding that strategic peninsula to France, along with Dunkirk. The New England[13] enemy of the Stuarts and former enthusiastic Cromwellian diplomat who, in 1661, had delivered three regicides, whom he had protected in Holland, to be hanged at Tyburn, was now one of the geniuses of the Restoration era. He dreaded the two million Netherlanders whose foreign trade yielded them a billion gulden a year and whose great bank at Amsterdam loaned money at low rates of interest all over western Europe; he would, therefore, fight Puritan Holland at every turn and make Stuart England the greatest economic power in the world: hence his name is perpetuated in the Downing Street of our day. Martin Noell and Thomas Povey, marvellous

---

[12] Mahan, A. T., *The Influence of Sea Power upon History*, 90-101.
[13] George Downing was a nephew of the great Governor John Winthrop of Massachusetts, one of the first graduates of Harvard College and first cousin of Governor John Winthrop of Connecticut. He began as a Puritan preacher in Barbados, became a favorite of Cromwell in 1650 and Ambassador to Holland in 1657.

speculators and colonial experts whose business houses stood on "Old Jewry" Street, London, agreed with Downing and, having won a high financial rating under the Protector, they were promptly accorded a similar standing with the Cavaliers who surrounded Charles. Noell, Povey and Downing, with the crafty Sir George Carteret and the great Earl of Albemarle, all deeply interested in West Indian land holdings and participating in the profits of the sugar and tobacco trade, threatened all the while by the Dutch, knew in 1662 exactly what they wanted, and they drafted the economic policy which made England and her colonial possessions the nearest approach, perhaps, to a perfect autarchy known to modern history.[14]

The Navigation Act of 1651, as we have already seen, was designed to bring all colonial commerce into English harbors and strengthen a weakened British navy for probable conflict with the Netherlands. Charles II and his eager associates had hardly secured their positions in 1660 before the Cavalier Convention re-enacted the Cromwell Act of 1651 and declared its immediate application to Barbados and the tobacco plantations—greatest single cause for Sir William Berkeley's presence in London the following summer. In 1663 the Staples Act still further strengthened the Stuart programme. No other peoples might participate in British colonial commerce and no English shipmaster might sail the ocean unless two-thirds of his seamen were British subjects; and Cromwell's decree of 1654 that no ship of any nation might sail the North Atlantic without acknowledging British supremacy was renewed. It was no longer freedom of the seas or freedom of trade so often demanded of the Spanish, but absolute British control.[15]

[14] Andrews, Charles M., *British Committees, Commissions and Councils of Trade and Plantations*, Ch. III.
[15] Beer, George L., *The Old Colonial System*, I, Ch. II.

Under this policy London, Plymouth and Bristol merchants quickly established domestic control of all colonial trade, especially sugar and tobacco imports, and exports of clothing, farm supplies and household furniture. The customs income on sugar and tobacco quickly rose to £200,000 a year—exports of only sixty thousand planters and farmers in Barbados and the Chesapeake Bay regions! Additional revenue to his Majesty's treasury was derived from duties collected from indispensable French or Dutch products that must pass through English ports on their way to the colonies. All colonial raw stuffs were duly prepared for the English consumer at high, monopolistic prices, and the surpluses were "dumped" each year upon the continental market. The prices of tobacco and sugar for the producers promptly declined to half, even a third of the rates paid during the Cromwellian era of free or illicit trade. For twenty-five years the sugar and tobacco colonies suffered from a "depression" which drove West Indian small proprietors into piracy and hastened the Virginia-Maryland freemen into the western wilderness where they fished, hunted and fought the Indians. New Englanders alone profited from the system, and they were able to do so through the sales of fish, farm products and timber, all of which were needed in the West Indies and not wanted in England. They also developed a tobacco trade with the Dutch at New Amsterdam. They were the only lucky colonists during the following decades.

As this marvellously effective trade act went into operation, the King appointed eight members of his Privy Council to serve on a new Committee of Trade and Plantations. They were John Lord Berkeley, Sir George Carteret, Sir Nicholas Crispe, Sir Andrew Riccard, Sir John Shaw, Sir John Colleton, Martin Noell and Thomas Povey—Berkeley, Carteret, Colleton, Noell and Povey being the directing minds of the organization, all of them deeply interested in exploiting the King's colonial subjects.[16] Thus the members of the Privy Council who aided Clarendon in guiding the hands of His Majesty and the Duke of York were also the administrators of the far-flung commercial policy. This at the end of 1660.

In 1661 the same leaders of the new régime, aided by George Downing, still Ambassador to the Netherlands, gradually worked out another plan which went into effect in February, 1662. The greatest weapon by which the Netherlanders had won commercial leadership in all Spanish America had been the African slave trade. The Duke of York, Carteret, Lords John and George Berkeley, and the other members of the Committee on Trade and Plantations organized the Royal African Company and obtained from Parliament a charter which authorized them to operate for a thousand years. The Queen Mother, the Duchess of Orleans, the famous Prince Rupert, Sir James Modyford, cousin of Albemarle and later Governor of Jamaica, and other favorites of the Crown joined the clever Cromwellian merchants Noell, Povey and William Legge in this comprehensive scheme for driving the Dutch off the west coast of Africa and gaining a complete monopoly of the rich slave trade of the West Indies, perhaps of North America. It was thought to be another East India company which would make its stockholders rich enough to become members of the House of Lords:

> This trade would be of more public honor, interest and advantage than any other experiment in any part of the world; it would return £200,000 to £300,000 each year in gold and supply the plantations with Negro servants.[17]

Thus a second organization directed by the same men that controlled the Committee of Trade and Plantations

[16] Andrews, C. M., *British Committees*, etc., 49-51.
[17] *State Papers, Colonial,* Jan. 2, 1665.

STUART ECONOMIC NATIONALISM 177

was set up while Sir William Berkeley was in London. His brother was a dominating figure in the new company, and his cousin, George Berkeley, was a heavy stockholder. The African Company's stocks, face value £96,000, entered into competition with those of the East India Company.[18] But the great and dangerous slave trade adventure of the Berkeleys, Carteret, Noell and Povey had hardly had time to prove its worth before Clarendon, Albemarle, Carteret and other leaders of the Privy Council persuaded his Majesty (in 1663) to give them the hundred thousand square miles of Spanish territory which lay between the southern border of Virginia and the St. Johns River, North Florida—a promising domain, already mentioned, which had been granted to Sir Robert Heath in 1629. Clarendon, Albemarle, William Lord Craven, John Lord Berkeley, Anthony Lord Ashley (Cooper), Sir George Carteret, Sir William Berkeley and Sir John Colleton were the proprietors of the new realm. All of these men were members of the Privy Council, the Committee of Trade and Plantations, and nearly all were stockholders and directors of the African Slave Company; and several of them were directors of the East India Company. Downing, Noell and Povey, though deeply interested, were not among the prospective Carolina magnates.

It would be difficult to find a more complete system of interlocking directorates at any period of English or American history—a small group of interested men in substantial control of King and Parliament and in constant contact with experienced merchants and speculators who had made their fortunes under Cromwell and who knew how to manipulate affairs under Charles II. Rarely has any country ever fallen into the hands of a more able

[18] Donnan, Elizabeth, *Documents Illustrative of the History of the Slave Trade to America,* II, gives all needful documents bearing on African slave trade.

or more selfish group of leaders. All of them pretended to be orthodox Church of England Christians, but most of them were deists. All of them supported Charles II, although most of them had given support to Cromwell during the preceding decade, Albemarle, Cooper and Colleton being the most conspicuous. None of them failed on occasion to profiteer at the expense of the public and, although there were rivalries and hatreds in many bosoms, the group held firmly together till Charles, under pressure of Arlington, Buckingham and Downing, drove the aged Clarendon out of the country in 1667.

IV

If the comprehensive programme were put into effect, there would be thousands of religious dissenters who would be deported to the colonies where religious freedom might be allowed.[19] Of course Baptists and Quakers could not submit to the Clarendon Code. In order to control all colonial trade, more than a hundred commercial ships of a hundred to five hundred tons burden each, and manned by some five thousand sailors, would have to sail once a year to the West Indies and North America. It was no small undertaking, and, according to the records of the preceding fifty years, about one-fourth of the ships and sailors would be lost each year. Each summer the ships would leave London, Plymouth or Bristol and sail toward the Azores, thence to Barbados and Jamaica where they would dispose of a half of their cargoes and take on thousands of tons of sugar; thence over the stormy western Atlantic to the Chesapeake Bay where they would linger a month or two during each winter, selling the remainder of their goods and indentured serv-

[19] Lloyd-Thomas, J. W., *The Autobiography of Richard Baxter* shows how widespread was the dissenter feeling.

ants, and add thousands of hogsheads of tobacco to their cargoes. Late winter or early spring they would set sail for England across the North Atlantic, altogether twelve thousand miles, over the roughest sea Europeans had ever known.[20] It would be the finest schooling that seamen had ever had and admirable preparation for war, since there were always some fifteen hundred pirates in the Caribbean and central Atlantic region.

Nor was this all. If little England were to control all its own trade in the North Sea, on the Baltic, in the Mediterranean and over the vast seas *via* South Africa to India, there would be hundreds of other ships and crews under the control of English merchants. Hundreds of ships and tens of thousands of sailors watching every accessible harbor in the world and carrying British goods wherever there was a market, and bringing back such articles as the masters of the new régime would allow to enter their ports. It was to be a magnificent system under rigid control. There were to be as few imports as possible from Holland, France and Spain; the plantations were to furnish all possible raw stuffs; and nobody was allowed to take any money out of the country. A merchantman carried goods to the colonies. It took away raw stuffs. If Barbados or Virginia needed money their only source of supply was the Spanish silver pieces-of-eight which they could get only by trade with England's enemies. Since New England produced none of the raw materials desired in the mother country, the only promise of prosperity to that section lay in the trade along the North American coast and in the West Indies, where thousands of men needed lumber, fish and barrel staves. From the West Indies bold New England sea captains might sail across the central Atlantic at the right season of the year, buy Negroes along the African coast in spite of all oppo-

[20] No study of shipping and sailors for the period seems ever to have been made.

sition, and return to Jamaica or Barbados and exchange their cargoes for sugar and molasses which Boston later learned to convert into marvellous rum and which in turn was exchanged in the Chesapeake Bay region for tobacco which clever seamen might slip into Dutch and French ports at prices twice as high as could be obtained in London. The Atlantic was too vast and the American coastal plain too intricate to be entirely controlled by the Committee of Trade and Plantations, even under the most repressive statutes.[21] Hollanders and Frenchmen often broke into the autarchy, and pirates were always in the offing.

But the new African Slave Company with the great Duke of York himself as patron, stockholder and guide, might crowd the Dutch traders off the West Indian seas, out of the Virginia rivers, and strengthen the hands of the Trade and Plantations Committee. To that end two or three of England's best warships were stationed off the West African coast in 1662, and during the next year a score of new ships began to carry goods and trinkets to the Negro chiefs of Africa in exchange for slaves and even for gold and elephants' tusks. The slaves were to go to the British plantations at £18 each and the surplus of Negroes to the Spanish mainland in competition with the "wicked" Dutch.[22] To further the process, Albemarle's favorite kinsman, Sir Thomas Modyford, was supported against the population in Barbados and made Governor of Jamaica in 1663, soon to be the greatest slave market in the world; and Francis Lord Willoughby and Lawrence Hyde, son of Clarendon, were given the island of Surinam of the West Indies and a great stretch of South American coast for their private exploitation. The small farmers and ex-indentured servants, anxious to become

---

[21] *State Papers, Colonial,* Volumes XII and XIII, give ample evidence of trade difficulties.
[22] *State Papers, Colonial,* Jan. 2, 1662, and after.

landowners, of all the sugar islands, were to be carried to the great island of Jamaica or the mainland of North America where Sir John Colleton was trying to duplicate, at the mouth of the Cape Fear River, Lord Baltimore's prosperous performance on the Chesapeake Bay. If this gigantic African scheme succeeded, the proprietors of the hundred thousand square-mile Carolina realm might hold enemies in restraint and each receive returns approaching in volume those of the second Lord Baltimore from his growing Maryland domain.

Rarely has there been a more comprehensive and complicated economic scheme. If it succeeded, the colonies would suffer and the mother country prosper. Already the Carolina wilderness with perhaps a hundred thousand of the wildest Indians, was being settled by unruly Puritans and Quakers from Virginia and enterprising cattle raisers from New England; and these newcomers were practicing all the freedoms that were denied them under the Clarendon Code—freedom of religion, the right of all men to vote for legislators, free trade with Indians, New Englanders and the Dutch, and what Europe had not known in a thousand years: free lands. About the time the grateful proprietors of Carolina gave the name of the king to their new domain, John Locke, the youthful friend and private secretary to Lord Ashley (Cooper), began to work out a social philosophy for the frontiersmen of the new domain which would bind them to their new masters, satisfy the unhappy victims of the new slave system of the sugar island and the even more unhappy victims of the Clarendon Code in England. There were conflicting ideas and interests everywhere, but the astute Locke was not without success, as we shall see later, and he gradually became a sort of undercover guide to Shaftesbury, Albemarle and the Berkeley, somewhat as the famous Samuel Pepys was to Carteret, Downing and the lords of the navy.

When, therefore, Sir William Berkeley, honored with a proprietorship of Carolina, completely converted to the new economic order, with increasing prestige and two thousand pounds of Dunkirk money in his pocket, set sail for the plantations, the Virginia ideal of free trade and freedom of conscience faded from his mind.[23] Having forgotten his solemn instruction to contend against the "losse of Virginia liberties and oppose the invaders of our freedomes," he would now seek to fit the tobacco growers into the vast colonial autarchy which would give England her mastery of the "Seven Seas," make an end of Spanish dominion in North America, and put the pushy, if wealthy, Dutch traders again behind their sea dikes. And all the troubled Virginia planters and farmers gave their popular Cavalier Governor an enthusiastic welcome when he arrived at little Jamestown in December, 1662, to restore prosperity. Would the great plantation scheme work?

[23] Hening's *Statutes*, II, 17.

10

The First American "Recovery"

"The quantity of tobacco made in this country is become soe great and the value of it is reduced so low that it is most proper to cease planting for one year (1666)."—Hening, II, 224.

I

BEFORE SIR WILLIAM BERKELEY RETURNED IN THE autumn of 1662, Maryland and Virginia, sorely depressed by the closing of continental markets for their tobacco, had endeavored to stabilize their restless communities in contradictory fashions. In Maryland, Governor Josias Fendall, as we have seen, was compelled to surrender his office, and the popular assembly lost its supreme position as a law-making body. Philip Calvert, brother of the proprietor, took over the position and restored the Council to its former position as a little House of Lords; but in 1661 Charles Calvert, son of the proprietor, became governor and made his uncle Philip Secretary of the Council and a sort of director of all the county courts. Both of these men were ardent Catholics. They added other Catholics to the Council and made large grants of land to still other leaders of the same faith, so that a score of lords of manors, many of them kinsmen of the Governor, became the governing clique of Maryland.[1] The more prominent of these favorites of Lord Baltimore were Baker, Brooke, Thomas Gerrard, William Hawley, Richard Keene, James Neale, Henry Sewall and Christopher Rousby. Most of their manors were lo-

[1] Fiske, John, *Old Virginia and her Neighbors*, II, 136.

cated in Saint Mary's and Charles counties. Although Fendall was condemned to death because of his activity against the proprietor, the protest strength of the assembly was such that he was permitted to retire to his great estate in Charles county. However, Calvert and his fellows ordered a little later that only half the representatives of the people should sit at one time in the legislature. Thus fifteen hundred Catholics, acting in concert with the governor and Council, endeavored to govern fifteen thousand Puritans, liberal Catholics, Baptists and Quakers who spoke through the limited assembly. Maryland was about to become what the proprietors had hoped for from the beginning: a mediaeval state with all elements of society subordinated to its master. The young Governor, councillors and sheriffs received ample returns from the poor tobacco growers who sold their crops for a penny a pound, while they lived on estates of five to twenty thousand acres of land each;[2] but there were many free small farmers and frontiersmen always out of control, and never silent. The proprietor now claimed four shillings a year for each hundred acres of land, except from the lords of manors. That was twice as much as Virginia landowners were supposed to pay the King. There were also import and export duties which probably raised the annual income of the third Lord Baltimore in London to £10,000 a year. Although the majority of Marylanders were discontented under this planned Stuart autocracy, they enjoyed something like religious freedom; and since the Navigation and other trade limiting acts were not so easily applied to their exports, there were always chances of selling tobacco at two pennies per pound to Dutch traders who slipped into their harbors and against whom Lord Baltimore and his prosperous son made little resistance. During the two decades following 1660 there was an increasing activity of forbid-

[2] Forman, Henry C., *Early Manors and Plantation Houses of Maryland.*

den Dutch traders and Caribbean pirates in Maryland harbors.

The manorial system, the increasing power of a few great landlords and the influence of the orthodox Catholics seemed to be guaranteed. The majority of the population was thought to be under definite control. Would the planned economic system so carefully worked out at London between 1660 and 1664 be applicable? Certainly the aging Lord Baltimore, his ambitious son Charles, in Saint Mary's, and their Catholic kinsmen in the other counties were working in concert with Sir William Berkeley as he began his operations in Virginia in the winter of 1662.[3]

But before Berkeley began his more difficult task, the acting governor, Francis Moryson, member of the famous Lord Falkland family, and Henry Randolph, the first of that name in all the American plantations, had, under the direction of the House of Burgesses, revised all the statutes of Virginia in such a way as to guarantee the liberties which Richard Bennet and his fellow-workers of 1652 had applied to both the tobacco colonies: free manhood suffrage, the jury system, and the self-perpetuating county courts. The House of Burgesses was to remain the supreme authority. The Governor and council were to continue as a minor house of lords. They might argue and delay matters and submit statutes to the new Council of Trade and Plantations in London, but they were not to veto acts of the assembly. While religious freedom was not guaranteed in Virginia, as in Maryland, the penalties laid upon dissenters were not applied; and there was a local self-government in the so-called established church which continued the semi-religious freedom which had prevailed since 1620.

The little village of Jamestown was still to be the capital. There the representatives from all the counties from

[3] Mereness, Newton D. *Maryland as a Proprietary Province*, gives best account of these efforts.

the far-off Rappahannock region to Lower Norfolk were to meet before planting time in March and after the tobacco harvesting in September. Travel was still very difficult, and sometimes it required a week to ride horseback over the back-country bridle paths above the falls of the rivers and creeks, or row down the stream on which one lived to the Chesapeake Bay and thence up the milewide James River to the capital. The Council was to hold its legislative sessions while the Burgesses were in action; but its judicial sessions were to precede or follow legislative work. This meant that the leading men of the colony, the still unwelcome lawyers, frontier trading folk and even delegations of complaining Indians would assemble twice a year in the little boarding houses of Jamestown or be lodged in farm houses along the river. Greenspring Court, the Governor's mansion four miles out of town, was frequently the meeting place of the Council and general court—a little Hampton Court with a prison and gallows conveniently located.

Thus there was already a somewhat aristocratic society in the oldest of British American colonies. The Governor or members of the Council travelled up and down the James, York and Rappahannock rivers to preside over the self-perpetuating county courts and to assist simple-minded judges in the performances of their judicial functions. But sheriffs here, as in Maryland, were appointed by the governor with informal approval of the Council. These gentlemen planters were still the masters of great tracts of land and modest mansions at strategic points along the rivers from the site of Norfolk of our day to the site of Mount Vernon.[4] The councillors and their fellows were the leaders, but not the absolute masters, of tenants and indentured servants. All the ten or

[4] Nugent, Nell Marion, *Cavaliers and Pioneers,* I, 1623-1666, gives revealing list of land patents and grants.

twelve councillors received £200 a year for their voluntary attendance of conferences at Jamestown, the Governor receiving £1,200, all exempt from taxation. Thomas Ludwell of Jamestown, secretary of the colony, collected many fees and lived quite as handsomely as Philip Calvert of Maryland. On each of the rivers the older councillors were collectors of import and export duties from which considerable personal incomes were derived; and there were abuses on the part of these dignitaries which resembled those of the Maryland lords of manors. The most prominent of these economic leaders of the Stuart era was Captain Thomas Willoughby, who lived on the southern side of the entrance to the Chesapeake Bay and controlled a vast Indian trade. Edmund Scarborough, owner of thousands of acres in Accomac county, where he in war time enjoyed a monopoly of salt-making from sea water, was hardly less powerful than Willoughby. Richard Bennet, still living on the banks of the Nansemond River, was the most powerful of the southside leaders. Further up the James River, on the southside, was the great estate of Nathaniel Bacon, kinsman of the British philosopher. He was a member of the Council from 1660 to 1684, and his modest seventeenth century mansion still stands in the neighborhood of Smithfield. On the site of the famous Westover of the eighteenth century lived the clever councillor, Theodorick Bland, brother of John Bland of London who wrote booklets on free trade and argued with the King himself against the Clarendon-Colbert economic nationalism. He was the first Adam Smith of England. Colonel Abraham Wood, explorer and Indian trader, was still the commander of the frontier militia on the present site of Petersburg, and an occasional attendant of Council meetings. On the northern shore of the York River, where Yorktown now stands, still lived the Puritan ex-governor, Edward Digges, the first scientific agriculturist of all the British colonies;[5] and a few miles northwest of this experimental plantation, near the site of West Point, lived the aged ex-secretary of the Council and sturdy warrior, William Claiborne. Bennet, Bland, Claiborne, Digges and Wood were economic and religious opponents of the new Stuart autocracy, and their influence was too powerful to be ignored by the governor.

On the frontier region along both sides of the Rappahannock there were other interesting planters whose attitudes were friendly but not enthusiastic. Ralph Wormely, long a member of the Council, owned a great estate on the southern bank of the lower Rappahannock, and his beautiful home was, toward the end of the Stuart régime, a second governor's mansion. Near him lived Sir Henry Chicheley, brother of Sir Thomas Chicheley, master of ordnance after 1670 and an intimate of Charles II in London. For twenty-five years Sir Henry was counselor and sometimes acting governor of the colony. Both of these officials were also masters of harbors and collectors of revenue. In the same section, his house fronting one of the navigable inlets of the Chesapeake Bay, lived Richard Lee, founder of one of the most famous of Virginia families. He was a fairly wealthy man and a member of the Council from 1660 to 1664. Of hardly less importance were John Carter and Richard Smith, active assistants of Governor Berkeley, who also held great tracts of land in Lancaster county. On the fertile peninsula between the Rappahannock and the Potomac lived William Fitzhugh, Giles Brent, Margaret Brent, George Mason and John Washington. Fitzhugh was the master of a vast estate, 1670, and a law partner of Giles Brent, former Catholic Governor of Maryland. Margaret, his sister, had, as we know, served for a time as Governor of Mary-

[5] Bruce, *Economic History of Virginia*, I, 365, indicates part of his experiment activity.

THE FIRST AMERICAN "RECOVERY" 189

land; but she had retreated in 1645 to tolerant Virginia where she carried forty indentured servants and became the mistress of a great estate before 1660. Mason and Washington were frontier militia captains who were known throughout the tobacco country for their embittered warfare against the Indians.

One sees that Virginia still bore the character it had developed under the Cromwell régime: the Puritan southside; the more aristocratic planters north of the James and on both sides of the York rivers; and the more vigorous Rappahannock people, famous a hundred years later as the Northern Neck revolutionists. Although there were scores of men who owned ten thousand acres of land, some even twenty thousand, there were no manors or manorial courts or family chapels as in Maryland.[6] The leaders of these sections served as councillors or burgesses, and their experience and interests gave them far more popular authority than the lords of manors enjoyed in Maryland. Although these eminent men enjoyed privileged positions and often exercised decisive influence over county courts and church activities, they are not to be compared with feudal lords in Europe. There were always scores, even hundreds, of smaller landlords in each county who had worked their way up from the status of indentured servants and were rarely submissive to their "superiors."

Under such influences the burgesses, the Council and the acting Governor, Moryson, had decided in 1662 to make all churches more closely fit the British model than had been the practice during the Cromwell decade. The vestries, hitherto elected annually by the members, were henceforth to be self-perpetuating, not unlike the county courts. That is, the vestrymen were thereafter to hold office for life and choose, with the approval of the pastor, new members to fill vacancies as they came. They were

[6] Nugent, Nell M., *Cavaliers and Pioneers.*

also to select two of their numbers to serve indefinitely as wardens, whose business it was to administer church affairs, collect tobacco to pay pastors' salaries, and discipline unruly members or carry their cases to the county courts. Since the bishop of London did not appoint the preachers and the colony did not pay preachers' salaries, the vestrymen were still the guiding authority of each church; and a minister who did not please his church members was apt to lose his income and also his glebe estate. Thus the churches of Virginia, in spite of the new regulations, were much the same as under the Cromwell régime. The pastor's salary was fixed at eighty pounds sterling a year,[7] twice the English rate, and he was to have the same glebe rights as before, and perquisites which gradually merged into the ownership of slaves. However, the preacher was to be paid in tobacco, and when the price was very low his eighty pounds was hardly equal to the Englishman's forty pounds sterling. A minister must preach every Sunday; the Sabbath day was to be observed as in Massachusetts; everybody must meet in church each January 30 to bemoan the terrible crime of beheading his "saintly" Majesty, Charles I; and all must meet again on May 27 to thank God for the restoration of Charles II. If one failed to attend these commemorative services, he must pay a fine of fifty pounds of tobacco for each offense, and a Quaker or a Baptist must pay twenty pounds sterling.[8] A clergyman who married persons without a license was to be fined 10,000 pounds of tobacco; but licenses cost 200 pounds of tobacco, which was to be given to Secretary Ludwell. The preacher was also to receive 200 pounds, the clerk of the county court 50 pounds and the recorder the same amount —500 pounds of tobacco for the privilege of marrying!

---

[7] The amount of salaries to be paid was fixed by the Assembly but collection and payment remained under control of the vestries.
[8] Hening, II, 45-53.

THE FIRST AMERICAN "RECOVERY" 191

And there were similar regulations designed to prevent newcoming freemen or freed indentured servants from settling on other people's land. Quit-rents to his Majesty must be paid promptly, as in Maryland to the proprietor—but this regulation was never strictly enforced in Virginia.[9] Every man must work without wages once a year to build or improve highways. If anyone refused to carry a letter to his neighbor, as it was carried across the colony, he was penalized heavily; and a physician who neglected a patient had to appear before the county court to explain. A woman servant who bore an illegitimate child had to add a year to the period of her indenture. If a servant ran away and was caught it also meant an extra year of work.

Although these measures seem drastic, they were in no sense as severe as European penalties upon serfs and other helpless folk. Neither a "witch" nor a heretic could be put to death in either of the tobacco colonies. But if children were not baptized at proper age, parents were to pay a fine of 2,000 pounds of tobacco; if a woman indulged in gossip about her neighbors she might still be publicly "ducked" in the river or creek nearest to her county court. Untrue gossip meant two "duckings." If five or more Quakers or Baptists met in a private house or barn to worship God their own way, each one was to be fined 200 pounds of tobacco. If these heretics continued their secret worship, and it were discovered, they were to be banished, which meant that more people would be ready to settle on the Albemarle lands of Sir William Berkeley and his fellow-proprietors of Carolina—another parallel to Lord Baltimore's freedom of religion in Maryland. These and other regulations agreed to in the Virginia assembly of 1662 all looked in the direction of a closer social and religious control. However, a law of 1663 reasserted the old claim that a Virginian could not be sued

[9] Bond, Beverley W., *The Quit Rent System* shows this clearly.

in courts for debts due English creditors except for recently imported goods.

The same assembly that enacted all these reforms undertook, before Sir William's return, to remedy the distress of the people due to over-production and the Stuart trade decrees. In the hope of producing silk, every landowner was ordered to plant ten mulberry trees for every hundred acres, heavy fines to be applied for neglect. Every county court must order the people to reduce tobacco plantings, and every farmer must cultivate and harvest two acres of corn or wheat per worker. No one might export wool or hides upon penalties as high as a thousand pounds of tobacco for each offense. And, since the people had largely ceased making their own clothes and shoes during the Cromwell prosperity, women were to be given prizes for the best handmade cloth; and shoemakers were to be awarded similar honors when they produced good shoes.[10] These regulations revealed the willingness of the Virginia population to apply remedies to cure the great depression which followed the Restoration; and in Maryland there were similar, if less comprehensive, acts of recovery—the distress there not so great.

II

With these recovery measures already enacted Sir William Berkeley began his scheme of economic control in December, 1662. The Council and the burgesses seemed to be ready to do anything further which he suggested. They ordered the building of thirty-two brick houses in Jamestown, each of the nineteen counties to build one of the new houses. Well-to-do planters and members of the council and burgesses were persuaded to build houses at their own expense in the little capital or in the neighbor-

[10] Hening, II, 41-124, gives all the statutes bearing on these problems.

Emmett Collection, New York Public Library

EDWARD, EARL OF CLARENDON

hood. All the tobacco produced on both sides of the James River for a distance of forty miles was ordered to be stored in a new warehouse in Jamestown where all ships must sell exports from England and take tobacco in return. Other areas were to be brought under similar control. In addition to the private house building on the part of the well-to-do, there was a general annual tax of thirty pounds of tobacco laid upon each individual. As soon as these recovery measures became effective, towns were to be built in Accomac county, on the lower York, the Rappahannock and Potomac rivers, where all tobacco was to be sold and where ships were to dispose of their cargoes. There were thus to be great warehouses and substantial brick residences in five towns. The two major objectives were recovery from the depression and strict control of commercial relations.

Sir William assumed the rôle of general superintendent of public works and economic recovery. Either in his office in Jamestown or on his Greenspring estate, he showed men how to reconstruct Virginia. He planted two thousand mulberry trees—in accordance with the law of the previous session of the assembly—and imported silkworms in the hope that the tobacco colonists might produce silk for fashionable English folk, and close England to French silks. He also began the planting of flax and hemp. What the governor did every other landlord undertook to do, perhaps with less enthusiasm. While this work went on, Sir William compelled the churches to apply the self-perpetuating system decreed by the assembly of March, 1662, and pressed members of the Council to attend county courts and control the selections of sheriffs who were in Virginia, as similar officials in Maryland, to represent the central authority: an imitation of sheriff control by the Crown in England. The law which compelled all Virginia farmers to report under oath the amounts of tobacco they sold was to be enforced through the sheriffs. The purpose of this stringent measure was to prevent illicit trade with privateer and Dutch ship captains who lingered in Maryland and Virginia harbors.[11] If all these regulations were actually applied, Virginia was expected to become self-supporting, have a smaller annual tobacco output, and the various sections would be brought into complete subordination; and, all the other colonies co-operating, England hoped to erase importing from other nations.

With these basic measures agreed to, the assembly adjourned. Meanwhile Berkeley was making land grants to settlers in the Albemarle region of upper Carolina where some two thousand frontier people were located on small tracts of land, and perhaps a score of more wealthy planters were already the masters of larger estates, strategically located on peninsulas or the higher banks of bays and rivers. There were Puritans, Baptists, Quakers and Church-of-England folk—perhaps a majority without any religious connections at all—scattered over the wild region, engaged in Indian trade and growing tobacco which swift-sailing New England ships carried over the shallow sea entrances to Dutch traders in New Amsterdam. Sir William was acting for the proprietors, to whom the King had granted the vast domain all the way to the Savannah River. The busy Governor appointed his James River friend, William Drummond, a cultured liberal of Cromwellian tendencies, to the governorship of the new settlement.[12] While he pressed his recovery programme in the spring of 1663 he boldly announced that there were to be no more elections of members of the burgesses except for the filling of vacancies, and called the assembly into session, after the manner of Charles I, early in September. He and Charles Calvert were convinced then that they could limit or even forbid the planting of tobacco in

[11] Hening, II, 176.
[12] Ashe, Samuel, *History of North Carolina* I, pp. 64 and 69.

THE FIRST AMERICAN "RECOVERY" 195

both colonies for the year 1664. But the assembly had hardly begun its work before an indentured servant, Berkenhead by name, in Gloucester county, reported a planned uprising aimed at the overthrow of the new Berkeley régime. The assembly, attended by the foremost planters of the colony, Bacon, Bennet, Bland, Chicheley and Wormeley of the council, and William Claiborne, Robert Ellyson, Gerard Fowke and Peter Jennings of the burgesses, was greatly excited. It freed Berkenhead, gave him ample reward for revealing names of people engaged in the conspiracy and hastened him and colony officials off to Gloucester county where several people were caught, condemned, their bodies quartered and their heads put upon chimney tops to warn men against further opposition. The conspirators were denounced as wicked Cromwellians.[13] A few new statutes were passed tending to stiffen the control of the people; and at the end, Henry Corbyn, Thomas Ludwell and others were commissioned to meet Philip Calvert and Henry Sewall of Maryland to agree upon an order approved by Charles II for suspending tobacco planting; and both colonies agreed as a result of their conferences to forbid tobacco growing the next year.

While the Governor of Virginia received a handsome salary, was the owner of great tracts of land on the Rappahannock and in Lower Norfolk county, expected profits from Carolina, and was becoming the dictator of his forty thousand fellow-farmers, there was another element in the new colonial picture which needs to be reviewed if one would understand the plantation problem. In Jamaica and Barbados sugar prices had fallen so low that hundreds of small farmers and thousands of tenants were giving up their homes and begging to be transferred to unsettled areas where hunting and fishing might prevent starvation. Since transfers could not be promptly

[13] Bruce, Philip A., *Economic History of Virginia* II, 29-31.

made, many of these desperate folk joined the pirates of the Caribbean region and began to prey upon the commerce of the central Atlantic.[14] But Francis Lord Willoughby of the great Parham speculative family of England, owner of a huge area of land in present-day Venezuela and master of the sugar island of Santa Lucia, was Governor of Barbados and commissioned to do there what Berkeley was to do in Virginia. His task was to restore prosperity to islands on which there had been a score of millionaires, in our money, under the Cromwell free trade régime, islands that had yielded taxes to the British treasury of £200,000 in 1659 and where Chesapeake Bay farmers had sold barrel staves and foodstuffs at profitable prices. But there was to be no more free trade. The sugar merchants in London, Plymouth and Bristol, like the tobacco importers of the same cities, had set up a monopoly and hence were able to sell refined sugar to English consumers at prices ten times as high as they paid the West Indian planters, who received less than the cost of production. Whatever surplus there was at the end of each year was "dumped" to the continent at whatever return could be had. The men who controlled the Jamaica-Barbados region were, as we have already seen, members of the Council of Trade and Plantations, the Privy Council of the King, the new African Slave Company and proprietors of the Carolina realm. The Duke of Albemarle, Sir George Carteret, the Earl of Clarendon, Ashley Lord Cooper, Martin Noell and Thomas Povey, the last two not of the council, played the most important rôles.[15]

Jamaica was to have been restored to Spain by Charles II in return for the assistance which he had received when he regained the throne. The Earl of Arlington had negotiated the treaty in which this was promised, but neither

---

[14] *State Papers,* September 9 and November 4, 1663.
[15] Cruikshank, Brig. Gen. E. A., *The Life of Sir Henry Morgan.*

he nor other members of the governing group were embarrassed when this promise was ignored and Jamaica was made the trade center of the reformed plantation system. Sir Thomas Modyford, named in a previous chapter, was about to become Governor of the island. The homeless Barbadians were to have there 400,000 acres of land, free trade for a time and freedom of religion; and unemployed Irish folk were to be sold to newcomers on terms of five to seven years service, the same opportunity the unemployed had received in all other colonies. Jamaica was to be the distributing centre for African slaves; it was to have a post office for all the colonies; and the first bank of all the American settlements was to be set up at Port Royal, the emerging capital.[16] While some of these measures were not immediately applied, Governor Modyford and Henry Morgan, soon to become the greatest of West Indian pirates, drew all kinds of people to the island and in a few years gave it the greatest reputation of all the plantations south of Virginia. It was ten times as large as Barbados. But the complex Stuart economic and plantation recovery scheme could not be made successful unless two other items of the programme were applied: the Dutch settlements on the Hudson River must be annexed and their profitable slave trade between West Africa and the Caribbean settlements, Spanish as well as French and English, must be seized. This of course would mean war. And war might defeat the whole colonial programme.

While the Governors of Maryland and Virginia applied their agricultural control, and the Governors of Barbados and Jamaica tried to work out their recovery and forbade popular elections of new assemblies, thus modelling the sugar and tobacco settlements after the Long Parliament of Charles II, George Downing, interested in the Royal African Company and still ambassador

---

[16] *State Papers,* February 18, May 10 and 23, 1664 and later dates give interesting pictures of this hopeful relief settlement.

THE OLD SOUTH

to Holland, now demanded British access to the Dutch slave zone of Africa.[17] Jean de Witt and the Netherlands assembly refused all concessions. Hence in October, 1663, Captain Robert Holmes, a second Sir Francis Drake, sailed to the coast of Africa with a fleet of a dozen vessels. He took possession of the island of Goree and other strategic posts along the coast from which his lieutenants proceeded into the Negro country to capture and purchase slaves for the West Indian markets to take the place of the poor white workers. Early in 1664, as Holmes' ships sailed away to Barbados with their shrieking slaves, the great Dutch Admiral, Michael de Ruyter, appeared off the coast of Africa, recaptured the Dutch slave trading posts and all but ruined the new British Slave Company. Meanwhile, the Duke of York had authorized Colonel Richard Nicholls and Sir George Carteret [18] to take three warships, with three hundred men, into the eastern end of Long Island Sound and there negotiate with Governor John Winthrop of Connecticut, son of the great Massachusetts Puritan and cousin of George Downing, for the assistance of 1,300 New England militia with whom he would move upon New Amsterdam, the Dutch authorities at home busy with their slave trade defense in West Africa. On August 19, 1664, Governor Peter Stuyvesant surrendered the strategic Dutch region under protest against such an act in time of peace. The Duke of York retained the Hudson River area for himself, gave it his name and presented the New Jersey country to his friends, John Lord Berkeley and Sir George Carteret. This meant an Indian trade for the Duke of York which amounted to £10,000 a year, and it stopped the illicit sales of Maryland tobacco to the New Amsterdam merchants. The eastern area of North America from Nova Scotia to Florida

---

[17] See preceding chapter, pp. 19-20.
[18] The *Diary* of Samuel Pepys gives interesting views of this richest man of England, especially entries of July 4, 1663, and April 12, 1667.

was now in English possession.[19] These performances: the attack of Captain Holmes on West Africa and the seizure of New Amsterdam, caused the outbreak of the second English-Dutch war in the winter of 1665. And in the spring of the same year, the great Admiral de Ruyter sailed for Barbados where he destroyed a score of British ships, took shiploads of slaves to the Spanish colonies, and then brought the European war into the mouth of the James, where Colonel Richard Bennet raised a regiment of militia and checked the depredations of the Dutch sailors—representatives of the very free trade which Bennet advocated all his life. After lingering a while in the Chesapeake Bay, perhaps loading tobacco in the holds of some of his ships, the Admiral moved upon New York in the hope of restoring the strategic colony to his own people. Somehow he learned of the war bitterly waging in the North Sea. He hurried *via* Newfoundland to the west coast of Norway where he heard of the horrors of the struggle and slipped cleverly on August 6 into the mouth of the Ems River: the plantations were free for a time. There had been terrible fighting on the North Sea all summer; but even worse was the poor man's plague which had devastated London at the rate of five thousand deaths a week and spread quickly into Amsterdam and the Hague. The two greatest commercial countries in the world seemed on the verge of collapse—would war go on?

While Sir William Berkeley, Charles Calvert and their divided peoples pressed their first recovery experiments in 1664, they learned that Lord Baltimore had forbidden his Marylanders to limit their planting—loyal as he proclaimed himself to Charles II. So their first recovery scheme was defeated. Then came the news of the fall of New Amsterdam, the story of Captain Holmes and finally

[19] Trevelyan, G. M., *England under the Stuarts* gives excellent map of the Stuart North America.

the actual invasion of Admiral de Ruyter and the active resistance of Richard Bennet. Would the Chesapeake Bay become a Dutch possession? There would be no need of limiting tobacco crops in that case for some time to come; but the great Admiral had hurried across the Atlantic, as we have noted, and the next English news was the story of Dutch defeat—followed by the sad picture of the London plague of 1665. England seemed to be in as bad a plight as when Charles I lost so many battles in 1644; and Holland was in no better condition.

However, Louis XIV, thinking it a good time to subordinate the English people, had authorized his fleet to assist the Dutch. The Earl of Albemarle, just appointed Admiral, hastened the famous Prince Rupert, with twenty warships, off to engage the French while he attacked de Ruyter. It was June 1, 1666, second year of the great war. A terrific four-day battle followed, the English losing seventeen of their warships and 8,000 men killed or captured. The Dutch lost 2,000 men and four ships. Sir William Berkeley's nephew and three other Admirals were killed. Albemarle's prestige was broken; and it looked as if de Ruyter had broken the British sea power. Louis XIV sent expressions of admiration to the Dutch commander.[20] Joost Vandel, the greatest Netherlands poet of the time, wrote:

> Christendom by God's blessings rare.
> Henceforth must all your fleets be free
> On every coast, from east to west,
> Thus quench this fury waterpest,
> Hell's serpent out of British sloughs.

There was, however, one more desperate conflict in August, 1666, and Admiral de Ruyter was compelled to retreat hastily into the poverty-stricken harbors of his

[20] Grinnell, Milne G., *Life of Admiral de Ruyter*, 122-133; also Mahan, A. T., *Influence of Sea Power in History*.

own country—the Earl of Albemarle again master of the Seven Seas! His bankrupt Majesty had hardly ceased rejoicing at this victory when the greatest fire known to English history raged four whole days in London. Was the Almighty visiting his wrath upon the King, his mistresses and the corrupt favorites of the Restoration? Many people in New England, the tobacco region, and the West Indies asked this question in the winter of 1666 and 1667; and half of England was of similar mind.

Before the Virginians learned of the unexpected victory of England in the summer of 1667, there came a terrific hail storm, described in Chapter I, which did immense damage to the greatest tobacco crop ever planted; but late in August a cyclone of wind and rain of immense weight and speed swept first from the northeast, then from the west, and finally from the southeast. The rivers rose to unprecedented heights and swept over all the valleys toward the Chesapeake Bay, doing more damage than the former hail storm; but when the wind and rain shifted to the southeast, the waters of the Bay rolled up the rivers and over the valleys and destroyed thousands of houses, throwing vessels that had been left in the harbors upon high land. Two-thirds of the tobacco crop was destroyed, corn and wheat ruined, and the people were threatened with starvation. It was the worst of Virginia calamities since the Indian war of 1644; and the whole world was in tragic plight,[21] another war for economic control!

While British public opinion was so despondent, and the colonists from Barbados to Maryland wondered whether there would ever be a better time, Louis XIV, whom all Europe began to fear, coaxed Charles II and his "cabal" to begin peace negotiations at Breda; and to complete the pressure, Jean de Witt joined the aged de Ruyter and sailed once more with a sizeable fleet into the Thames, destroying British war vessels, many of whose

[21] Bruce, I, 395.

officers and sailors had refused to fight because their wages remained unpaid. London seemed once more to be doomed, the people fleeing again to country districts. Would there be a Dutch William the Conqueror? It was at this most depressed moment that Sir George Carteret loaned the helpless Charles II £280,000; the sailors went to their posts again and de Ruyter was unable to force the surrender of the devastated British capital. Although the French dictator was counted a friend of the Netherlands, the Peace of Breda, 1667, guaranteed to defeated England all the islands and mainland of North America which she had claimed or seized since Cromwell came to power, left her Far East possessions untouched, and did not deny her claim as mistress of the Seven Seas.[22] It was plain that the French monarch was counting on British assistance in his coming campaign for the annexation of the Spanish Netherlands, the seizure of western Germany and the domination of Spain and her vast American holdings. Two of the greatest French military men before Napoleon I, Louis Condé and Henri Turenne, were organizing and equipping a vast army for the planned campaign as soon as Charles II was ready to give naval assistance. France was to dominate Europe and South America; and England, if she became Catholic, was to dominate North America!

III

The New England and the tobacco colonists were more than half aware of the dangerous European drift. They were, however, seeking escape from their own troubles. Sir William was still granting tracts of land to dissenters in upper Carolina; and when his friend, Drummond, gave up his governorship of unruly Albemarle, he ap-

[22] Trevelyan, George M., *England under the Stuarts*, 356-58.

pointed another personal friend, Samuel Stephens, to the same post and lent all possible aid in developing the new colony. New Englanders were shipping tobacco and deerskins out of the settlements at more profitable rates than others. And when the new Governor died, in 1669, Sir William hastened to marry the distressed widow, Frances, of the well-known Culpeper family, in a few months; Berkeley thus became the master of other improved areas of Carolina land. Within a few months (1670), he urged his friend, the Earl of Arlington, to appoint his wife's kinsman, Alexander Culpeper, surveyor-general of all the lands of Virginia and upper Carolina. This brought a new figure into Virginia history, Thomas Lord Culpeper, a brother of Alexander, who had been removed from the governorship of the Isle of Wight in 1669 because of his parading a new mistress about the island, leaving his famous and disgusted wife at Leeds Castle, Kent County, England. Charles II had promised Lord Thomas £12,000 for his father's helping him back to the throne in 1660; and a year after Sir William's favorite was appointed to the Virginia surveyor-general's office, Lord Thomas was promised the governorship of Virginia and made lord proprietor, with the Earl of Arlington, of the Northern Neck.[23] It was too much favoritism even for Sir William, who was not quite ready to die.

Nor was this all. Governor Modyford of Jamaica, Sir John Yeamans of Barbados, and John Vassall of New England had been most busy during the Dutch war trying to locate helpless West Indian whites and active New Englanders into another area of Carolina—the Cape Fear valley, where Indian trade and cattle raising were most promising. And of course English, Dutch and French privateers and pirates were busy all the while carrying sugar and tobacco to Europe, delivering slaves to Barbados and the Spanish mainland, and on every pos-

[23] *State Papers, Colonial,* June 26, 1671.

sible occasion seizing ships of any nation with Mexican gold or silver in their holds. There was intense piratical activity under the screened stimulation of the Governor of Jamaica and the active leadership of Henry Morgan. Nor was there real opposition in the harbors of New England or the Chesapeake Bay. Men were trying everywhere to make money, and Barbados alone shipped £800,000 worth of sugar a year to England; the local tax of 4½% and the tax at English ports was three times as much.[24] Jamaica was hardly less successful, distributing slaves for the African Company, producing moderate quantities of sugar and shipping logwood from Yucatan to Europe, where there were half-free markets for this new kind of wood. The Virginia tobacco planters yielded the King a tax income of more than £100,000 a year, and Lord Baltimore received a proportionate amount. But only a few of the larger slaveholders of the sugar colonies and some of the land speculators of the Chesapeake Bay settlements were fairly prosperous, a prosperity which was probably due to illicit trade in war time. Although the Virginia burgesses had voted Sir William 45,000 pounds of tobacco a year to maintain a personal, uniformed guard to protect him against expected attacks, the same burgesses continued to insist upon their absolute and unlimited right to levy taxes. The increasing number of self-made planters who figured in the House of Burgesses added constantly to the suppressed opposition to the Governor. Moreover, the growing dislike of the self-perpetuating Long Parliament and the continued imprisonment, even execution, of dissenting preachers in England increased emigration to Virginia and caused people in the county courts to jeer the name of Charles II and clamor for the right to elect new burgesses. In the hope of subordinating his opponents, Sir William and the Council induced the burgesses to enact a

[24] *State Papers, Colonial,* April 20, 1671.

law in the autumn of 1670 which limited the suffrage in elections to fill vacancies, to men who owned land or had a fixed income. While the terms of the law were rather easy to meet, it was the first denial of manhood suffrage in either of the tobacco colonies. And at the same time, Charles Calvert and his Catholic lords of manors were so afraid of opposition in Maryland that they allowed no meeting of their assembly during the period of 1666 to 1669. When the unruly Maryland assembly men sat down together in 1669, they lowered taxes and tried to limit the profits of the Governor and his Lordship in London; they allowed a dissenting preacher member to denounce the Governor and Council, and then adjourned presenting a list of grievances against their lordships. The delegates were forbidden to re-assemble; but when the election of 1670 was ordered, the Virginia example was imitated: no Marylander might cast a vote unless he could prove that he owned fifty acres of land or a visible property worth £40. This was a plain violation of the Maryland charter, and it was done simply on the Governor's order. There can hardly be a doubt that these limitations were bitterly resented in both colonies, yet they became the fixed practices of Maryland and Virginia for a hundred years to come. It looked as if Sir William, with his uniformed guardsmen about him, and Charles Calvert, with the support of his lords of manors, were fixed masters of the two colonies that were destined to play great rôles in American history.[25]

But European behavior again disturbed all the planter colonies. In 1667 Charles II had caused the Earl of Clarendon to be tried for treason because the Dutch war, which he had opposed, had been so terrible. Instead of executing the greatest of his Restoration friends and managers, the King allowed him to spend the rest of

[25] Mereness, *Maryland as a Proprietary Province*, Chapter II, and Hening's *Statutes*, II, 280.

his days in exile.[26] In 1670 Charles entered into a secret treaty with Louis XIV to aid him in his great campaign against the rest of Europe. The English monarch was to receive about £150,000 a year and 6,000 French troops in case of a Protestant uprising; and both Charles and the Duke of York were in due time to become Catholics. Europe was to fall under the sway of Louis XIV and accept again the Catholic religion—though no one could call any one of the three monarchs a Christian. While this treaty was entirely secret, its main items leaked out, and the privy council was superseded by a little group of royal intimates of whom Lord Ashley was the cleverest statesman. This friend and patron of John Locke, ignorant of the King's promises to Louis XIV, worked his way to the position of prime minister, although he remained chairman of the Board of Trade and Plantations and was busy all the while with the sugar and tobacco colonies and expanding the new Carolina domain. He became the Earl of Shaftesbury in 1672 and, being a bitter enemy of the Netherlands, he was ready to go to war for Louis XIV! He even went so far as to cry aloud in the House of Lords: "delenda est Carthago" (the Netherlands).

When the last great Dutch war broke in 1672, the tobacco and the sugar planters of America were by no means ready to see Louis XIV destroy the Netherlands. Yet Dutch war vessels entered the Chesapeake Bay again and destroyed what vessels they could find; in 1673 there was another attack, and, moving northward, the story came back that New York was again New Amsterdam. The prospect of England's defeat was good, and the Virginians were inclined to welcome the event. The King sent Sir John Knight, of the navy, to the West Indies

---

[26] The next year the great Earl of Albemarle passed away; it was in 1669, Sir George Carteret was condemned by the House of Commons for corrupt practices.

and the Chesapeake Bay to ascertain whether the colonists were about to revolt. He reported:[27] "The people say openly that they are in the nature of slaves, so that the hearts of the greatest part of them are taken away from His Majesty, and His Majesty's best, greatest and richest plantation is in danger, with the planters' consent, to fall into the enemy's hands." This was true of New England, the Chesapeake Bay and Barbados. If the war, almost as terrible as that of 1666 to 1668, continued another year, all the colonists might actually revolt. The Stuart system was immensely unpopular—in spite of all promises, there had been no "recovery" during the twelve years of dictatorship. The Americans longed for the Dutch freedom of trade and dreaded the danger of Louis XIV's dominating all Europe, though they hardly wished annexation to another country.

[27] *State Papers, Colonial,* October 29, 1673.

11

The Albemarle Overflow

"For the persons that at present designe thither expect liberty of conscience and without that will not goe."—
Sir John Colleton to the Duke of Albemarle, 10 June 1663.

I

THE VIRGINIANS HAD NOT CONCLUDED THE FIRST phase of the controversy with the Marylanders before their more enterprising and restless souls explored the wild and tangled region which Armadas and Barlow had pronounced as of "so strong a smel as if we had been in some delicate garden." These eager people entertained the vague hope of discovering some of the hundred and eight members of Sir Walter Raleigh's lost colony of 1587; and they also hankered for the profits which any traveller might make by the trading of trinkets with the curious natives camped about favorite fishing and hunting grounds south of the "dismal" swamp. It was a maze of bays, inlets and meandering rivers, bearing the Indian names of Chowan, Pasquotank and Perquimans; and there were wonderful necks and marsh-screened promontories on the banks of the rivers fit for the establishment of mediaeval manors. Moreover, there was the romantic lure five hundred miles further southwest of powerful tribes supposed to carry supplies of gold and silver to the Spaniards at Saint Augustine. One might at any time discover a gold mine!

It is not surprising then that Sir John Harvey, the unwelcome governor of Virginia, should have offered a patent from his royal Majesty to Henry Lord Maltravers of East Greenwich manor, England, and urged him in the spring of 1637 to assume the neglected rôle of Sir Robert Heath and thus found a palatinate on the southern border of Virginia. Such a venture, if successful, would pre-empt the region against the French and the Spanish as Baltimore's work was barring the way of the Dutch settlements on the Delaware. But the bitter struggle between the Crown and the turbulent leaders of the House of Commons in London defeated for two decades whatever efforts Sir John Harvey and Lord Maltravers may have directed toward the occupation of the southern wilderness. And, as so often happened in the later development of the United States, restless border people and poverty-stricken farmers, without the help of government, contrary to law and at the risk of Indian attack, "squatted" upon the fertile necks and peninsulas of the southern rivers, built themselves cabins, opened a few acres of land, planted Indian corn and turned their cows and swine into the woods. At the very moment the Virginia borderers began to occupy the lands beyond the headwaters of the Nansemond, the new Dutch republic finished breaking the monopoly of the Spanish empire over the South Atlantic, proclaimed again universal free trade and increased their operations in every West Indian port. They were ready to give twice as much for tobacco as the English had been paying; they took pork and venison and lumber to Barbados; and because of the civil war in England they gave evidence of a new era of prosperity. It was not the sixteenth century flood of Spanish gold; it was a new and free commercial era.

Nor was the Virginia situation unfavorable. Edward Bland of the Bland reservation on the south side of the James River and Theodoric Bland of Westover were but kinsmen and representatives of John Bland, the great free trade advocate of London. All of these leaders took increasing interest in the development of what was soon called the Carolina country. Richard Bennet, soon to become Commonwealth governor at Jamestown, was of the same party. These men proclaimed the right of self-government, freedom of conscience, free trade with the world "as Englishmen have enjoyed," and the right to bargain with Indians for land and thus escape the payment of quit-rents: the land belonged to him who improved it. Nor were the Blands alone in the movement. Thomas Willoughby of Willoughby's Point, kinsman of Lord Willoughby of Parham, and Francis Yeardley of Cape Charles, both crossing the ocean frequently to sell their cargoes, were ready to pay good money for pork, bear and beaver skins. What these great folk forwarded smaller men pursued with similar zest. In 1652 Roger Green, a "clarke," undertook to seat a hundred men on the banks of the Chowan and received a promise of a thousand acres of land. The next year Yeardley, having heard a marvellous story of the remains of Sir Walter Raleigh's colony,

> dispatched a boat with six hands to build the [Indian] king an English house, and two hundred sterling with which [in a little while] they effected and purchased and paid for three great rivers and in solemn manner took possession of the country.[1]

With these enterprising chiefs still another leader, later of decisive influence in shaping the course of Carolina history, associated himself. I refer to George Durant of Northampton county, some twenty-five years old and son of the vigorous William Durant described in the preceding chapter, when he began to traverse the new domain in search of eligible sites for homes of Virginia emigrants who found the older colonies on the Chesapeake Bay stifling to their sense of liberty and equality.

[1] Saunders, William L., *The Colonial Records of North Carolina*, I, 18, hereafter cited as *Colonial Records*.

Married to Ann Marwood of Virginia, and already acquainted with the marvels of Carolina, George Durant moved in 1659 to a projecting peninsula on the Chowan River which was known thereafter as Durant's Neck and was the centre of liberal and even radical social teaching and example the next half a century.[2] It was but a little while before his friends, George Catchmaid, John Harvey and John Jenkins, joined him and, with their increasing neighbors, composed the dominant element in the new society.

It was the period of Dutch prosperity in Barbados and Jamaica where some hundreds of sugar planters had become dominating masters. These new-made rich men, led by Daniel Searles and James Modyford, were now demanding freedom of conscience, self-government and freedom of trade with all the world. Oliver Cromwell and his merchant friends were not a little embarrassed lest the overseas settlements get entirely out of hand. But he was too busy with Europe to send great fleets to America; and entrepreneurs were everywhere active. Francis Lord Willoughby, Sir John Colleton, and Sir George Carteret were investing their means in sugar plantations in the West Indies, sending trading outfits to Africa and offering freedom to their emigrants. Virginia was a commonwealth and, just before Cromwell's death, Barbados received a charter of self-government. Why might not the venturesome settlers on the Chowan River set their own political patterns?[3]

And that was what they were doing. The newcomers seized lands and then made bargains with the natives. They brought servants after the usual manner, agreeing to set them free a few years later, each with two suits of clothes, a few tools, a cow, some pigs and fifty acres of

[2] Samuel Ashe, *Biographical History of North Carolina*, I, 257, gives a somewhat different story.
[3] Harlow, *Barbados*, Ch. III.

land, no quit-rents to the crown, no two-shilling export tax on tobacco. There was no church to define good conduct or say whether servants or free people should marry. Since there was no minister, two witnesses before a substantial citizen of the little republic was sufficient to regularize the marriage relation; and there was no ten or twenty-shilling minister's fee. Children needed not to be baptized and the dead people were buried on convenient hilltops. Men of Quaker or dissenter emotions built log cabins or made bush arbors and there prayed in silence or read from the Bible such passages as fitted their theories of life. It was a sheltered if ill-governed community. The wide stretch of swamp and inaccessible pine land barred the constable and the tax gatherer from Virginia; the Tuscarora Indians to the southwest, so long as they were friendly, protected the settlement from sudden invasion. The shallow calm waters of the great bay enabled venturesome New England or Dutch small craft to take away the products of their labor. The promise was too good to be true.[4]

II

The story of the resignation of Richard Cromwell had hardly reached the Carolina frontier before the news of the return of Charles II to Whitehall was reported. The Virginia royalists were about to regain control at Jamestown. These were ominous facts for the idealists of the mid-seventeenth century. There was consternation in Massachusetts. In Maryland, as we have seen, the representatives of the people united with Josias Fendall, the governor, to overthrow the proprietor and rewrite the Maryland constitution—without real punishment when the movement failed; and Sir William Berkeley reas-

[4] R. D. W. Connor, *History of North Carolina,* I, Chapter III.

sumed the governorship of Virginia on condition that he hold the office as a gift of the people. James Modyford, recently installed as elective head of Barbados, yielded to the Stuart restoration with great reluctance; nor did the thriving slave traders in Jamaica willingly surrender to the appointees of the new régime in London. In all the West Indian settlements, as on the mainland of the continent, the more idealistic tenets of the early Cromwellian movement had become second nature. Would Charles II intervene?

The answer was to be given by Sir William Berkeley, who returned to England in the early summer of 1661, as we have seen in Chapter VIII, and there argued rather gently for the Virginia policy of free trade. London offered a strange atmosphere: the royal household, the great merchants of London and the heads of great county families were uniting in a far-reaching speculation which, as we shall see, involved the defeat of Jean and Pierre de Witt and their great mercantile party of Amsterdam, the capture of the Dutch African slave trade and the strictest subordination of all the American plantations to a new British mercantile system. When Sir William returned to Jamestown in the autumn of 1662, he was one of the group of famous lords and earls to whom the Sir Robert Heath domain was to be formally granted the next year as a palatinate;[5] he was the official spokesman of the proprietors to the Carolina freemen. Berkeley was a convert to the new British imperialism. As soon as the governor had pressed through the burgesses at Jamestown a curious building programme to relieve the terrible depression which had followed the Restoration, he turned to the larger plan of regulating the production of tobacco in Maryland and Virginia; he then endeavored to enforce

[5] The chiefs of these proprietors were the men who had restored Charles II to the throne: Ashley Cooper, later the famous Earl of Shaftesbury; Edward Hyde, already Earl of Clarendon; George Monck, Earl of Albemarle; Lord John and Sir William Berkeley, brothers.

the law against dissenters and to expel even eminent Quakers of the south side. This increased the number of emigrants to the no man's land over which he was to rule as a deputy proprietor. Thus strenuous orthodoxy in Virginia would increase the Governor's power and profits as one of the lords of Carolina. In the autumn of 1664, as already noted, he journeyed across the swamps to the Chowan settlements with authority to settle and regulate the affairs of the colony.

Much as Sir William liked to govern by decree, he was bound by the instructions which his Majesty had issued upon the advice of all who hoped to make the new settlements successful. There was to be a governor and a group of six councillors. The freeholders were to choose two representatives for each tribe or parish "to make their own laws, so as they be not repugnant to the laws of England." The freeholders who paid their own fare to the new colony were each to receive a hundred acres of land in free and common socage. Man-servants who were carried into the new country were at the close of their indentures to receive thirty acres of land and become freemen; women were to receive smaller portions. All masters and servants were to have their lands free of quit-rents for five years. These were to be the terms for newcomers as prescribed by the lords proprietors under their first charter. The settlers who, like George Durant, had already seized or bought lands from the natives, must take out new titles and adjust their claims as best they might to the clauses of the new constitution, paying small fees for the services of surveyors and neighborhood clerks. If the governor and council met with the representatives of the freemen and enacted laws for their own guidance and social betterment, these laws were to apply one year without question and become invalid only upon veto of the proprietors in London.[6] Such an assembly as could thus be brought to-

[6] *Colonial Records,* I, 24-26, 34.

THE ALBEMARLE OVERFLOW 215

gether in Carolina would inevitably assume authority to govern and tax themselves as they saw fit.

Under these circumstances, Sir William Berkeley appointed the liberal-minded tobacco planter, William Drummond, a Scotchman who lived on the north bank of the James River, as Governor of Carolina, henceforth called Albemarle, for a term of three years. It was not an unfit appointment, for he was deeply interested and was in full sympathy with the local planter-farmer community. The area of the Albemarle country was now roughly described as forty square miles on both sides of the sound, extending as far west as the mouth of the Roanoke River. Durant, Catchmaid and the other leaders who had been on the ground four or five years participated in the little government as councillors; and all the freemen sat in the first meetings of the assembly. It was a pure democracy for many years. Berkeley made no effort to organize a church or to regularize men's social behavior or to lay taxes on imports or exports. There was a single county the first five years, with the usual county court and clerk. Thomas Woodward, well-known to Charles II, and whose son, John, was to be a prominent officer in the British service, was appointed surveyor-general, and he sent assistants into the wilderness to step off tracts of land for newcomers and measure ten to thirty acre strips for indentured servants at the expiration of their terms.[7]

Sir William Berkeley officially dissolved all connection with Virginia, but retained a lively sense of his part in the new palatinate with beginnings already making at the Cape Fear River and far-reaching schemes taking form in the minds of Sir John Colleton of Barbados and Sir Peter Colleton, an even greater figure in London, men who had probably spent many hundred pounds in exploring and advertising the Carolina country. But in spite of

[7] *State Papers, Colonial*, V, 187, 1005.

the high hopes of great men, the dissatisfied and distressed farmers of the Chesapeake region did not hasten across the borders to take up lands and begin to grow tobacco. The new regulations discouraged them. The Barbadian farmers, so rapidly crowded out of their holdings by the pressure of the new slave system, did not seek homesteads in Albemarle. Abemarle, Clarendon and Ashley Cooper, with vast holdings in the West and ships engaged in the sugar and trade, were disappointed. Thomas Woodward, the wise surveyor-general, diagnosed the case:[8]

> Sir Francis Bacon says planting of counties is like planting of woods, you must count on losing your profits for twenty years; the principall thing in the ruin of plantations hath been the hastee drawing of profit in the first yeares.

Judging from the great philosopher's statement, Woodward urged that the possession of land was the only objective of Albemarle's immigrants, and that the laws and practices of Virginia and Maryland gave prospective settlers better terms than Sir William offered in the new and isolated country. George Monck was about to have his name perpetuated for hundreds of years in the new country; but the unruly democracy on the banks of Albemarle Sound required conciliation if he and his heirs were ever to receive any profit.

III

Before the Albemarle problem approached a solution, some New England explorers and traders seized lands near the mouth of the Cape Fear River about half-way between Virginia and the Spanish claims on the Saint

[8] *Colonial Records,* I, 99-101.

Johns River. It was a promising region. The climate was so mild that cattle might range the forest unprotected during the winter. There were swamps and marshes in which grass and reeds remained green throughout the year; some of these were huge peninsulas that might be fenced off at little expense; and there was a large island, in the middle of the river, some twenty miles from the coast. There were small tribes of natives, offshoots of the Cherokees from the west, Saponas who lived some miles up the river and the Yamasees who had strayed away from the great southern tribe of the same name. These Indians offered a fair trade in skins and, on occasion, a pious New Englander might seize a few of the older children and sell them for slaves in Jamaica or Barbados where they might memorize the shorter Catechism.[9] Hence in 1660, the easterners made a small settlement near the mouth of the river, fenced off some peninsulas of land, put neat cattle and hogs into the woods and began to rive staves for the sugar planters as well as to cut choice timber for West Indian markets. But the New Englanders had no more than made a beginning before the restoration of Charles II. Under the new dispensation, Governor John Modyford and John Yeamans of Barbados, more interested here than on the Albemarle Sound, organized a movement looking toward the development of this middle portion of the great Heath domain. For reasons not quite clear, the New England settlers abandoned their venture, left their cattle in the swamps and warned people against an attempt to live in the country. It was here, as elsewhere, a time of serious economic distress. The price of sugar had fallen to one-fourth its former value and cattle were hardly worth slaughtering. Barbados was perhaps in the worse plight of all the colonies. Their poor whites were without employment and not unwilling to venture into the mainland wilderness, two

[9] Ashe, *History of North Carolina*, I, 76-77.

thousand miles away, in preference to starvation on their wonderful island.

In London there was increasing enthusiasm for colonial empire, and the reports of the Barbadians led the new proprietors of the Heath domain to issue propositions to Thomas Modyford, still governor of Jamaica, and Sir Peter Colleton, one of the most enthusiastic of the West Indian adventurers, similar to those that were sent to the Albemarle people; it was a new land of promise. But the proprietors still wished to maintain effective control.[10]

> Some people here [London] propose that we shall make choice of a governor without their [the colonists] consent; if your people desire the like, it shall be done; more freedom than this [the same as that of Albemarle] we can not give.

It was the same story everywhere: independence, political, religious and economic, save for the mere matter of the governship, else emigrants could not be induced to take the risks involved. But Henry Vassall, of whom we know too little, was urging the New England claims in London while his brother John, a most enterprising commercialist, labored in Jamaica and Virginia for the same cause. There was, in consequence, something of a compromise between these interests in 1664, and the Cape Fear venture was renewed. A great country was pre-empted on both sides of the river, renamed in honor of the king, and John Yeamans, then Sir John, was appointed Governor at the same time Berkeley commissioned Drummond head of the Albemarle country. John Vassall was made surveyor-general while Henry Vassall continued to represent the interests of the colony in London.[11] Robert Sanford was to keep the records and collect the fees that multitudes of newcomers were expected to pay. The new region

---
[10] *Colonial Records*, I, 47.
[11] *Dictionary of American Biography.*

was to be known as Clarendon county in honor of the great and somewhat liberal chancellor and historian then trying to unite cavaliers and commercialists in support of the new Stuart mercantile system. The county was to embrace a thousand square miles of swamp and pine forest. Advertisements were published in London and hundreds of emigrants were reported as hastening to the new land of promise. At last the Governor gathered a council about him in the Carolina woods, and the settlers met with them in a sort of general assembly to make laws for all concerned. The landless folk of Barbados brought cotton seed and Indian corn. They cleared new fields and shipped timber to the sugar islands. Indians were seized and sold as slaves; a dangerous application of un-Christian principles. A little later at a moment of semi-famine and when Governor Yeamans was eagerly expected to arrive with ample supplies, the natives fell upon settlers who ventured into the woods; they killed cattle and hogs and brought the colonies to the verge of despair. In November, 1665, Sir John's long-expected ship anchored at the mouth of the Cape Fear when a great storm swept up the coast, wrecked the ship and all its store of provisions, guns and ammunition. The officers and the incoming settlers escaped drowning only to add to the number of hungry and half-naked people in the little colony. Sir John patched his broken ship and set off for Barbados for other immigrants while he sent a sloop, which had escaped the storm, to Virginia for supplies. On the return of the supply-sloop another storm swept up the Atlantic coast and the little vessel went down a few miles from the mouth of the river. A part of the crew escaped to tell their second dismal story. Many thousand pounds of good New England, English and Barbadian money and a considerable number of lives had been lost in the venture.[12] Complete ruin was imminent.

[12] *Colonial Records*, I, 147-49, 159.

Late in 1665 the councillors still on the ground united with the settlers and prepared a petition of their sad complaints to the proprietors and awaited a reply. During the next summer Robert Sanford, their recorder of deeds, explored the Carolina coast all the way to Port Royal and found many delightful and screened inlets and bays where the natives were eager for trade. And, although the little farmers on the Cape Fear River reported that they made two crops of "Indian wheat" that year and were shipping quantities of timber to West Indian markets, they were dissatisfied and uneasy. It was a bad time: the Virginians were threatened with ruin, the second Dutch war was at its worst; the Duke of York had lost a great naval battle in the Thames; and the fleet of Louis XIV lay off the coast of northern France waiting to take command in the south Atlantic, in case Charles II lost his fight with the Hollanders. Under these circumstances, the proprietors yielded to all the demands of their distressed Cape Fear colonists,

> liberty to worship God in their own way; election of thirteen persons whereof the lords will appoint governors; an assembly which should have the sole power of making all lawes; every man and woman that transport themselves to have 100 akers and every woman servant and slave 50 akers.[13]

But these enlargements of former concessions came too late. The Indians were still hostile, though not powerful; the lure of the southern bays and inlets was strong; and the "rude rabble" made ready to mutiny. Neither the great Duke of Albemarle nor the Earl of Clarendon was in a position to grant the two hundred sterling needed and the Vassall brothers gave up their colony.

Even John Vassall, unable to get assistance either from London or from Barbados, yielded at last, and the colo-

[13] Abbreviated from *Colonial Records,* I, 154-55.

nists wandered in the late summer of 1667 through the wilderness to upper Albemarle, or to Nansemond, Virginia, whence a disappointed adventurer wrote:

> You have heard of the unhappy loss of our Plantation on Charles river; the people that came to us made it their business to exclaime the country unfitt for Christian habitation; the rude rable ware daily ready to mutany against me; which enforced mee to stop the first ship and carry us all away, especially such weak persons as were not able to go by land. The charge and trouble and loss of my estate there have soe ruened mee as I am not well able to settle myself heare or any other place.

Thus other Cecil Calverts had failed to develop their palatinates and emerge as great lordships in the society about Charles II. Emigrants from New England, Barbados or England all, like the wanderers from the south side of Virginia, refused to cooperate without the guarantee of the cardinal rights of self-government and religious freedom. Some of them hunted their way through the wilderness to the Chowan settlement while others escaped northwards on passing boats.

IV

One of the curious turns in the colonial course of things was now taken. John Locke, a young amateur physician, protégé of Ashley Cooper and for that reason secretary to the board of proprietors, prepared his first essay in political philosophy. For the dissenters, democrats and runaways who were occupying the better sites along the upper Carolina rivers, he wrote the most elaborate constitution that has ever been attempted in any American settlement.[14] The proprietors called his scheme the *Funda-*

[14] Lord Ashley, later Earl of Shaftesbury, may have dictated part of the impossible document.

mental Constitutions, embracing a hundred and twenty solemn injunctions not to mention eleven rules of precedence to be applied whenever the shirtsleeve legislators sat down in some Albemarle home or tavern to do business with the grand representatives of the august lordships, Albemarle, Clarendon, Craven, Shaftesbury and their "successors for all time."

The greatest social philosopher of England and intellectual master of the American revolutionists of 1776 now declared that the purpose of his scheme was to reflect perfectly in the wilderness of Carolina the England of Charles II whom most Americans already distrusted if they did not hate: "the province (must) be made the most agreeable to the monarchy under which we live and avoid the (possibility of) a numerous democracy." There were to be as many huge counties in the region between Virginia and the Saint Johns River as there were proprietors. A deputy of the senior proprietor was appointed in London and called a landgrave when he took up his residence in Albemarle; he should be the supreme master of the Carolina palatinate which was to be divided into seigniories of twelve thousand and baronies of four thousand acres each. These proffered grants should embrace two-fifths of each county and remain forever the property of the emerging Carolina gentry. Three-fifths of the county area should be disposed of to all comers on such terms as the executive committee of the proprietors, sitting in the cockpit in London, should prescribe; that is, the land should be sold outright to freemen or leased on payment of a penny an acre quit-rent. Thus two-fifths of the area would be held by the landed nobility and three-fifths by the plain people, freeholders, tenants and servants. The landgraves or casiques, as the second-grade of landlords were called, would co-operate with the governor and be the supreme authority in the province. The same individuals would serve, as often as there was need, as a court

Emmett Collection, New York Public Library
GEORGE MONCK, DUKE OF ALBEMARLE

Emmett Collection, New York Public Library

JOHN LOCKE

of last resort, a committee of which would have control, as Carolina lords of the admiralty, over the navigable waters of the region—all the larger mansions were to be on prominent fronts of great rivers. In each county or precinct, as the earlier civil units were called, there was also to be a court which should hear disputes not involving life or limb or more than fifty pounds sterling in value. On the twelve thousand-acre baronies there were to be leet courts, not unlike those in operation in southern Maryland. Through the elaborate system there were the usual administrative officers, sheriffs, clerks, surveyors and constables, all to be landlords and prospective members of the gentry. This was intended to be an ideal social system according to the views of British liberals of that day.[15]

At the moment Locke prepared this constitution, the Earl of Clarendon, chancellor of the exchequer, who had succeeded to the first place among the proprietors, became involved in a conflict with the King, was charged with treason and hastened into exile where he died three years later. John Lord Berkeley was the next in order of precedence and thus became the non-resident governor or third palatine, who appointed Samuel Stephens, the second governor and palatine of Albemarle where the new land system could hardly be applied. Ashley Cooper, another proprietor with increasing investments in the West Indies and several slave-trading ships on the Atlantic, slowly succeeded to the supreme place in the royal favor, and in 1672 was made chancellor of the exchequer and earl of Shaftesbury. Albemarle, Clarendon and Shaftesbury were, and had been, tolerant, if not indifferent, as to men's religious views; and all of them also entertained the historic English attitude toward the House of Commons as the supreme power in the realm. This atmosphere and these attitudes of the greatest figures in Restoration Eng-

[15] *Colonial Records*, I, 187-206.

land gave Locke liberty to insert two guarantees in his constitution which went far to satisfy the Carolinians of all creeds. He stipulated:[16]

> There shall be a parliament consisting of the landgraves and one freeholder out of every precinct, chosen by the freeholders. They shall sit all together in one room and have, every member, one vote.

Although the elected legislators were to be the owners of five hundred acres of land each and only freeholders were to exercise the right of voting, it was further decreed that freedmen, as they worked out their terms of service and took possession of their little tracts of land, were also to be accorded the right of suffrage. As the population increased the parliament would necessarily be dominated by the common men of the new country and the proprietors, never more than twelve in number, would not be able to exercise successfully in London the veto so carefully reserved to them. The basic idea of this parliamentary co-operation in Albemarle was the granting of taxes for common purposes, and this was analogous to the terms on which Sir Edwin Sandys had authorized the assembling of the Virginia House of Burgesses in 1619. Although the governor and resident palatines, the landgraves, casiques and delegates of the masses were, in case of sharp disagreement, to sit in separate rooms and act as mutual negatives, there was no means of raising a colonial income without the consent of the assembled commoners. The parliament of the grand new realm was, therefore, but a modified popular control over which so many battles had been fought in Virginia and Maryland. Without this grant of power to the masses, it was everywhere agreed that immigrants could not be induced to buy or permitted to "squat" on the lands and grow the expected tobacco or cotton.

[16] *Colonial Records,* I, 199.

The next and more willing concession of Shaftesbury, Locke and their colleagues was a wider religious liberty than Baltimore had been able to practice in his palatinate:[17]

> No man shall use any reproachful language against any religion; and since charity obliges us to wish well to the souls of all men, and religion ought to alter nothing in a man's civil estate, slaves may enter themselves and be of what church any of them shall think best . . . ; and also that Jews, heathens and other dissenters may not be scared and kept at a distance; any seven persons agreeing in religion shall constitute a church, . . . ; [so long as] every man recognizes: a, that there is a God; b, that God is publicly to be worshipped; and c, that it is the duty of every man to bear witness to the truth.

But everybody must be a member of some church and in time the Albemarle parliament might, under another clause, make the British state church a tax-supported institution; and thus individuals might then in Carolina, as in Virginia, be compelled to support a religion in which they did not believe. More in harmony with the attitude of the settlers was the declaration that it "shall be a base and vile thing to plead in court for money; nor shall anyone plead another man's cause till he hath taken an oath that he doth not plead for money or other reward." Here was unexpected revelation of the English distrust of lawyers which had chacterized the Puritan movement and which so often took the form of a legal veto in Virginia. The author of the future *Essay on Government* closed this constitution of a hundred and twenty clauses with a series of rules of social precedence among the half-clad and barefooted pioneers of the Albemarle wilderness, rules which were also to apply in every other settlement to be made in the region.

[17] *Colonial Records,* I, 204.

While the august lordships of the court of Charles II worked toward their model constitution and the Londoners slowly recovered from the terrible plague of 1665, the great fire of 1666 and the naval disaster of 1667, the cautious William Drummond and Thomas Woodward, who had been hanging about the cockpit, returned to their lonely offices on the Chowan where men fought the more elemental battles of nature. In a little while Samuel Stephens as deputy of Lord Berkeley succeeded Drummond, held assemblies in private houses, and witnessed the growing prosperity of the community. When the second governor died in December, 1669, Peter Carteret, kinsman of the great seaman and capitalist, Sir George Carteret, just then expelled from the House of Commons for corrupt practices, succeeded Stephens as spokesman of the senior proprietor and served three years as governor of Albemarle. At the same time the Earl of Craven appointed John Jenkins his deputy; Shaftesbury named John Willoughby, son of William Lord Willoughby, governor of Barbados, as representative of his interests; and Sir Peter Colleton made Captain Daniel Godfrey his lawful spokesman. These were all to serve in the supreme council under the "grand" constitution. Another and a more interesting representative of the new aristocratic order appeared in the person of John Culpeper, brother-in-law of Lady Berkeley and member of the great family in England headed by Thomas Lord Culpeper. He was the legal spokesman of Sir William Berkeley. He would also sit in the Governor's council as representative of Sir William Berkeley. There was some commotion in the simple community about this hasty success; but there was no way to block the procedure, and a representative of both the Culpeper and the Berkeley families took his place for a time in John Locke's upper Carolina "aristocracy." To complete the picture, Sir William paid court to Lady Stephens; they were soon married, and the Governor of the older Dominion was thus able to add other tracts of land to his vast Virginia estates.[18]

Carteret promptly gave notice that their lordships in London had modified the new constitution so that Albemarle lands might be as easy to obtain and hold as Virginia lands. He called the assembly to meet in September, 1670, with the new landgraves, Jenkins, Willoughby and the rest. George Durant, John Harvey, Valentine Byrd, Thomas Cullen and others of the self-made planter leaders were in their accustomed places on the popular side of the assembly. The fundamental constitution was applied in so far as it might be; Thomas Woodward was instructed to lay off the wilderness in twelve thousand-acre tracts, awaiting the appearance of great landlords; Albemarle county was divided into four precincts bearing the names of Chowan, Currituck, Pasquotank and Perquimans. Each precinct was allotted five delegates in the assembly which continued to meet with the governors and palatines in legislative capacity on the north side of the sound till 1691. From that date, the governor and so many of the ten councillors as were willing to do so met as an upper house of assembly while the delegates from the precincts chose their speaker and other officials, and quietly ceased to name the five members of the council provided in the grand charter. Thus the legislative and administrative organs of Albemarle assumed the forms so well known in Virginia. The four older precincts continued to send five delegates each while the new precincts, created by act of assembly from year to year further west and south, were permitted only two delegates each, thus giving advantage in law-making to the older as against the new communities—a practice which has prevailed in many states of the United States till the present day.

---

[18] These relationships are revealed in *State Papers*, V, in scattered letters and reports. The *Dictionary of American Biography* and North Carolina biography fail to give adequate sketches.

With the legislature duly established, the governor and council served as a supreme court till 1683 when the proprietors, troubled with the recurrent democratic conflicts of the colony, ordered the appointment of four "able and discreet men" as justices of a supreme court who were to meet three times a year. When this body came into existence between 1700 and 1702, its functions were expanded considerably into the administrative field; and one of its members served, with local appointees of the proprietors, as a court of admiralty in the hope of checking the depredations of pirates and other less violent criminals. With a governor serving for a short term, a council proposed in the colony but approved in the cockpit, without the many prerequisites of Virginia and Maryland councillors, and a House of Commons with the right of initiative in legislation, the Albemarle community was the most democratic of all the southern settlements. At the beginning of these developments, when the proprietors were still filled with the hope of a great palatinate south of the Chesapeake and expectant of enormous profits from the growing slave trade, sugar refining and tobacco planting, Sir Peter Colleton revealed a little of the spirit of the time and the relationship of John Locke to the adventure in a letter which closes as follows: [19]

> If Locke will draw a description of Albemarle such as might invite people without seeming to come from us, it would very much conduce to speedy settlement and be a great obligation to the writer.

V

There was a comparatively speedy settlement. But the Virginians declared in formal legislative resolutions: "Carolina (was) a subterfuge for the late rebels, tray-

[19] *State Papers, Colonial,* VII, 714.

tors and deserters" of their troubled commonwealth. This was only saying what might as well have been said about all the communities on the North American coast. The unfortunates, even prisoners, from Barbados, from New England, even from England and Ireland were appealed to during the hard and terrible wars which followed the Restoration to try their chances on the banks of the Albemarle rivers; and like the unfortunates who went to Australia in the nineteenth century, they became good commonwealth builders. On the borders of the winding streams that flowed southwards into the sound from the coast almost to the falls of the Roanoke, a hundred miles inland, and on the southern side half-way to the valley of the Neuse River of our day, there were lonely settlers with great or less stretches of land pre-empted, but rarely paid for, entrepreneurs, freemen and freedmen. Their terrain was definitely described in 1691 by the authorities in London as all that country north and east of the Cape Fear. Some of the land was rich and productive, more of it was what came later to be called the "piney woods" and not very fertile; but everywhere there was a chance to earn a living, and escape Europe, the first consideration for most of the people who crossed the Atlantic in the seventeenth and early eighteenth centuries.[20]

Their economy was as simple as it had been in Virginia and Maryland. The forest and the rivers maintained the newcomers till they could clear a few acres of land. Then each settler produced from a thousand to twenty or thirty thousand pounds of tobacco a year. As soon as it was known that these remote planters had tobacco for the world market, enterprising New England shipmasters sent light-draught vessels over the shallows at the entrance of the Carolina sound, loaded with such goods as frontiersmen and eager-eyed Indians thought they

[20] Catherine Albertson, *In Ancient Albemarle*, Chs. IV and V, give persons and local descriptions.

needed: axes, hoes, rough, ready-made clothes, trinkets, guns and ammunition. In exchange they took tobacco, bear and beaver skins, and salted venison in great quantities to Jamaica, Barbados, England and the United Netherlands. As the settlers rarely paid for their lands and never permitted an export tax on their shipments, a penny a pound for tobacco and a shilling per skin gave them sharp advantage over the planters on the Chesapeake Bay who paid two shillings per hogshead export tax on all their tobacco and considerable fees for the handling of other goods. The Navigation laws of England were not observed in Carolina for thirty years after their enactment and even when there was an attempt to apply them, as we shall see later, inspectors and collectors were unable to compel obedience.

There were six individuals or partnerships in Boston alone that engaged in the profitable and unlawful trade of Albemarle Sound through the second decade of Carolina history; as the great war against Louis XIV became intense, greater numbers of New England traders made fortunes from their southern and West Indian trade. The older settlers like Durant and Catchmaid, John Harvey and Valentine Byrd were in close harmony with the eastern economic interests. All fought shy of English or Chesapeake shipmasters. Their intricate river system protected them from his Majesty's patrol and war vessels, like that commanded by Sir John Knight or the famous *Quaker* "ketch" commanded by Captain John Allen. The tobacco crop of Albemarle amounted to two thousand hogsheads a year in 1677 and, selling at a better price than the Virginia product the same year, the return value in imports was at least twenty thousand pounds sterling. Zachariah Gillam, an English trader who had learned the way into the Albemarle Bay, swore in court, 1679: [21]

[21] *Colonial Records*, I, 294.

rather than goe away with his ship empty, he sold his goods for tobacco and skins which came for England and paid his Majesty near two thousand pounds customs, which his Majesty never before received since that province was seated.

This was a single ship's work. Such profits must have been tempting and one may suspect that needy Stuart customs officials were not eager to break up a trade which yielded the crown handsome returns and left Shaftesbury and the other proprietors to shift for themselves. Still less might the New Englanders, who sometimes praised the "pious work" of pirates in their pulpits, be expected to give up their rich opportunities half-way down the coast to Jamaica. They of all men gave Carolina the surest guarantee of a profitable market.

A tobacco business that yielded twenty thousand pounds a year was not to be spurned by such poor folk as the Carolinians. Luckily there were as good as no taxes to be paid. The governors lived more off their lands than their salaries. Even the judges of the supreme court received meagre stipends before the year 1700. The county officials likewise lived off their lands and their fees for registering deeds and other legal papers. Not only were the expenses of government negligible; the cost of living was more negligible. Nowhere in America was it more easy to get one's meat from the streams or the forests. And there were everywhere little "patches" of land planted to potatoes, turnips and peas. A few acres of Indian corn would supply the needs of a family with ten children, two steers, and a dozen hogs. Collards grew here better than in Virginia; and this easy-grown vegetable remained a fixed item of the southern diet for two hundred years. The Albemarle country was only another James and York river region.

With all these advantages, the Quakers and squatters

on the Albemarle Sound were uneasy during the years that followed the close of the first great Dutch war. Sir George Carteret and his partner, Colonel Charles Berkeley, were the masters of the Dutch and Swedish settlements along the Delaware; the same enterprising speculators were associated with the Earl of Shaftesbury in land and slave-trade speculations in Barbados and Jamaica; and in 1671 John Berkeley succeeded Thomas Woodward as surveyor-general of all the Carolina lands and settled in Charlestown. Durant, Catchmaid and Byrd might any day find their trade with New England and all their land titles called into question. In northern Virginia Sir William Berkeley was similarly engaged in land speculations where he had been commanded by the King to deliver all the region between the Rappahannock and the Potomac to Thomas Lord Culpeper, brother of the surveyor-general of Carolina and of Alexander Culpeper, surveyor-general of Virginia. But while these developments made men uneasy and led to violent Virginia protests in London, the Governor of the so-called Dominion endeavored, as we have seen, to enforce the Clarendon code [22] whereby every Virginian must submit to the ordinances of the Church of England; he also sought to enforce the statute of 1670 whereby only freemen were permitted to vote; and he only allowed elections to the burgesses when vacancies from death or resignations required, and thus maintained a "long burgesses," like the Long Parliament under which Charles maintained his reactionary régime in England. These attitudes and measures, described in a previous chapter, sent scores of families to upper Carolina, which only added to the resolute popular will of the new community.

But a worse threat appeared in 1675 when, on account of ruthless treatment of the Indians all the way to Boston, the Meherrin tribes northwest of the Chowan com-

[22] Trevelyan, *England under the Stuarts*, 341.

menced relentless war upon the exposed settlers. The accustomed militia training had been neglected and there were insufficient supplies of arms and ammunition. The existence of the colony was threatened. The sudden and unexpected appearance of Zachariah Gillam, the English buccaneer and tradesman already mentioned, with a supply of arms, gave the means of defense and saved the colony from extirpation. Meanwhile the repressive measures of Sir William Berkeley had driven all southern and western Virginia to arms. William Drummond, the ex-governor, joined Giles Bland, William Byrd I and Nathaniel Bacon in the fierce war of 1676. The Carolinians were everywhere sympathetic and when the revolutionists were defeated at the end of the year, other Quakers and dissenters trekked southward. With Virginia in turmoil on the north and all the great colonial speculators of London and the West Indies engaged in the founding of a great and model colony farther south, the humble Quakers, dissenters and squatters of Albemarle were allowed to live with or without religion as they liked. Religious freedom, the third item of their decalogue, was now openly conceded by the proprietors, then under the domination of Shaftesbury, who was willing to fill the new region with dissenters and other English "criminals" so they made tobacco, agreed to pay quit-rents to the proprietors and customs duties to his Majesty.

However, the earnest George Fox, who travelled and preached in Albemarle in 1672, and the equally resolute Quaker, William Edmundson, who made a second campaign there, reported that there were no meeting houses. Whatever religion George Durant professed in England, he was not distressed at the absence of churches in Carolina at the time of his death in 1694. There was probably occasional religious worship in private houses throughout these thirty years and there is evidence that Quakers, Puritans, Episcopalians and Baptists were rather numerous. But it must have been a "semi-godless" community. Yet there was a distinct sense of social morality for Thomas Miller denounced the king of England about 1672 as a filthy whoremonger, and the people applauded. Of all the early settlements in North America, that on the Albemarle Sound was the freest in each of the cardinal points of seventeenth century democracy. No man needed to observe either the Clarendon code or the thirty-nine articles. John Locke's perfect reproduction of Stuart England slowly became a crude and unruly democracy ignoring grand constitutions, and oblivious of the interests of Shaftesbury, the great London politician and statesman.

12

The First American Civil War

> "I thank God there are no free schools nor printing [in Virginia], and I hope we shall not have these hundred years; for learning has brought disobedience, heresy and sects into the world and printing has divulged them."—Sir William Berkeley, 1676.

I

WHEN LOUIS XIV LOST HIS WAR WITH THE DUTCH, because of the heroic flooding of strategic areas of Holland with sea-water, and when the young William of Orange rose, like his great ancestor a hundred years before, to the leadership of Protestant Europe, the Virginians and Marylanders were delighted. During the eight years of 1666 to 1674 thousands of unemployed English and Irish folk, with scores of well-to-do leaders, settled in these tobacco colonies. The "sale" of English people for terms of years had been forbidden by Charles II, but the decree had been violated. Two of the most important of the free newcomers were Giles Bland, son of the distinguished John Bland and nephew of Theodoric Bland of the Virginia council, and Nathaniel Bacon of the Lord Bacon family and a nephew of Nathaniel Bacon, a close friend of Sir William Berkeley. Both these young men were resolute opponents of the Stuart régime, as also of the French domination of Europe; and they soon became eminent opponents of the Berkeley dictatorship. Bland suspected the Governor to be a grafter on a huge scale, because he had not enforced the law to inspect vessels leaving Virginia rivers; and Bacon soon became a friend of the first William Byrd, the young frontier leader and Indian trader who had succeeded Abraham Wood. Practically all the planters and people south of the James River were in opposition once more—awaiting their opportunity to do what had been done to Sir John Harvey in 1635.

Nor was this all. During the summer of 1673, when the Virginians were most troubled about the effects of the war in Europe, they learned of the King's grant of the Northern Neck, the most popular area of the whole colony, to Arlington and Culpeper: it included all the region, not already settled, between the Rappahannock and the Potomac, some six million acres of land. It was designed to be a new Maryland carved out of Virginia.[1] But to make matters worse, Lord Culpeper, Lady Berkeley's cousin, was to become Governor and overlord of all Virginia for a period of thirty years—after Sir William's retirement. Culpeper, who had been vice president of the reorganized Board of Trade and Plantations—also connected with the African Slave Company—was familiar with plantation affairs, and he longed to become another Lord Baltimore.

But before the Virginians became aware of the Culpeper plan, Giles Bland, collector of customs on the James River, reported Sir William's profiteering at the public expense and started a movement which may have been intended to enforce the recall of the Governor. He called the attention of the Board of Trade and Plantations to the fact that Berkeley had never enforced the King's decree that all ships must give bonds for their strict observation of the Navigation acts, and reported payments of good sums to the Governor for his indulgences, also great profits from his monopolized Indian trade. This started a commotion in southern Virginia. When the matter was brought before the council, Berkeley was able to get a

[1] Harrison, Fairfax, *The Proprietors of the Northern Neck,* 73-88.

vote of condemnation of Bland. The House of Burgesses supported the "injured" Governor at its session of November, 1674, although popular sentiment was clearly against him. Bland was bold enough to denounce publicly the Governor and Council, and went so far as to refuse to fight a duel with Thomas Ludwell, who had challenged him; and he even nailed the Secretary's challenging glove to the State House door with a contemptuous note attached. Both houses of the assembly, in obedience to Berkeley and Ludwell, condemned Bland and ordered him to pay a fine of £500.[2] It was a sensation of the first order, and the matter was appealed to the Privy Council in London, the Collector of Customs of the upper James River being too influential to be thrust into prison.

The population of Virginia and Maryland was now most restless: "they complain of unjust taxes, the poorer sort paying as much as he that hath 20,000 acres, the charge of the burgesses (elected in 1662) of 1,000 pounds of tobacco a day against their counties."

While all the colonists were troubled at the prospect of Louis XIV and Charles II bringing the Netherlands under French control; and the tobacco settlers were still hoping for the abandonment of the drastic trade decrees of 1660–63, the powerful Iroquois Indians of western New York killed or expelled practically all rival natives from the Susquehanna valley. The Susquehannocks and fractions of other tribes undertook to settle on the Potomac and in the coveted Northern Neck. Guerrilla warfare broke out at once in the neighborhood of present-day Georgetown, and frontiersmen and women were scalped, killed or carried away as captives. Terrorized ex-servants and freemen immigrants abandoned their little farms and took refuge among the older settlements. The forts and scattered frontier guardsmen from the falls of the Potomac to the upper James River were unable to protect

[2] *State Papers, Addenda,* April 28, 1676.

the people. In 1673 Sir William Berkeley authorized county lieutenants to collect volunteers and pay themselves by capturing and selling as slaves as many of the hostile Indians as possible; but this had not been successful and there was a general Indian hostility all the way from the Hudson to the Roanoke.

These troubles in northern Virginia and Maryland tended, of course, to rouse the people against what they thought were their indifferent and autocratic executives. In September, 1674, when Sir William's hand-picked burgesses met in Jamestown, their first act was to protest unanimously against the making of Lord Culpeper a proprietary governor and part owner of all the region between the Rappahannock and the Potomac. They were unwilling to have a new governor with the huge salary of £2,000 a year, the right to collect for himself the long unpaid quit-rents and to own all lands abandoned by planters and farmers who gave up their eastern possessions in order to take up better lands to be wrested from the Indians. They declared that the King had violated their charter of 1609—as he had—and that he had no right to re-grant Virginia sovereignty without the approval of the burgesses. It was a strong democratic protest which Sir William and all his council were compelled to support; and the staunch royalists, Thomas Ludwell, Francis Moryson and Robert Smith, all members of the council, were hurried off to present the unanimous Virginia grievances to the Board of Trade and Plantations, and even to his Majesty himself. For months in the year 1675 these distinguished planters of the Berkeley régime were arguing in London at the same time the scandalous charges of Giles Bland were being pressed by no less a personage than John Bland. Lord Culpeper, then acting head of the Committee of Trade and Plantations, was in an embarrassing position; and his Majesty, surprised that the Virginians could be so persistent in their protests, delayed his decision till other and worse events came.³

The frontier warfare of 1673–74 in both Maryland and Virginia had hardly relaxed before the news of King Philip's war in New England, June, 1675, made all the colonists think that all the Indians were co-operating in a grand effort to destroy settlements from Massachusetts to southern Carolina. Although Charles Calvert and Sir William Berkeley authorized frontier leaders like William Byrd at the falls of the James River, George Mason of the Northern Neck and John Allen on the Maryland frontier to keep their volunteers under arms, there was no adequate protection. The controlled Virginia assembly made no protests against the failure of Sir William to take more vigorous action. In September, 1675, the war broke out afresh on both sides of the Potomac, and Major Thomas Truman of the Maryland Council and John Washington of the Northern Neck, as already noted, slaughtered both hostile and friendly Indians in ruthless manner; however, there was no evidence of real victory. In early January, 1676, there came fresh reports of Indian atrocities; and about the end of the month two-score frontier Virginians were murdered in a single day. When Sir William Berkeley announced once more that there was nothing to be done till the burgesses met in regular session two months later, all sections of the colony were ready to revolt, even to assume control of the government.

Thus Maryland and Virginia, with their populations increased to 70,000, had been remodeled. Their governors, like most officials in England, had received great profits at the expense of their peoples; they controlled the councils almost without resistance, and the legislatures were little "Long Parliaments"; neither the general ("su-

³ *State Papers, Addenda,* May 12 and October 12, 1675; also Hening, II, 518-28.

preme") nor the county courts were independent. The church in Virginia was under Sir William's direction, and in Maryland the Catholic minority was still in control of the government and always contending against the Puritan-Baptist-Quaker majority. The secretaries of both colonies, Ludwell and Philip Calvert, drew large incomes from fees of all sorts; the sheriffs and clerks of county courts abused their positions in the same way, and even the preachers knew how to profiteer. Sir William Berkeley boasted of his system and declared there should be no freedom of press or public education.[4]

II

When the distinguished commissioners of Virginia, Ludwell, Moryson and Smith appeared in London in the winter of 1674-75 to contend with his Majesty against Lord Culpeper and for the parliamentary rights of their far-off colony, English political and religious affairs were in the saddest plight they had been in since 1649. The Earl of Shaftesbury, the most popular English leader among the Americans, was removed from the presidency of the Board of Trade and Plantations and superseded in the high office of Chancellor by the clever and corrupt Sir Thomas Osborne, Earl of Danby. Shaftesbury was beginning his long struggle in the House of Lords for a newly-elected House of Commons to replace the disreputable Long Parliament. Danby was negotiating huge gifts to Charles II from Louis XIV for the purpose of maintaining a standing army in England, and at the same time successfully pressing the marriage of Mary, the daughter of the Duke of York, with William of Orange, the savior of Protestant Europe! While Danby bribed members of Parliament and secured gifts from Louis XIV

[4] Hening, II, 517. Berkeley's survey of Virginia, 511 to 518.

THE FIRST AMERICAN CIVIL WAR 241

for the King, Shaftesbury organized active dissenter, liberal opposition in the greater cities and several of the western counties. He was the leader of the same element that had given Cromwell his power thirty years before. He was so powerful that the French Ambassador offered him a bribe of £10,000 if he would support his monarch; and Shaftesbury was one of the few leaders of the time who indignantly refused a bribe. Before the Virginians could get their grievances to the King, Shaftesbury was ordered to leave London—and when he refused to go, he was thrust into the Tower.[5]

It was from this troubled England—actually moving toward the revolution of 1688—that Nathaniel Bacon and Giles Bland had come to Virginia in 1673. They were of the emerging party of liberalism which slowly acquired the name of Whigs and for several decades did more to save both England and Europe from the dictatorship of Louis XIV than any other force whatsoever. With influential connections at home, Sir William Berkeley had made Bacon a member of his Council and Bland collector of customs on the upper James. These young leaders brought wealth enough with them to become masters of large plantations between Jamestown and present-day Richmond. Twenty miles west of Bacon's estate young William Byrd had become the master of a large area of land at the falls of the James River, having inherited it from his mother, the wife of a Cromwellian Indian trader; and Byrd had quickly become captain of the militia which held that part of the frontier against Indian invasions, just as the deceased Abraham Wood had done for many years on the site of present-day Petersburg. Before 1676 Byrd had also become an Indian trader, with contacts all the way to middle North Carolina. Bacon was twenty-nine, Bland was hardly older, and

[5] British *Dictionary of National Biography*. There is, I believe, no really good biography of Shaftesbury.

Byrd was only twenty-two, all ambitious young liberals who were disgusted with the corrupt autocracy which had grown steadily worse for fifteen years.[6]

When still another Indian invasion was threatening in April, 1676, Bacon, Byrd, James Crewes and Henry Isham, all of Charles City or Henrico counties, held a conference in Bacon's house, Charles City county, and decided to rally the farmers of the upper James River region for a campaign west and southwest of the falls of the James and Appomattox rivers. The people rallied, supplied themselves with arms and a few days' rations, and marched, some three hundred strong, under Bacon's command toward the North Carolina border. Sir William Berkeley was so angered that he collected as many of the cavalry about Jamestown as he could, denounced Bacon as a traitor, and advanced toward the falls of the James in the hope of defeating the uprising and capturing Bacon. He did not succeed. But when he returned to Jamestown toward the end of April the news of Bacon's heroic victory over the Indians on the Roanoke River was being discussed with great enthusiasm. William Drummond, the first governor of North Carolina, and Richard Lawrence, a graduate of Oxford and a clever opponent for years of Sir William's autocracy, were the leaders of the Jamestown opposition; and all the way to Norfolk most of the people were shouting approval of the brave young Bacon and Byrd. On the Rappahannock, where Giles Brent, George Mason and John Washington had made similar moves against the Indians, there was a similar approval of the Charles City uprising. Public sentiment of all sections of the country was so outspoken that Berkeley authorized a general election for a new House of Burgesses.[7]

It looked as if Bacon would compel Berkeley to do for

---

[6] Bassett, J. S., *The Writings of Col. William Byrd*, Introduction.
[7] Stanard, Mary Newton, *The Story of Bacon's Rebellion*.

THE FIRST AMERICAN CIVIL WAR 243

Virginia what Shaftesbury had tried in vain to force Charles II to do in England. Bacon and Crewes were elected to the new House of Burgesses which was to assemble in Jamestown early in June. When Bacon approached the capital in a boat on the James River, his friend Lawrence, also a member of the new assembly, warned him at night that he was to be arrested by the Governor; but he appeared on the little public square in due time, was arrested, went through the form of an apology and took his place among the new lawmakers— also remained for the moment a member of the Council. Arthur Moseley, Lower Norfolk; Robert Beverley, Middlesex; Thomas Mathews, son of the Puritan Governor, Samuel Mathews, Stafford; George Mason and Richard Lawrence were leaders of this assembly. Under the leadership of Bacon and his fellow-reformers, manhood suffrage was restored to the people, church members were given their right to elect their vestries and frequent free elections ordered; investigation of official abuses was decreed, long terms of office forbidden, trade with Indians stopped, some of Berkeley's friends denied the right to hold office, and even the sale of spiritous liquors no longer permitted.[8] Since the Council was denied the right to annul acts of the burgesses, the measures were regarded as a restoration of the democracy which had prevailed in Virginia since the dismissal of Sir John Harvey. What the Virginians had done had been contended for in Maryland under the leadership of Josias Fendall and the more eminent assemblymen there since 1669; and there was reason for Bacon to expect cooperation there and pressure in London for democratic reform. Of course these revolutionary statutes of Virginia would be submitted to the Board of Trade and Plantations in London, where the Virginia commissioners were still contending against the proposed proprietorship of Lord Culpeper. There was

[8] Hening, II, 356-365.

so much unrest in England and so many members of the House of Lords, like the Earls of Essex and Halifax, were pressing for a new parliament that Virginia and Maryland had a fair chance to recover all they had lost, except freer trade.[9] The restless majority in Maryland, ready to listen to the advice of the former Governor, Fendall, and others, was almost as resentful against Charles Calvert as were the Virginians against Berkeley.

Before the *reformer* burgesses adjourned to their busy tobacco farms, they made Bacon commander-in-chief of an army of a thousand men which was to drive the threatening Indians far into North Carolina or beyond the Blue Ridge Mountains in the upper Potomac region. But Berkeley refused to sign the necessary commission and planned once more to arrest Bacon; and he even placed secret agents on the banks of the James River instructed to kill his young opponent in case he did not surrender. But Bacon escaped again, and in a few days led some hundreds of volunteers back to the capital and obtained both his and a score of other commissions for the officers of the new army. He had hardly finished this arbitrary, if patriotic, task before a new Indian invasion was reported in the upper York River region. While Bacon advanced into the wilderness northwest of present-day Richmond, Berkeley, supported by a minority of the Council, went to Gloucester county and raised a company of volunteers which he hoped to increase sufficiently to attack Bacon on his return. When his recruits deserted, Berkeley crossed the Chesapeake Bay to Accomac county, where he expected the Scarboroughs and perhaps reactionary Marylanders to come to his assistance. When Bacon returned from his half-successful chase of the Indians into the wilderness south of the falls of the Rappahannock, he denounced in violent language Sir William Berkeley,

[9] Mereness, Newton D., *Maryland as a Proprietary Province*, different chapters.

THE FIRST AMERICAN CIVIL WAR 245

Robert Beverley, Sir Henry Chicheley, Richard Lee and other northern Virginia leaders who were reported to be skeptical of him, some even hostile. With Berkeley's strength increasing in the Rappahannock region and the news spreading about the colony that Charles II was about to send an army to suppress his movement, Bacon called a conference of his friends in the house of Otto Thorpe, near present-day Williamsburg, on August 3, 1676.[10] Drummond and Lawrence, wiser leaders and better informed about Virginia attitudes than Bacon, urged that Sir William be forced to give up his abused position and that the cautious Sir Henry Chicheley of the Rappahannock country, be proclaimed the new governor. William Byrd, like Robert Beverley, had deserted his revolutionary friend; but two eminent members of the council, Thomas Ballard of James City county, and Thomas Swann, master of the great peninsula just south of Jamestown, seemed loyal and took part in the discussion. A number of less prominent leaders like John Beale and James Bray were also active supporters. Bacon declined to proclaim Chicheley governor, denounced Berkeley again, called upon his followers everywhere to take an oath of solemn loyalty, agree to fight the King's troops in the name of the King, if they came; and then issued writs for the election of a new House of Burgesses to meet in September, 1676, and decide who was to be Governor, as had been done in 1635, and call on the peoples of Maryland and the Albemarle settlement to unite with them, set up a democracy for all the distressed tobacco region and then ask the approval of his Majesty in London. The revolutionary conference adjourned, Bacon crossed the James River and defeated another Indian invasion on the south side of the Appomattox and at the same time authorized his friend, Giles Bland, to seize some ships in the river at Jamestown, with William Carver

[10] Stanard, Mary Newton, *The Story of Bacon's Rebellion,* Ch. VIII.

of Lower Norfolk county and Captain Larrimore of England as captains. Bland hastened with his two assistant commanders and a few sailors to the western shore of Accomac county to capture Sir William. When they arrived, Carver naively accepted an invitation to talk things over with Berkeley; and while the conversation went on, Philip Ludwell, son of the famous Thomas Ludwell, still in London, approached Bland's ships in the harbor with a few assistants and quickly put both Bland and Larrimore in chains. When Carver returned, he too was seized and promptly hanged upon the order of the treacherous Governor. With these and other ships now under his control, and Bacon still fighting Indians under trying circumstances on the western frontier, Berkeley decided to sail for Jamestown and recapture his coveted little capital. He took the ships Bacon had sent to Accomac, kept Bland and Larrimore in chains, promised enormous rewards to recruits and sailors who would join him and, on September 8, he captured the little capital with some six hundred men helping him; he thought he would speedily make an end of the Bacon rebellion.[11]

Returning from another Indian chase, with less than one hundred and fifty half-defeated, half-naked and hungry men on September 13, Bacon rallied his little army at Berkeley's famous Greenspring home and marched that night to the edge of the little capital whence his friends Drummond and Lawrence had flown as the Governor had taken possession and given Bacon all possible information. On the morning of September 14, Berkeley saw that the only ways of escape from the swamp-surrounded village, except upon his captured boats, were barred by banks of densely packed tree tops pointing toward him. The revolutionists had a few big guns in strategic positions, and recruits were once more volunteering. Bacon was now bent upon defeating Berkeley without the loss

[11] Fiske, John, *Old Virginia and her Neighbors*, II, 74-75.

THE FIRST AMERICAN CIVIL WAR 247

of a single man, and he, therefore, resorted to the device of compelling the wives of prominent friends of Berkeley to stand in front of his defenses and thus warn the besieged Governor against attacking his foe. With little food and only foul and half-salt water to drink, the six hundred men around Berkeley began to desert, some entering the camp of Bacon, others returning to their homes in eastern Virginia. A little after the middle of the month, Sir William abandoned the town, with perhaps two-score of his followers, including Thomas Ballard and James Bray, who had been with Bacon at the Thorpe conference. Bacon ordered the complete destruction of Jamestown, and both Drummond and Lawrence, owners of homes there, applied torches.[12] Berkeley could hardly hope to return, and Bacon took possession of Greenspring. The assembling of a new House of Burgesses, which had been ordered August 3, did not take place, and the people were losing faith in their erratic leader. The destruction of their capital was too much for them. Northern Virginians were now decisively hostile, and the Marylanders failed to give support. To quell the rising opposition, Bacon killed one deserter at Greenspring and imprisoned no less persons than Sir Henry Chicheley and Richard Lee.[13] The properties of half a score of other eminent conservatives, including Robert Beverley, Thomas Ludwell and John Washington were seized or damaged as much as possible upon the orders of Bacon as he began to realize that his cause was failing. The last week in September Bacon decided to march toward Gloucester county once more, where he expected to meet opposing forces organizing in the Rappahannock country, and perhaps appeal to Marylanders. With his energies weakened by the amazing campaigns of three hot months, and aware of the bank-

[12] Fiske, II, 76-78.
[13] Hendrick, Burton J., *The Lees of Virginia*, 39-41.

ruptcy and chaos which confronted him in all parts of Virginia, Bacon was taken seriously ill about the time he abandoned Greenspring. On October 1, he died suddenly in the house of a friend in Gloucester county. There was no possible successor in his little army. Richard Lawrence secretly buried the remains of his adored friend at some unmarked point in the York River. It had been a sadly managed uprising of the masses; but the sudden death and secret burial of Bacon gave it a popularity as described in romantic and poetic writings ever since. It was the end of the first revolution in North America, the first bloody attack upon a minor autocracy of Charles II against whom more than half of England was ready to revolt, the great Earl of Shaftesbury still in the Tower and half the House of Lords protesting in vain.

III

While Sir William Berkeley, on his second retreat in Accomac, awaited anxiously the coming of a regiment of British redcoats which Charles II had promised, he learned that Bacon was dead and that Lawrence, Ingram and a few score resolute rebels were making their way into New Kent county on the south side of the York River where they hoped once more to rally the discontented farmers to their side. But Captain Drew and the men and boys whom Bacon had left at Greenspring were abandoning the Governor's mansion and inviting his return. With conditions more favorable than they had been since the upheaval began, the Governor hurried Robert Beverley, beginning a curious rôle in Virginia history, with a little company of soldiers, into the old York neighborhood and there captured a score of Ingram's men, including the outstanding leaders, Colonel Thomas Hansford and Edward Cheesman. Beverley carried these

THE FIRST AMERICAN CIVIL WAR 249

men promptly to Berkeley's camp, where Hansford was hanged. Cheesman's wife urged Sir William to put her to death instead of her "innocent" husband.[14] The Governor insulted the woman shamefully, but left the husband in prison, where he escaped hanging by sudden death. With prospects so good, Sir William, accompanied by the released Sir Henry Chicheley and Robert Beverley, Edward Hill and Philip Ludwell, entered the James River, captured the elder Bacon's "castle" on the south side of the river in Surrey county and quickly scattered Ingram's forces. Ingram, Lawrence and a few others escaped and were never heard of again; but Sir William lingered about the region, using English boats and sailors to assist him in capturing the revolutionists. On January 11, 1677, he called his councillors to sit in conference with him as a court martial. No less persons than Nathaniel Bacon, senior, Thomas Ballard, Robert Beverley and the famous, aged William Claiborne, and several others, were present. Some of these distinguished persons had sat in conference with the revolutionist Bacon at Otto Thorpe's house, August 3. Thomas Hall, a well-to-do farmer of Lower Norfolk, was ordered to be hanged; on the next day Thomas Young, Henry Page and James Wilson were likewise ordered to be executed. A week later about half the councillors reassembled at the house of James Bray where William Drummond, captured in the Chickahominy Swamp, was brought before them.[15] Sir William said: "Aha, you are very welcome; you shall be hanged in half an hour." The former Governor of North Carolina replied: "What Your Honor pleases," and was promptly put to death. Still other men met the same fate.

But as Berkeley had ordered the election of a new House of Burgesses and it was to assemble in his Green-

[14] Stanard, Mary Newton, *The Story of Bacon's Rebellion*, Ch. XIV.
[15] Hening, II, 545-46.

spring mansion, he returned about January 20 to the desolate region where the new-built houses of 1663 no longer existed, or were in ruins. The Governor claimed that his personal losses were more than £10,000; and it can hardly be doubted that the devastations were even worse for poorer folk all over central Virginia.[16] It happened to be an unusually cold winter, and the number of people who were in desperate circumstances was probably many times greater than the deaths due to the Indian and revolutionary war. As Sir William returned to his home, Charles II's commission, composed of Herbert Jeffreys, Sir John Berry and Francis Moryson, came into the James River with a shipload of soldiers, six or eight hundred others lingering at Barbados. Three other of his Majesty's warships awaited events in the James River. Although Berkeley greeted the officers of the little army with enthusiasm and was delighted to find that his beloved wife was also returning from London to his half-ruined estate, he was resentful that his Majesty had sent over three distinguished men to take control of the colony and, if possible, restore order and even prosperity. The most welcome of the commissioners to the people was Francis Moryson, who had labored with some success two years in London to save Virginia from the proprietary plans of Lord Culpeper. There were no houses on the north side of the river for the soldiers, not a public building or church in Jamestown; and the boat on which they came was under orders to return as promptly as possible to England. Thomas Swann, an opponent of Berkeley, who had lent aid to the Bacon revolutionists and who had refused to sit in the Governor's Council, acting as a court martial, invited the commissioners to his home at Swann's Point on the south side of the river. It was five or six miles from Greenspring, where the representatives of the King naturally ex-

[16] *State Papers, Colonial,* 1677-79, give details pp. 44-54.

THE FIRST AMERICAN CIVIL WAR   251

pected to be at home; Swann's Point was also a place where the commissioners almost daily heard the revolutionists tell their sad story.[17]

But Berkeley was not in a mood to listen to his Majesty or the commissioners. He thought fate had scored for him and, in spite of the persistent hatred of most of the people, he expected to rally his Council and control the burgesses who were to assemble on February 20. And no less persons than Sir Henry Chicheley, Giles Brent, Richard Lee, Ralph Wormeley and John Washington of northern Virginia were on his side, though not enthusiastic. Nathaniel Bacon, Thomas Ballard, John Custis and William Claiborne of the York region, who had hesitated to support him against the young Bacon, were now ready to sit again in his Council. Though hardly a man south of the James River but agreed with Thomas Swann: the Blands, whose kinsman was soon to be hanged at Greenspring, and William Byrd, who was elected a member of the new House of Burgesses. Before the commissioners, far more popular than the group around Berkeley, announced their instructions from the King.[18] Sir William gathered eight of his councillors, all but one from central and northern Virginia, to condemn to death, or banish, scores of the men who had fought with Bacon, Giles Bland, James Crewes, Charles Scarborough and John West the more prominent ones. The Council continued its work as a court through the month of February, banishing participants in the revolt and confiscating property to amazing extent for the benefit of Berkeley, his friends and servants.[19] This he did after the manner of the Cromwell and Stuart courts in England thirty years before. The

[17] *State Papers, Colonial,* 1677-79, 38, 44.
[18] Who was soon to say: "The old fool, Berkeley, has put more people to death in that naked country than I did for the murder of my father"; but one must not forget John Lord Berkeley was still an intimate of the King.
[19] Hening, II, 546-54.

protests of the commissioners were ignored. When the burgesses met on February 20 they chose Augustine Warner, a member of the Council, Speaker, and Robert Beverley, another councillor, Secretary. The majority of the new burgesses repealed all the statutes of the assembly of June, 1676, and promptly passed the most drastic acts of attainder and confiscation, finishing what the Governor and Council had begun; and on March 8 they made no protest when Sir William and the Council decreed that none but freeholders might serve as jurors in the many confiscation proceedings which were to begin that spring all over the colony. When the county courts brought people charged with cooperation in the Bacon revolt before them, the defendants were to stand on their knees with halters about their necks, confess "treasons and rebellions", and have their property taken.[20] There was no doubt that Berkeley, Philip Ludwell, acting secretary of the council, Warner and Beverley were masters of what was left of Virginia—hundreds, perhaps a thousand of poor folk slipping over the borders into Carolina or the wilds of the Indian country.

When the Council and the burgesses came thus into regular session and were duly organized, the commissioners presented their credentials and urged just and moderate treatment of the people and legislators who had felt compelled to defend themselves against the Indians and had reformed in June, 1676, the shameful abuses which Sir William had approved or permitted to be practiced for twelve years. They had hoped to do what they had urged for weeks upon the Governor and Council: to apply in Virginia what Shaftesbury had been imprisoned for trying to apply in England. It was a curious thing: a King's commission trying to correct abuses, bribery and dictatorial methods in Virginia hardly half as bad as the

[20] Hening, II, 380-83; 556.

abuses, bribery and autocracy in London.[21] Sir William denounced the high-toned representatives of his Majesty, and both he and the two houses of the assembly ignored the commissioners and pleaded that they were in no sense as ruthless as Charles I had been during the sixteen-forties. The session was hardly over before the King's definite authorization of the commissioners was given: that Sir William must give up his office, go home on the first boat that sailed and leave Herbert Jeffreys in charge of affairs.

At last Sir William informed Jeffreys that he would sail on the *Rebecca* for England on April 20, and that Captain Larrimore, whom he had imprisoned in Accomac the preceding August, would command the vessel. The *Rebecca* was delayed a day or two, and his Majesty's representatives paid the Governor a formal visit on April 22 to say farewell and perhaps to hasten his departure. When Sir William's carriage was about to take them home from Greenspring, the common hangman of the place was ordered to escort them to the river at Jamestown. The commissioners were so indignant that they dismounted and walked four miles to the place where they were to take their boat to Swann's Point. They made a sharp protest at the indignity, saying they had seen Lady Berkeley peeping out the palace window as the hangman had offered his services. Thomas Motley, acting Governor of Maryland, wrote Lord Baltimore that Berkeley's system was so hated in Virginia that there would be another revolt if he remained.[22] And this view is fully sustained in the mass of petitions and complaints which every county and hundreds of individuals presented to the commissioners as Sir John Berry and Francis Moryson were making ready to return to

[21] *State Papers, Colonial*, 1677–80, pp. 26-28.
[22] *Ibid.*, May 22, 1677.

London early in May. No other American colony ever gave so complete a picture of political and social conditions as these members of the commission presented to the Board of Trade and Plantations that summer.

Sir William finally bade farewell to Lady Berkeley on May 5, gave her his will and testament which meant that she would be the wealthiest woman in America, and then sailed with Francis Moryson for England. He was half ill, but resolute in his public declaration that he would return with the King's approval in a few months. His health was hardly improved by the fact that Francis Moryson was on the same ship and master of hundreds of anti-Berkeley documents. But as he was to take up his residence again in the London palace of his brother, John Lord Berkeley, there was some chance of the seventy-one-year old dictator sailing again for his beloved Greenspring. He reached the palace on June 16 and died there on July 9.

Virginia was at last free; and Herbert Jeffreys, still living at the home of Thomas Swann, was the reform Governor. Would he restore the democratic system for which men had fought so long?

13

Charles Town

> "Substantial men and their families must make the plantation which will stock the country with Negroes, cattle and other necessities."—The Earl of Shaftesbury, *State Papers, Colonial*, Dec. 16, 1671.

I

THE THREATENED FAILURE OF THE NEW ENGLANDERS and the Barbadians to maintain their settlement on the Cape Fear River, 1663–66, caused a group of men on a small boat to explore the harbors and rivers of the Carolina coast between present-day Charleston and Port Royal. Robert Sandford and Henry Woodward, were the leaders. They entered the mouth of Ashley River, came into contact with friendly Indians who showed them the resources of the region and expressed the hope that they might persuade the English people to make a settlement there. The explorers then went farther south and found other Indians near Port Royal who were equally friendly. The whole area from Charles Town harbor to the mouth of the Savannah River was most appealing to Sandford and Woodward, and they wrote descriptions of the beauty of the islands, the fertility of the mainland, the marvellous forests, the abundance of fish in the waters and wild animals in the woods. These reports renewed the interest of the Carolina proprietors in their colonial undertakings, which had not been too successful for them in Albemarle. Ashley Cooper, whose history we have already reviewed, was most concerned, and John Locke, his liberal young secretary, took the lead in proprietary affairs a little after the close of the horrible second Dutch war. The enforcement of the Stuart Navigation and Trade acts of 1660 and 1663 increased the depression in Maryland and Virginia and rendered most of the white workers and farmers in Barbados helpless and homeless, ready as we have seen to migrate anywhere and even to become pirates under the leadership of Henry Morgan of Jamaica. At the same time the enforcement of the Clarendon code under which so many religious dissenters were executed in England caused thousands of church people, Baptists, Presbyterians and Quakers to be ready to cross the terrible Atlantic, even in the winter. Under these circumstances the proprietors, half of whom were deists at heart, renewed their plans for founding a second Carolina colony. John Locke rewrote the famous charter under which an aristocracy in a wild country was to be created, with great plantations on the banks of many rivers, smaller manor places intermingled and freemen farmers to compose two-thirds of the population that was to be.[1] Perhaps thousands of Englishmen and Barbadians would migrate and in a few years make the proprietors wealthier "palatines" living in London than Francis Lord Willoughby, recent governor of Barbados and the greatest speculative landlord of all the West Indies.[2]

When Sandford and his fellows returned to the Cape Fear settlement a little before its abandonment, they left the brave Henry Woodward with the friendly Indians near Port Royal there to speak with the natives and study the relations of the many tribes of the Savannah River and along the borders of the later Florida country. He remained about a year in that remote and dangerous country, and was then captured and carried to St. Augustine where he joined the Catholic Church and

[1] Andrews, Charles M., *Colonial Period of American History*, III, Galleys 88-90. This proof has been kindly loaned me.
[2] McCrady, Edward, *History of South Carolina, the Proprietary Government*, Ch. III.

GEORGE FOX *From an old print*

Emmett Collection, New York Public Library

learned that the Spaniards preached their religion to the natives and helped them resist the Westo Indians who had been expelled from Virginia in 1656 only to become for a time the most powerful of southern Carolina tribes. Imprisoned in 1668, he escaped the same year to become a physician on a West Indian pirate ship, hoping some way to get back to England and report the conditions and promises of lower Carolina.

August 17, 1669, Ashley Cooper and his hopeful fellows hurried off three ships, the *Albemarle*, the *Carolina* and the *Port Royal*, under command of Captains Florence Sullivan and Stephen Bull, for Carolina with ninety-three passengers—one of them with sixty-three servants. Two months later the expedition reached Barbados, where other settlers and servants were to be taken on board; but on November 12, a storm swept over the harbor and destroyed the *Albemarle*. Thomas Colleton and Sir John Yeamans, who was asked by the proprietors to be the first governor of Carolina, lent all possible assistance and furnished a small ship to take the place of the *Albemarle*. The ships sailed northward toward Bermuda in November, Sir John Yeamans on board, but the expedition was once more overtaken by a heavy storm. The endangered ships entered the harbor of Nevis Island where they found Dr. Henry Woodward, who had escaped from his storm-wrecked pirate ship the preceding August. Woodward now joined the Carolina settlers. After lingering a time at Bermuda, the ships sailed again, but on January 12, 1670, the *Port Royal* was destroyed by another storm near the Bahama Islands—many lives lost. Under these depressing conditions Sir John Yeamans returned to Barbados and appointed the aged William Sayle first governor of Carolina. The *Carolina* and two small ships with the surviving passengers and servants on board sailed from Bermuda on February 26, 1670; but another storm broke upon them and one of the boats was thought to be lost. The others arrived at Port Royal on March 17, where Governor Sayle and his colleagues, Joseph West, deputy for the Duke of Albemarle, Stephen Bull, representative of Shaftesbury, and three others called upon the freemen of the colony to elect five representatives to sit with them in the Council, a prospective parliament. Paul Smith, Ralph Marshall, Samuel West and two others were chosen. It was the first governing group in South Carolina. Because of the reported dangers from Indians and Spaniards, the Governor and assembly decided to move northward to the mouth of the Ashley and Cooper rivers, as they were soon to be called —the famous Charleston harbor of later times. They reached their final destination during the early days of April, and their lost ship with most of its passengers joined them on May 23. What a troubled journey, August 17, 1669, to May 23, 1670! Two of the three larger ships had been lost; some additional settlers had been taken on at Barbados; but just how many were lost or how many began their operations in the first settlement on the south bank of the Ashley River can not be given. The story reveals once more the risks and disasters of seventeenth century colonial endeavors.[3]

The Kiowha Indians who occupied the region south and west of the new settlement, welcomed the newcomers because they hoped for protection against the Westo natives who occupied the area about Port Royal and westward toward the Savannah River. Governor Sayle and his fellows hoped to use both tribes of Indians against probable attacks of Spaniards who had not acknowledged the proprietors' rights to settle the region south of the Cape Fear. It was the beginning of anxiety and warfare which continued almost uninterrupted nearly half a century, a struggle between the Carolinians, the Indians, the Spaniards and later the French settlers at Mobile

[3] Salley, Alexander S., *Narratives of Early Carolina*, 116-124.

CHARLES TOWN 259

and New Orleans. But in the early years the first problem was actual self-support, the proprietors unwilling to continue to send large sums of money to their representatives, Sayle, West and their other prospective landlords —"landgraves and caciques." Foodstuffs came mainly from the rivers, the forests and the Indians; cows and hogs for breeding purposes were first imported from Virginia, later from New York. Lumber, barrel staves and ship timber were soon being sold to Barbados and London. But there was no real farming, after the manner of Virginia and Maryland, before 1690, and the proprietors lost immense sums of money. Their curious notion of having a great landed aristocracy, 48,000 acres each for landgraves, 24,000 for caciques and 12,000 for the owners of manors, like those of successful Maryland, was perhaps a cause of their losses.

The aged Governor, an earnest Puritan of Bermuda who had lived long in the West Indies, studied the Carolina country from the Cape Fear to the Savannah, and hoped to found a strong settlement to resist the Spanish encroachment toward the north. He tried seriously during his short term to make his Albemarle Point a strong fortress against all opponents. John West, the representative of the Earl of Albemarle, in whose honor their little town was named, and Stephen Bull, the spokesman of Ashley Cooper for whom the two protective rivers north and south of the Charles Town, founded a little later, were named, were co-operative with the Governor; and two-thirds of the population, drawn in 1670 and 1671 from Barbados, Bermuda and New York, and said to be "irreligious and reckless," were ready always to follow his lead. They insisted upon their right to elect a "parliament," to assist Sayle in organizing a free church and to select a pastor from Barbados or even Massachusetts. Like Virginia and northern Carolina, they would have no lawyers in their colony and were disposed to ramble over the wonderful lowland forests, take possession of the most promising lands along the banks of rivers and trade freely with the Indians; but the natives, under Spanish influence or provoked by ruthless treatment, began quite early to rob the distant settlers and were making ready to do in Carolina what had been attempted in Virginia in 1622—kill every newcomer. This caused men to cling to their little Albemarle town; the region round about seemed to them:

A new land of Canaan where the winters were mild, the summers not hot, the land flowing with milk and honey; the woods may be called a garden over which millions of ducks darken the sky and where hogs, sheep and goats are always fit for the knife.[4]

II

Half true as the above quotation of a contemporary letter was, due to imports of cows and pigs and goats from Virginia and New York, Governor Sayle, John West and the other spokesmen of the distant proprietors were confronted with serious dangers, when "His Excellency" passed away in March, 1671. There was a shortage of food and actual danger of serious Spanish-Indian attacks. Therefore, when John West was elected governor of the colony, then numbering 263 men able to bear arms, less than a hundred women and sixty-two children, he managed to get his council and assembly to order every family, except busy carpenters, to plant two acres in corn or peas, and compel slothful or unwilling persons to become the servants of active landowners. This application of the early Virginia system had a decisive influence during West's early governorship, 1671–1672. The fees of local officers were sharply limited, the

[4] *State Papers, Colonial,* March, 1671, Shaftesbury letters, No. 85.

wages of "artificers" were rather liberal and new-coming servants from England and Barbados were to have land-grants in due time; and liquors were not to be sold except upon licenses granted by the Council. Although there were protests against certain injustices practised under these laws, there was a real application which relieved food shortage even in the summer of 1671, promised ultimately the payment of interest on the proprietors' loans, and, above all, held the population together in a way that promised fair security in the event of attacks.

But the crops of 1671 were not harvested before the Kusso Indians, a small tribe south and west of Albemarle Point, with the promise of Spanish assistance and the co-operation of other natives, began to attack frontier Carolina settlers. The idea was to destroy the settlement and kill every Englishman, although they had urged the English more than once to come into their country. The colonists, fairly organized for military resistance and aware of the dangers ahead, seized two Kussos who happened to be in their town and, with guns on their shoulders, invaded the Indian villages the last days of September. They surprised and defeated the natives, took many prisoners whom the soldiers were permitted to sell as slaves, in payment for their service—a practice authorized by the proprietors.[5] A treaty of peace followed, but the Carolinians were not sure enough of themselves to establish farms far from their little capital on the Ashley River.

Before the end of the year, Sir John Yeamans, the landgrave of Barbados who had failed in his Cape Fear endeavors and had declined to accompany the colonists in 1670, appeared at Albemarle Point and claimed the right to be the governor in spite of West's success and increasing popularity. John Culpeper, a kinsman of Lady Berkeley, land speculator of Barbados, and other West In-

[5] Rivers, William J., *A Sketch of the History of South Carolina*, Ch. 4.

dian freemen and Negro slaves had accompanied Sir John to Carolina. West refused to surrender his office, and called upon the colonists to elect another assembly. The result was a general refusal to recognize Sir John Yeamans as their governor, in spite of the provision in the charter which had made him the owner of a vast tract of land there. This was a parallel to the Virginia popular control of 1635. Sir John was not in a position to seize the authority he claimed, but he set his servants and slaves to work on his land along the Cooper River and began profitable trade with Barbados. He procured skins and furs from the Indians, set up a sawmill and shipped large quantities of lumber, staves and timber to West Indian settlements. He even exported foods at a profit at a time when the Governor and the Carolina people were still anxious about their scarcity of provisions.

While the Carolinians were resisting the pressure of Sir John Yeamans and slowly fixing themselves in their dangerous zone, the proprietors, under the general pressure of Charles II and Louis XIV in their secret alliance for the conquest of the Netherlands and the subordination of Germany, changed the charter of 1669 so that dissenters from England, Barbados and even New England must abandon their religious freedom and their claims to self-government. Lord Shaftesbury, speaking for his fellows, proclaimed Sir John governor, appointed John Culpeper surveyor of the Carolina lands and made the former governor, West, "superintendent of plantations and registrar of contracts"—a patriotic secretary of the commonwealth and assistant to the Governor as William Claiborne had been for many years in Virginia. But the assembly refused to recognize changes in the charter, declined to allow the Council to suggest all the laws they might enact, while the people distrusted and opposed their new governor so vigorously that he retreated to Barbados.[6] Culpeper tried, however, to apply Shaftesbury's plan for building the town of Charles Town at Oyster Point between Ashley and Cooper rivers; but he was even more unpopular than his retiring chief. He retreated to Albemarle in a year or two, where he later played a peculiar rôle. Aware of the speculative blunders of Sir John and the natural resistance of the Carolinians, the proprietors reappointed West to the governorship in 1674, and the enforcement of the changes of the charter was not insisted upon. The trying years of the founders now merged into more prosperous ones and the colonization greatly improved.

The Earl of Shaftesbury, now Chancellor to Charles II, still the owner of vast estates in Wiltshire and Dorsetshire, southwestern England, and master of great areas in Barbados and Bermuda, was in 1674 much inclined to emigrate to his estates on the Ashley River, where he hoped to do more in the great Carolina country than the Lords Baltimore had done in Maryland.[7] His friend, Woodward, had been seeking in Carolina and Virginia to discover mines, make trade treaties with the many and rival Indian settlements on the Savannah River and even in the high mysterious mountain region where furs of similar value to those of the famous Six Nations of New York were to be found. Abraham Wood, a self-made landlord of Virginia, in command of Fort Henry (Petersburg) and some hundreds of frontier soldiers, sent his assistants, James Needham and Gabriel Arthur across the Roanoke River southeast of present-day Danville into the Yadkin valley and thence over the Blue Ridge and Great Smoky mountains to the Cherokee villages. Although Needham was slain by Indians on his return to Wood's headquarters, Arthur made trade ar-

[6] *State Papers, Colonial*, June 20, 1672.
[7] *Ibid.*, May 3, 1674.

rangements which later became most important and which so irritated the little Carolina colony that they undertook to prohibit Virginia's southwestern activity, especially when the Catawbas of upper Carolina became commercial allies of the "Old Dominion."

When Woodward's knowledge of frontier possibilities—trade in furs and skins which might replenish the losses of the proprietors—was repeatedly submitted to the Earl of Shaftesbury before 1676, there was a renewed interest in the Carolina adventure. Although Shaftesbury had been imprisoned in the Tower of London more than a year for his opposition to the King, he organized a Carolina trade association of his fellows, the aged Earl of Craven and the sons of the deceased first proprietors, Albemarle, Clarendon and Sir John Colleton, each of whom contributed £100. Woodward was to make treaties with the Indian chiefs on the Savannah and, even in the Spanish zone, forbid Carolinians to trade with the natives except their neighbors along the coast, discover gold and silver and make reports in a secret code so that nobody might learn of his discoveries.[8] It was the beginning of the long struggle with the Spaniards which more than once endangered the very existence of the Carolinians, and of an Indian trade which matched the famous New Amsterdam activity of 1640-50. It was also the beginning of hostility toward Virginia and wars with certain Indian tribes that continued more than half a century.

The increasing Indian trade of the proprietors and the profits of selling natives as slaves in the West Indies caused Shaftesbury, Craven and their fellows to think they might recover their losses and even obtain real profits from their vast land grant. The majority of immigrants who had come as indentured servants were then

[8] Crane, Verner W., *The Southern Frontier*, 1670-1732, pp. 15-20. Best account of this problem that has been written.

CHARLES TOWN 265

earning their own livings on fifty-acre tracts of land but, like Virginians, they were unable or unwilling to pay their quit-rents to their London masters. In fact, a penny per acre, as prescribed in their contracts, was almost half a dollar per acre in present-day currency. Although horses, cows, goats and hogs everywhere roamed the grassy meadows and woodlands, hardly costing their owners anything, the New England and West Indian markets had not yet developed. However, the common people were now self-supporting, and they might one day be so numerous as to give value to the great tracts of land that lay west of them. In fact, land about Charles Town, as Oyster Point was beginning to be called, was actually selling as high as $25 per acre.[9] There was an increasing lumber business, and the Negro slaves, in exchange for Indian captives, were of increasing value. Negro slavery was more popular in lower Carolina than on the Chesapeake shores, because they could be purchased by shipping Indians to the West Indies and also because blacks worked well and seemed to need no clothes.

III

Before the Earl of Shaftesbury was imprisoned for his democratic tendencies and John Locke made uneasy about his ideas of freedom, there was reapplication in England of the severe Clarendon code. The bishops of the Established Church were bent upon making all dissenters orthodox state church members. The King and his brother, the Duke of York, pressed successfully for the liberty of the Catholics whose chiefs were Jesuits; and both the Church of England and the Crown were in the late sixteen-seventies persecuting and imprisoning the Scotch Presbyterians as never before. John Maitland,

[9] McCrady, 185.

i.e., the ruthless Earl of Lauderdale, an intimate counsellor of Charles II, was the dictator of Scotland. In this tense era Titus Oates, a Baptist in his early life, then a Jesuit propagandist who turned dissenter again in 1678, reported a plot on the part of the Catholics to murder the King which so aroused religious fears and political hatreds that the King was compelled to dissolve his eighteen-year-old House of Commons. The election which followed revealed two parties, Whigs and Tories, some of whose leaders were of the most violent, even murderous, tendencies. Charles II and his hated brother would assist Louis XIV to make all Europe Catholic. Outstanding members of the House of Lords, also the Commons, would make England and Scotland a solid Church of England area. Equally influential men demanded the right of religious freedom for Baptists, Quakers, Presbyterians and even Unitarians—later more important in New England. Charles II had no son and was approaching the end of his libertine life. The Duke of York was expected to become King. He would compel England and Scotland to accept his arbitrary system, religious and political. This even increased England's anxieties. But the Duke of York had two daughters, grandchildren of the Protestant Earl of Clarendon who, as we know, had been banished from England in 1668, although he had done as much as the Earl of Albemarle to restore Charles II in 1660. Both these daughters were members of the Church of England; the older was Mary, wife of William of Orange, who had defeated the French dictator and his wife's brother, Charles II, in 1672–73 and who was trying in 1678–80 to unite the Netherlands, northern Germany and Austria in an alliance for the maintenance of religious freedom in all Europe. The hostilities of religious groups, the hatreds of party chiefs and the persecutions of 1678–82 caused scores of thousands of Englishmen to plan to cross the dangerous Atlantic where they might have religious freedom, homes of their own and even democratic government.

One of the effects of these persecutions and imprisonments was strange enough. William Penn, son of Admiral Penn, released from the Tower a little before Shaftesbury entered the famous place, was becoming a Stuart leader, although he was an ardent Quaker and the author of a marvellous book on religious freedom, for which he had been imprisoned; but he was the heir of a handsome income from his deceased father. In 1676 he purchased the proprietary rights of the Sir George Carteret heirs to New Jersey and began to hurry Quakers off to his place of refuge. Four years later he was a more ardent Stuart champion and was made absolute master of the vast area west of the Delaware River, soon to be called Pennsylvania. He hoped to make of his new, wild realm an even greater proprietary state than the Lords of Baltimore had made of their "Catholic" Maryland— and all the world knows how successful he was.[10]

When Penn was persuading his Quaker friends to migrate for religious freedom to his lands in New Jersey, the aged Earl of Shaftesbury and the heirs of his fellow-proprietors thought they might add tens of thousands of dissenter immigrants to their burdensome Carolina settlement. It was the same situation which assisted the King in 1625 and Lord Baltimore in 1633 in making their tobacco settlements on the Chesapeake Bay appealing. Human freedom was to the orthodox proprietors of Carolina in 1678-80 quite as promising as it had been at earlier dates, and they made liberal grants of lands to Benjamin Blake, of the Cromwellian Admiral's family; Daniel Axtell, kinsman of the famous Axtell who guarded the royal palace in 1649 to prevent the King's escape; Joseph Morton and scores of less distinguished people of the southwestern counties of England. Blake, Axtell

[10] *Dictionary of National Biography* gives a good Penn sketch.

and Morton were made landgraves. And this new migration to Carolina was so appealing that Thomas Colleton, of the wealthy Barbados family, joined his fellow-landgraves and added considerably to the number of freemen and servants on their way to the new world.

Before these new people arrived, the people of Albemarle Point had decided to move their little capital to the north side of the Ashley River. They called the place Oyster Point. In the spring of 1680 a little government house was built and thirty residences were soon afterwards erected. The good old Governor West called the place Charles Town, a name that became Charleston a hundred years later. The people were urged to become more religious and set up schools for their multiplying children. These settlers from New York, the West Indies, England and Ireland were intermingled, healthy still and no longer in danger of starvation. They had not yet had a serious yellow fever attack from the West Indies. Some men owned 700 head of livestock and had found markets in New England and Barbados for their surplus products. The Council members were still the representatives of the great proprietors in London, but they and the Governor co-operated with the assemblies elected by freemen and owners of fifty-acre tracts. It was a promising self-government with none of the violence and persecutions which plagued the peoples of Europe.

The proprietors were so hopeful at last that they once more changed the Carolina constitution. The Governor and council were to enact and enforce laws for the good of the people without the consent of the legislature, even without awaiting the approval of the proprietors. If the council in Charles Town did not thus act promptly and also correct the laws of the popular assembly, the grand jury of Berkeley county might enact needful statutes and enforce them;[11] and great landlords might be excused

[11] McCrady, 191-93.

from paying rents on their lands if they made sufficient explanations. These concessions were made to encourage persecuted gentlemen of England to migrate to Carolina. In spite of the solemn instructions from the proprietors to Governor West and his fellow-councillors, the colonists all but unanimously rejected every constitutional change and insisted upon the right of their assembly to make laws and reject proprietary changes; but they did accept the division of lower Carolina into three counties: Berkeley, the Charles Town area; Craven, the region about the great Santee River to the north; and Colleton, the dangerous country of which Port Royal was to be the capital.

When Benjamin Blake and his distinguished fellows with some hundreds of freemen and indentured servants arrived in 1682, Governor West and other popular Carolina leaders were ordered to retire, and Joseph Morton became the new chief. The popular retiring Governor, who had done so much to make Carolina a successful colony, was discredited by charges that he had been engaged in selling Indians as slaves to the West Indian planters, a practice which the proprietors had ordered more than once. In spite of these mistakes on behalf of the newcomers from England and Barbados, the Carolinians continued to spread over the better lands north and westward, and they undertook, like the Virginians in 1630, to build strong fortifications west of their new capital between the Cooper and the Ashley rivers. The embankment and wall between the rivers were watched by trained militia. The streets were a hundred feet wide and straight. Their first church was neatly built on brick foundations and surrounded by a palisade, and the first Church of England pastor, Atkin Williamson, was actively engaged before 1682; and other denominations held their meetings, but seem to have had no regular preachers. The total population of Charles Town was not more than 500;

the settlers of the whole colony numbered about 2,000, eight or ten landgraves, perhaps a score of caciques. Would there be a Carolina aristocracy like that of Barbados and more profitable to their proprietors than the slavery system of Barbados was to the Crown of England?

Before these newcomers were fairly settled, Henry Erskine, i.e., Lord Cardross, released from his long prison term in Edinburgh and because he was an uncompromising Presbyterian, he applied to the proprietors for tracts of land in Carolina and was promised thirty plots of 12,000 acres each in the dangerous lower Carolina region, Port Royal to be its county seat and export town—a rival of Charles Town.[12] There would be more landgraves, caciques, freemen and servants, all stern Scotch Presbyterians. Alexander Dunlop, the Hamiltons, Montgomeries and scores of simpler folk joined Lord Cardross as he sailed in 1683 from Glasgow for the Carolina coast. There were ten thousand other Scotchmen ready to settle at Port Royal. Would the proprietors at last succeed in their great and costly adventure? But Charles II had dismissed his second troublesome parliament. He would govern England as he wished; and the sixty-two-year-old Shaftesbury was once more ordered to be tried for treason—because he had fought for parliamentary supremacy. Sick and hopeless as to his country's future, this greatest English statesman of the second half of the seventeenth century escaped his enemies in London, took up his residence in free Holland, the country which he had helped Louis XIV try to destroy in 1672–73, and there passed away on January 21, 1683. Thus the chief of all the proprietors, the closest friend of poor John Locke and the one who had lost perhaps a hundred thousand dollars on the Carolina adventure, died in Amsterdam at

---

[12] *Dictionary of National Biography;* Rivers, William J., *History of South Carolina,* 142-43.

the moment all his fellows were sure their great Scotch-American adventure would be more than successful. But human hopes in the seventeenth, as in the twentieth century, were disappointing.[13]

Before Lord Cardross and his first shipload of settlers reached Port Royal, the proprietors informed their unpopular Governor Morton and his Charles Town opponents that the Scotch settlement was to be a new state, his lordship was to be Governor and the new Scotch colony was to elect its own legislature. Charles Town was also asked to send to Port Royal five or six heavy guns to assist the newcomers to resist expected Spanish or Indian attacks. The proprietors could hardly do otherwise for their "ten thousand" Scotch settlers and their distinguished lordship Cardross. But the Ashley-Cooper river people, contending for popular government, had practically forced Governor Morton to submit to them, and both the councillors and the assemblymen were bitterly opposed to the independence of the lower Colleton region. Even the eminent new settlers in upper Colleton, Axtell, Blake and their fellows were unable to persuade the Carolina assembly to allow their county equal representation before the Cardross settlement. The exasperated proprietors wrote Morton in 1683: "Are you to govern the people, or the people you?" That was the issue, and the farmers and traders of the thirteen-year-old colony were determined, as were the Virginians of 1630–1662, to govern themselves. Under these circumstances Morton lost his position in 1684, and Sir Richard Kyrle, an Irish immigrant, took his place. Kyrle died in a few months, and the councillors chose West once more for their leadership. While the popular ex-Governor, who had been in England, was returning, Robert Quarry, secretary of the province, served as acting governor.[14] Dur-

[13] Trevelyan, *England under the Stuarts,* Ch. XII.
[14] McCrady, 201.

ing those troubled times Lord Cardross and his one hundred or more fellows settled in lower Colleton, built themselves cabins on the shores of Port Royal and began to lay the foundations of their American Scotland. But they fell at once into difficulties with their Indian neighbors, who were in a sort of alliance with the Spaniards. Henry Woodward had been in London in 1682 and received instructions to make other explorations and trade agreements among the natives all the way across present-day Georgia, with the Westos on the Savannah and the far more powerful Lower Creeks further southwest. Lord Cardross himself had planned some such commercial arrangements; and he promptly arrested Woodward, the most famous explorer in all the southern colonies. That added to the troubles with the Charles Town settlers, though they too had quarrelled with the proprietors because of their relations with Woodward and the thousands of Indians ready to trade with anybody who did not capture and sell them for slaves. His lordship had not been in Port Royal a year before he was ordered by the Carolina Council to appear before them and learn that the constitutional rights granted in 1669 did not allow him and his distinguished new colony to set up an independent state, even on the dangerous Spanish-Indian borders. Lord Cardross refused to meet the Carolina authorities, and continued to urge more immigrants from Scotland who would at once make Port Royal more important than Charles Town. His fellows, Dunlop, Hamilton and Montgomerie continued their work, clearing land and trading with the Indians. They named their little village Stuart Town.

But decisive influences in Europe, as so often before, greatly affected the policy of the Charles Town colony. Even before the Scotch Presbyterians had sailed for Port Royal, Louis XIV began to persecute the Huguenots of his country so violently that thousands of French dissenters from Catholicism began to seek homes in friendly Holland or persecuting England. Under these circumstances Jean Bazant and Richard Gaillard brought scores of their troubled fellows into Carolina and received ample grants of land north and west of the Ashley-Cooper region. In 1680 two shiploads of Huguenots had reached Carolina, Rene Petit and Jacob Grinard obtaining lands for them. These vigorous people hoped to produce silk and wine on their new lands. About the time James II came to the throne of England, Louis XIV revoked the famous Edict of Nantes under which perhaps a million French Protestants had flourished nearly a century. If these cleverest people of France did not become Catholics their property was to be taken and scores of thousands were to be killed. Four hundred thousand refused to surrender and managed to get out of France in spite of all the ruthless border warfare and persecution. Thus during the very year when Port Royal was thought to be a new state within the older state, some five hundred of these Protestants landed in Carolina. The Bacots, Du Bois, Doveaux, Du Ponts, Guerards and Hugers were their leaders from whom many distinguished Carolinians of later generations descended. They settled on Goose Creek, the great Santee River and also in upper Colleton county, building churches of their own and later contending for equal rights with the older settlers. Thus Colleton county of the south, Berkeley in the middle section and Craven county to the north were duly organized and the populations of all the rival sections were led by more aristocratic families than any other mainland colony of the seventeenth century.[15]

Before the close of the second decade of their existence, the lower Carolinians had become far more important than the more numerous Albemarle settlement three

[15] McCrady, 181, 238; Hirsch, A. H., *The Huguenots of South Carolina,* an excellent detailed account.

hundred miles to the north of them. All the proprietors, hoping to found an aristocracy and to earn fortunes for themselves, had passed away; and England had ceased to co-operate with Louis XIV, which caused English migration almost to stop—persecution also discontinued. There were now perhaps a score of landgraves and caciques along the banks of the Ashley and Cooper rivers, and Charles Town was already the greatest village of all the settlements south of New York. The great number of Indian tribes in the western up-country and between the dangerous Savannah River and the Spanish zone gave South Carolina a different character from that of Virginia or Maryland. Men must be armed and ready to fight. This Indian problem caused hundreds, perhaps thousands, of captives to be taken and sold or exchanged for Negro slaves in Jamaica and Barbados. These facts gave the Council members and chiefs of the more aristocratic families opportunities for a trade that had hardly been matched in New York and along the upper Hudson River—the slave system even beginning. This and the use of Negro slaves caused the larger landholders, even the ex-indentured servants, to follow more aristocratic habits than either Marylanders or Virginians before 1680; but when English serfs or city unemployed could always become freemen owners of sizeable tracts of land in five years, the aristocracy could not be developed rapidly. The masses of people voted almost as freely as in Virginia before 1662,[16] and the various denominations, Church of England members, Huguenots, Presbyterians and even Baptists and Quakers, acting under the guarantees of the original charter, prevented religious persecution—even serious opposition. Governors, despite their landgrave social rating, were compelled to recognize the supremacy of the popular assembly, and they were several times, as had been the case in Albemarle and Vir-

[16] *State Papers, Colonial,* Dec. 12, 1681.

ginia, elected by the Charles Town assemblymen. Thus government was almost a local affair, unlike the other southern governments, with Berkeley county majorities in control of things. The concentration about Charles Town, the grave dangers from the Indians and Spaniards and the influence of commercial men were the causes of this. The grand, original plan had substantially failed; however, the Carolina folk were beginning a career which was to influence all southern history almost as much as Virginia.

14

The Emerging Carolinas

> "Our laws against privateers neither discourage nor lessen them while they have such retreats as Carolina, New England and other colonies."—Sir Thomas Lynch, *State Papers, Colonial,* Feby. 28, 1684.

I

WITH TENSE RELIGIOUS STRUGGLES IN ENGLAND TOward the end of the Stuart régime, with wars on the continent of Europe still raging, and the governments of Spain, France, England and even Holland competing with one another in the West Indies and along the North American coast all the way to Boston, the enforcement of the Navigation acts was almost impossible. The limitation of the trade and crime of ome fifteen hundred pirate and privateer ships in American harbors was now far more difficult than in the Cromwell time. The people of every European master of colonies were forbidden, as we know, to trade with anybody in other colonies; but no government was strong enough to enforce such a policy three thousand miles away where the rivers and harbors were so many and complicated, and where all populations greatly needed commercial opportunities. Under these circumstances, buccaneers, pirates and privateers were more encouraged to enter harbors everywhere than they had been during 1640–50. At Barbados, Jamaica, Bermuda and along the Carolina coasts these semi-warring traders were most active. They were more active in the Chesapeake Bay, where tobacco exports were more carefully controlled than anything else. Even

THE EMERGING CAROLINAS 277

pious New Englanders kept some hundreds of small fast ships sailing the seas from their own harbors to the tobacco and sugar colonies, transferring products to Scotland, France and the Netherlands at higher prices than England paid. Then, with proceeds in hand, they slipped into African ports, where they picked up shiploads of Negroes and sold them in the West Indies or even to the hated Spaniards on the mainland. The Royal African Company, over which members of the Carolina proprietors, even high officials in the British Government, still presided, could hardly make any profits in competition with New England and West Indian pirates who escaped all taxes on their operations.[1]

Henry Morgan of Jamaica was for many years the greatest of these warring pirates. His attacks upon the Spanish settlements were the most murderous of all, and he seized gold in such quantities that he greatly interested Charles II, who profited from privateers and who pardoned Morgan when he was sent under arrest to London. He was proclaimed Sir Henry Morgan in 1674 as he returned to Jamaica to be Deputy Governor.[2] Though his interest declined, there were many other chiefs of pirate ships most actively engaged during the period when the two Carolinas were slowly working their way to stability. George Gallop, an English captain who tried to regulate trade in the West Indies, seized a Dutch ship in 1675 with 544 Negro slaves on board. This was said to be "more beneficial to Jamaica than all the prizes brought to harbor." The seizure of gold and silver on the way to Spain and the capture of Negroes in Africa during the second half of the seventeenth century were the most profitable activities of the West Indian region. But during the 1670's there developed a remarkable trade in log-

[1] *State Papers, Colonial,* Aug. 29, 1682, and many other references in this volume.
[2] General E. A. Cruikshank, *The Life of Sir Henry Morgan,* Ch. VII.

wood which tempted shipmasters quite as much as Albemarle tempted New England and Scotch traders. This peculiar hardwood was to be found anywhere in the Central America of our time. It belonged to Spain; but it would have required fifty war vessels and a considerable army if the pirates and wandering settlers from Barbados and Jamaica were to be kept from cutting and exporting at high profits this popular timber. London, Amsterdam and Hamburg bought increasing quantities of it.[3]

With these difficulties all over the West Indies, the southern colonists could hardly be expected to hold themselves entirely aloof. In Maryland the third Lord Baltimore who had deprived his freemen in 1670 of their right to vote was violating the Navigation acts, and earning larger profits than ever by shipping tobacco to other countries than England. Unlawful trade and pirate activity were so common that the King of England kept tax collectors in the Chesapeake Bay. In May, 1681, four ships sailed away, refusing to pay duties and earning for his lordship, then Governor, £2,500. The Virginians were at the same time in such a sad plight that they destroyed nearly half their tobacco crop in May, 1682, hoping to get better prices from English markets. Governor Nicholas Spencer reported that "the necessities of the inhabitants, owing to the low price of tobacco, have made them desperate." With most of the 80,000 Virginians in such condition, one could hardly be surprised to learn that the Virginia waters were also "infested with pirates to whom our nakedness lays us open." Thus in "old Virginia" there were similar difficulties to those in all other settlements, although the shipments of tobacco to English ports still yielded his Majesty more than £100,000 a year. Under these circumstances the British Government sent the famous Edward Randolph to the colonies in 1676 to make a survey of things and suggest remedies.

[3] Beer, George L., *The Old Colonial System,* Vol. II, Chs. VI and VII.

THE EMERGING CAROLINAS 279

He took up his residence in Boston and set himself the impossible task of enforcing British commercial regulations; but there was no such thing as success, and later he was held for months in a Boston prison. Then he travelled about all the colonies reporting the hopeless state of things and once more found himself in a Bermuda prison, both the New Englanders and the West Indian people regarding him as the worst of enemies in spite of the fact that he represented the Crown of England.[4]

When Sir Henry Morgan abandoned his piratical activities about 1676 and Sir Thomas Lynch became Governor of Jamaica in 1680, there was a real effort to regulate West Indian trade. The legislature of the island enacted rigid statutes and the King sent a real war vessel with soldiers on board to enforce the law. Sir Thomas Lynch warned the Government in London once more that all other British colonies must enact similar statutes—especially the Carolinas; and in consequence war vessels were stationed in the Chesapeake Bay and competent officials placed in command. There were arrests and seizures of ships all the way from Boston to Charles Town, some pirates hanged, their bodies left in the air for months as warning; but there was no real success anywhere during the stormy period of 1678 to 1690. With war or semi-war in Europe, promising trade along the coasts of North and Central America and all colonists advocating free trade, even the drastic efforts of 1680–1690 failed.[5]

II

Under these circumstances the two little Carolinas worked their ways slowly another ten years toward rec-

[4] *State Papers, Colonial,* May 26, 1681, May 8, 1682, and on many other occasions give ample evidence.
[5] Beer, II, 71-75.

ognized self-government and trade profits. As we have already noted, the Albemarle people simply refused to pay quitrents for their land; tobacco duties of one penny a pound, fixed by the Lords of Trade in London, were counted unlawful, and rarely, if ever, paid; and there was no effort to apply the Navigation acts against the sales and purchases of ship captains who slipped into the intricate bays and winding rivers on which lived the remote frontier and farmer folk. When the Carolina proprietors tried to govern Albemarle by way of Charles Town where more eminent men lived, and sent governors there to enforce British statutes, resistance increased. Thomas Miller assumed the governorship in July, 1677, Timothy Biggs his chief assistant. They began to arrest and imprison prominent people, surrounding themselves with armed guardsmen as Sir William Berkeley had done for years. About the time popular armed resistance began, George Durant, one of the founders of the colony, returned from London, where he had warned the proprietors against threatened Albemarle domination. Durant at once organized the people, with the curious John Culpeper, recently trying to act as governor in Charles Town, for their leader. Governor Miller was charged with trying to control the precinct elections, and both he and Biggs were thrust into prison. Before the end of December the government of the people was re-established; but Thomas Eastchurch, a delayed appointee of the proprietors, more disliked by Durant than the imprisoned Miller, announced that he was on his way from Jamestown to his post. He would be the master of the Carolina freemen. But the Albemarle people sent troops to the Virginia border to arrest Eastchurch if he tried to enter the colony. The new "Governor" called on the Virginia authorities for troops to march into Carolina. When he was about to depart with trained soldiers, he fell ill and died in a few days. Durant and his fellows were again popular masters of the colony, as they had been fifteen years before; and they re-established their "government of the country by their own authority and according to their own model." [6] It was another of the many seventeenth century efforts to set up democracies by the southern colonists. The Stuart dictatorship idea was never accepted in any of the southern communities.

John Jenkins was now made acting Governor by the legislature. Thomas Cullen was speaker of the new assembly and his chief co-workers were William Crawford, Thomas Jarvis, William Jennings, Alexander Lillington and Richard Sanders, well-known names in North Carolina history a hundred years later. The Governor's Council, supposed to be dominated by appointees of the proprietors, and the palatine court—its members officially called landgraves or caciques—were acting in concert with the popular assembly and all were hopeful that the liberal Earl of Shaftesbury would persuade the proprietors to recognize their right to self-government. With New England ships, or even buccaneer captains, taking their tobacco away, with a surplus of foodstuffs, now and then going to the West Indies, and fifty-acre land grants to all ex-indentured servants, the upper Carolinians were in better condition in 1679 than the Charles Town colonists or even the Virginians. There were a few men like Valentine Byrd and George Durant who owned Negro slaves as well as white servants on four or five year contracts; but unlike the gentlemen of lower Carolina, they were not called landgraves or caciques. The people ridiculed these pretentious names. The tobacco output was 800,000 pounds a year, and the royal tax under the unapplied ruling of 1673 amounted to £3,000, one pound sterling per capita, equal to thirty dollars a year in present-day money. The proprietors had been entitled to a shilling a year for every fifty-acre grant. No governor or

[6] Ashe, *History of North Carolina,* Ch. X.

collector of export or import duties under the Navigation acts had ever been able to send a tenth of the above-named sums to London. Here, as in Virginia, the masses of the people could not meet the claims laid upon them, even when they had agreed to do so in the matter of quit-rents; and the proprietors had realized the disappointing facts.[7]

New Englanders were far more active in the upper Carolina and West Indian trade in 1670–90 than had been possible during the late Cromwell period; and their commercial leaders were most sympathetic with the Albemarle farmers who claimed practical independence in political as well as economic life. The most resolute and successful of them were Mordecai Bowdoin, Zachariah Gillam, Caleb Lamb and John Winslow. In spite of all the efforts of British officials, these traders sent their loaded ships regularly to Ireland, Scotland, Holland, France and Spain—returning as often as not loaded with slaves for the West Indian markets. Once, as we know, Gillam entered the Albemarle Sound when Indian attacks were most dangerous, and he delivered arms and ammunition enough to save the settlers from disastrous attacks. Later Gillam was indicted in an English court for violations of the Navigation acts, but he argued his case so ably that he escaped penalties. New England commercial activity was most helpful during this semi-revolutionary period.[8]

When Durant and his fellows won control, as indicated above, they built a staunch log prison near the home of the well-to-do William Jennings and lodged the royalist, Miller, and the Quaker leader, Biggs, there under guard till they could decide what to do with them. The clever Biggs escaped and hurried off to London to

[7] Only Barbados and Jamaica were able to meet the demands of the royalist collectors.
[8] Ashe, I, 116-17.

urge the overthrow of the popular government in Albemarle. This disturbed Durant and Jenkins, and they persuaded their legislature to hurry a commission to argue their case before the proprietors in London. Biggs did his best to have Durant and his government overthrown, but John Culpeper appeared before the authorities in London in 1680 and in spite of his own irregularities in Charles Town and even Albemarle, he argued the Albemarle claims before the Earl of Shaftesbury and his fellows.[9] The situation in London was almost revolutionary; and Shaftesbury had but recently been released a second time from the Tower. Catholics had been forbidden to come within ten miles of London, contrary to the King's wish, and the Scotch were, as we know, under the drastic dictatorship of Lord Lauderdale. The Whig Party, which Shaftesbury had done most to organize, was not unpopular with his fellow-proprietors who were helping dissenters escape to both Carolinas. When the Albemarle "revolutionists" were indicted before the proprietors, Shaftesbury argued that the Carolinians had not violated their charter, and he asked his fellows to recognize the work of Durant and acting Governor Jenkins as lawful and patriotic. This was an acknowledgment of the two Carolina claims, viz., that their charters did not stipulate that the Navigation acts were to be applied to them without their approval. After natural delays in troubled London, the proprietors appointed Henry Wilkinson as successor to Jenkins, but asked him to select judicious men for his advisers and new judicial leaders to serve on the palatine court, i.e., the supreme court of the little colony. They were to restore some of Miller's property, allow Biggs to dwell peacefully in Virginia and persuade the colonists to pay some of their quit-rents to the proprietors and tobacco taxes to the Crown. It was a recognition of the popular leadership,

[9] Andrews, Charles M., *Colonial Period*, III, Ch. 15.

George Durant still serving as attorney-general to the governor.[10]

But the new Governor, Wilkinson, was so closely connected with the Earl of Shaftesbury in the Whig scheme to prevent the Duke of York from succeeding his ill brother that he was thrown into prison and never allowed to go to Albemarle. Then the least satisfactory of all Albemarle governors was appointed: Seth Sothell, who had bought the Earl of Clarendon's share in both Carolinas. On his way to the upper Carolina settlement, he was captured by Algerian pirates, who held their rich victim in prison three years. This left the upper Carolinians to apply the proprietors' gentle reforms as they saw fit. They selected Jenkins again for their acting Governor. He named the clever Robert Holden as collector of customs for the King and proprietors. When Landgrave Sothell appeared in 1684 and took office, he at first governed fairly well; later as a lord proprietor he seized other people's land and tried to be an autocrat. In 1689 he imprisoned, without due process of law, George Durant and Thomas Pollock because they opposed his methods. Once more the people revolted and under the leadership of Pollock captured Sothell on his great Pasquotank plantation and shut him up in a log house as Durant had done to Miller some years before. The Governor was then forced to resign upon the demand of the proprietors. In a few months he migrated to Charles Town where he claimed the right to be governor in spite of his dismissal in Albemarle.[11] He was a proprietor.

Curiously enough, Lady Berkeley entered into the upper Carolina picture at this time. Her first husband, Samuel Stephens, the second governor of Albemarle, left her large tracts of land in that region. Her second husband, Sir William Berkeley, gave her all his property in Vir-

[10] North Carolina *Colonial Records,* I, pp. 300, 326, 333.
[11] Ashe, I, 138-40.

From an old portrait. Photo by H. P. Cook

LADY BERKELEY

THE EMERGING CAROLINAS 285

ginia, including the confiscated properties of several revolutionists of 1676, whom he had killed, the famous Greenspring manor estate and his proprietary rights to the Carolinas. In 1679 she married Philip Ludwell, Secretary of the Virginia Council, in spite of protests by the Lords of Trade and Plantations about his brutal performances in the struggle of 1676. Having no children by any one of her husbands, she was the freest and the richest woman in all America and more influential than Governor Jeffreys from 1677 to 1679. Both before and after her third marriage, she was interested in governmental work, at times directing Virginia legislation. In spite of her ladyship's wealth and political influence, Mrs. Drummond, widow of the first governor of Albemarle, and Mrs. Jeffreys, widow of the deceased governor of Virginia, sued Mrs. Berkeley in the English court for the properties she had taken from them. But she was a favorite of Charles II, and escaped for a decade the losses that were threatened.[12] Herself and third husband living at their historic Virginia manor house and owners of vast interests in the Carolinas, it was not surprising that the arbitrary administration of Seth Sothell in Albemarle invited their attention. In 1689 when the proprietors ordered the removal of Seth Sothell, they asked Ludwell to take his place as Governor of North Carolina—the first official use of this name. Greatly interested in Virginia and Carolina properties, Ludwell remained at Greenspring and appointed the popular Thomas Jarvis, an Albemarle farmer since 1659, to be the real governor; and the upper Carolinians continued their self-government with certain reforms and the approval of the new King of England—William of Orange. They now scattered southward over what was called Bath county and took the risk of encroaching upon the lands

[12] *State Papers, Colonial,* Jan. 14, 1681, and Nov. 25, 1682. Many other references to this interesting woman's activity.

of the powerful Tuscarora Indians between the Tar and
Neuse rivers. The people were now fairly prosperous.
There were twenty or thirty farmers who had become
masters of large estates and owners of a score of slaves
worth as much as £30 each. A good trader sometimes
earned as much as £300 a year; but "doctors and attorneys were scandals to their profession." Cotton was cultivated and woven into cloth, "some women keeping their
large families decently apparelled. Most of the houses
were of wood, some of brick; the women married very
young, and their houses were full of little ones." [13] This
was early North Carolina: 4,000 self-governing inhabitants, none too religious and not seriously afraid of the
tens of thousands of Indians on their western and southern borders.

III

In Charles Town the atmosphere was different. Before Lord Cardross set up his Scotch colony on the dangerous border land next to the Spanish realm, the older
Charles Town people, always afraid their Spanish opponents would lead Indians to attack them, had caused
their Indian allies, the Creeks and Westos, to break
across the Florida borders. The "Spanish" Indians were
so frightened that the Guales, a numerous tribe on the
lower Altamaha River—a strategic area—made alliance with the Carolinians and a considerable number of
them settled near Port Royal. When Lord Cardross
came, he induced a number of the natives to settle on St.
Helena and Hilton Head islands, 1684–85, off his coast,
where they might help him resist the new Governor Juan
Cabrera of St. Augustine, in case he or his "pirate" assistants attacked the new colony. This settlement of Indians in his neighborhood led large numbers of the Yama-

[13] Ashe, I, 152-53.

sees and even revolting Spanish tribes to abandon their former lands near the Lower Creeks in southern Georgia of our day; and in 1685 the little Scotch colony was regarded as their patrons and even dangerous to the Spaniards.

This unexpected activity of the Scotch caused the Charles Town traders considerable anxiety, the more when they learned that their little ships must pass through the new Scotch domain if they went into their Savannah waters. John Edenburgh, chief Charles Town Indian trader at the time, was called in March, 1685, into the presence of Lord Cardross and warned that no Englishman should trade in that region: "the Indians were his." Thus his Scotch lordship was to do in lower Carolina what Lord Baltimore had done to Virginians who were trying to trade with the Pennsylvania-New York Indians in 1630–40 over the Susquehanna route. This challenge to the Charles Town traders was hardly known to the people concerned before Lord Cardross's arrest of the famous Henry Woodward because he was found to be negotiating new trade arrangements with Indian chiefs west and south of the Savannah.[14] The fact that Woodward had authority from the proprietors to explore the Indian realm as far south and west as he could go did not satisfy Cardross, who released his prisoner only on condition that he keep out of his Port Royal-Savannah zone. This still further perturbed Governor Morton and his Berkeley county people; it was at this time that they ordered Cardross, Hamilton and Montgomerie to appear before the Grand Council at Charles Town and explain their challenging conduct. The Scots continued to refuse to recognize their "superiors" at Charles Town and at the same time renewed their demand for the shipment of big guns to their new Stuart Town settlement—sending William Dunlop as their representative to ex-

[14] Crane, 28-30.

plain events and dangers. Although the Carolinians practically recognized a state of war between the Scots and "Spanish" Indians on their southern frontier, they refused to send their dismounted guns. What Lord Cardross had done to Indian tribes on his southern border was worse than anything the Carolinians had done during the preceding decade. Woodward, making his last explorations as far west as the Chattahoochee valley, was condemning Cardross and his dangerous aggressions in his reports to their superiors in London; and the proprietors became uneasy about their Scotch settlement.

Under these circumstances Governor Cabrera of St. Augustine planned the invasion of Carolina in the summer of 1686, his lordship, Cardross, having departed for England whence he hoped to bring more colonists to his new Carolina "state." As we know, James II was on the throne, and there was a growing fear that all England would be ordered to reassume its Catholic religion, Louis XIV sending huge sums to help the new King. But Cardross lent a helping hand at once to James II's son-in-law, the able William of Orange, who had defeated the aggressive French dictator more than once. Would Orange overthrow his father-in-law? This delayed further Scotch migration to lower Carolina. It was thus a favorable moment for the Spanish recovery of their lower Carolina region. In September, 1686, Cabrera, with a hundred Spaniards and larger numbers of his distressed Indians, attacked the defenseless Port Royal settlement, killed most of the settlers and burned all the houses of Stuart Town. He then ranged northward to the Edisto River where he plundered the homes of Governor Morton and other more wealthy settlers, Charles Town being the major objective of their campaign. But there came a terrific storm which destroyed two of the Spanish ships, one of their commanders drowned. It seemed to the Carolinians that God Almighty had saved them! The whole colony had been greatly alarmed; but their Spanish enemies were so badly damaged that they retired with a remnant of their robberies to St. Augustine. The few surviving Scotch folk of Port Royal wandered northward and were gradually absorbed in the upper Colleton and Berkeley settlements.[15] The great Scotch undertaking had thus been defeated; and little Charles Town was again master of the Carolina realm. When Lord Cardross learned what had happened to his poor fellows, he gave up all hope and went to Holland to help the future King of England prepare his alliances with Germany and Sweden and make ready to invade England, the realm of his unwise father-in-law.

A year before these unfortunate blunders of Port Royal, the Lords of Trade and Plantations sent Captain George Muschamp to Carolina to enforce the Navigation acts and collect revenues and taxes for his Majesty, James II. Of even greater importance was Muschamp's mission to curb the pirates and privateers who dominated so much of colonial trade; but Muschamp's work was quite as difficult in Carolina as was that of Edward Randolph in New England. Long before 1670, pirates had slipped into Cape Fear, Charles Town and Port Royal harbors and traded at a profit with Indians. In 1672, as we have seen, Carolina settlers had been ready to sell Indian captives as slaves; and the proprietors had tried in vain to check this sort of trade because it upset their Indian agreements organized by Henry Woodward. With a vast wilderness all the way to the Mississippi, about which men heard in 1684, it was as difficult to regulate trade as it had been for a hundred years to check piracy in the West Indies. Carolinians began to make real profits from their Indian performances before 1680, and pirates could hardly be prevented from lending assistance. To apply strict regulations

[15] Crane, *The Southern Frontier*, Ch. II.

either to pirates or to all trade deals would have required, as elsewhere, large war vessels and trained English regiments, far more expensive than any possible British advantages. Muschamp was thus able to do nothing more than irritate Carolina's tradespeople and report stubborn disobedience to the proprietors.

It was this unhappy economic situation which prevailed at the time of the Cabrera invasion; and naturally Governor Morton and the Carolina assembly, i.e., the Council and the newly elected legislature—prepared in the autumn of 1686 to attack Saint Augustine with the aid of their Indian allies and drive the Spaniards off the Florida peninsula. An army three times as large as that which had destroyed Stuart Town was organized and ample appropriations were voted.[16] If they were successful there would be no more Spanish trouble and the expense of it all would be met by the capture and sale of hundreds, perhaps a thousand, "Spanish" Indians. The little Charles Town would then be able to show the proprietors at last what the proper policy in their vast domain must be. This movement was regarded as the more urgent since Woodward had returned from his last exploration of the country between the upper Chattahoochee valley to the upper Tennessee waters; but he was about to die. At this moment, James Colleton, brother of the former proprietor, appeared as the new Governor, with fresh instructions from London.[17] The new Colleton had been a wealthy resident in Barbados, like his father and brother. He was now also a landgrave of Carolina, owner of 48,000 acres of land. Governor Morton was at once retired from his post, and the campaign against St. Augustine was at once forbidden. This decision was almost unanimously opposed by the Carolina representatives of the proprietors and by the almost helpless people who had escaped murder in the

[16] McCrady, I, Ch. 10; Beer, 188-200.
[17] Rivers, *History of South Carolina*, 151-56.

Port Royal neighborhood. But the Spanish Government was in peaceful relations with England and about to join the Pope in secret relations with William of Orange— the Pope being anti-Jesuit. An attack upon St. Augustine might add to the troubles of Europe. Hence the Carolinians were warned simply to ask repayment of the damages they had suffered and the return of their captured slaves. A new Spanish Governor had arrived at St. Augustine, and Colleton readily accepted peace agreements under which no damages were repaid. The Carolinians had never been more disappointed and angry, especially as Muschamp chose this moment, April, 1687, to arrest a Scottish vessel because it was carrying away Carolina exports without paying duties—Irish, Scotch and Dutch vessels having been accustomed for years to trade freely with these settlers. The Carolina court refused to accept Muschamp's evidence, and the ship was released. A governor as well as a royalist tax collector must have arbitrary powers if they hoped to succeed in Charles Town; but Carolinians, like Virginians in 1676, would never submit without real resistance to such powers.

Under these circumstances Colleton tried to reveal personal prestige and the necessary powers. He behaved like a British duke, built himself the handsomest mansion in the little capital and boasted about the absolute support of his London superiors. He was to punish Governor Morton for too close agreement with the people, to arrest and prosecute all pirates and compel popular opponents to surrender. In order to do this, the minority of the legislature was urged to compel the majority to accept amendments to the constitution under which they or their predecessors had migrated to Carolina in 1669; but even the influence of Governor Colleton, Joseph Blake, William Dunlop, Paul Grimball and Thomas Smith was unequal to the task assigned. Having failed to get legislative support in 1687, Colleton, in the winter of 1688, presented an order from the proprietors which proclaimed, as in 1682, a new constitution. If this order became effective, the Governor and Council were to tell the people through their legislature what laws they must enact and obey. Since no agreement could be obtained from the new assembly, Colleton was ordered from London not to allow any more elections except upon extraordinary dangers.[18] It was a repetition of former attitudes; but no results were attained. The Governor in 1689 tried to collect quitrents for every acre of land held by settlers; he forbade all inland trade with Indians, trying to monopolize these benefits for himself; and he actually imprisoned a dissenter clergyman and fined him £100. A genuine uprising followed, and the people seized Paul Grimball, Secretary to the Council, and thrust him into prison, as the Albemarle people had done more than once with their highest officials. The Governor then proclaimed martial law, but he could not enforce it. At this critical moment, the curious Governor, Seth Sothell, of North Carolina, who had been thrown out of office there, appeared in Charles Town. Sothell was himself a proprietor of both Carolinas and he claimed the right to govern. The people gave him support in spite of his record; they overthrew the Colleton régime; and reannounced the sacredness of their original charter, although few of its clauses had ever been actually applied. Eminent leaders like John Harris, Ralph Izard and even the unpopular Muschamp announced their support of the people and agreed that a new assembly should be elected. The result was the expulsion of Governor Colleton; and no less persons than old Colonel Bull, Paul Grimball and Thomas Smith were denied the right to hold any civil or military positions. In spite of the resistance of Colleton and his fellows, the new Sothell régime went into office; and when a report of events reached the proprietors in London, Sothell was recognized as their

[18] McCrady, Ch. X.

lower Carolina Governor, in spite of their dismissal of him in Albemarle. But what had not happened in England during the Colleton struggle in Charles Town? William of Orange was on the British throne, as we have already seen, and James II was in Paris, where Louis XIV gave him a palace for a semi-royal residence. South Carolina legislators had done what the House of Commons had done, 1689–90, and the proprietors could not immediately repudiate the Carolina acts of assembly.[19]

Poor Colleton gave up his claims to office, was banished from Carolina and had to abandon his beautiful residence. Sothell, although recognized as Governor, was ordered home to London a little later to answer the Albemarle charges against him. He remained at his post, however, and governed lower Carolina better than either Colleton or Morton, contrary to his record in upper Carolina. He encouraged the people in their democratic attitudes, their growing trade with the Indians, and left Muschamp without his support as to unlawful trade and pirate activities. Through the years 1690–91 the farmers and traders were more active and prosperous than the Albemarle people had ever been. Increasing numbers of French and Swiss Huguenots, even unhappy New Englanders, were encouraged by Sothell to accept lands north of Charles Town or in lower Colleton. Although the proprietors continued to issue arbitrary decrees, they and their representatives in the Carolina Council saw the benefits of the co-operative work of the curious Sothell, governing Carolina in spite of his recall. There were now scores of great landlords and quite as many well-to-do if not wealthy Indian traders; there were Negro slaves on the greater places, indentured servants more numerous. Most of these men were or had been proprietors' appointees to the Council or had played popular roles in the legislature, which was now called the assembly. The total population approached

[19] *State Papers, Colonial,* Dec. 31, 1688.

3,000, most of them citizens of Berkeley county, the rest living in Colleton or Craven.[20]

During Sothell's service each of the counties was represented in the assembly by five delegates, the same sort of equal representation which had prevailed in North Carolina. The Albemarle people were asked to send their delegates all the way to Charles Town; but this was not practical. In a year or two the Berkeley people insisted that all South Carolinians must vote in Charles Town. That meant that a third of the voters must walk or ride twenty-five to fifty miles to cast their ballots. The former right of all freemen to vote was now modified so that only people who owned £10 worth of property could participate in elections. It is doubtful, however, whether there was any real disfranchisement before 1700. One of the reasons for requiring all voters to appear in Charles Town was to limit the influence of Huguenots, also the Scotch and New England Puritans living in Colleton and Craven counties. This was the beginning of the Charles Town demand to govern all Carolina which continued till 1808, the same thing that was done in Boston and Philadelphia. But aside from these limitations the popular constitution which now went into effect strengthened the people's control of affairs. The Governor and Council were to function in the same manner as similar officials had functioned in Virginia before 1662. The supreme or palatine court could not declare acts of the assembly unconstitutional, and the local courts were to function the same as the North Carolina courts. The *Habeas Corpus* measure obtained by the Earl of Shaftesbury for all Englishmen from Parliament and Charles II in 1679 was now made a part of both Carolina constitutions. No man could be arrested upon the order of the Governor or a sheriff; and jurymen were from that time on chosen by lot from scores of names on

[20] McCrady, Ch. XI; George Howe *History of the Presbyterian Church in South Carolina* gives detailed information.

slips of paper which were always duly stirred in a hat or box. There was no longer a chance to pack juries. The twenty-year struggle in lower Carolina thus resulted in a democracy almost as real as that of upper Carolina.[21]

When Sothell departed in 1691 for London, Philip Ludwell became the Governor of both Carolinas and named the popular Thomas Harvey Governor of North Carolina. The two colonies were thus vaguely united for a time. Lady Berkeley accompanied her husband to Charles Town, but she had sold her proprietary rights to the Carolinas and was probably not so influential as she had been in Virginia. During the two and a half years when Ludwell and Lady Berkeley governed both Carolinas prosperity prevailed south of Virginia and there were fewer complaints in London about their self-government. The former Spanish danger had almost ceased, but there was a growing concern lest the arbitrary Louis XIV should carry into effect the great La Salle plan of uniting all the Mississippi valley with Canada and making alliances with the hundreds of thousands of Indians west and northwest of the Carolina wilderness. The active Indian fur and slave trade, perhaps the richest commerce of all the British colonies, was in danger; and Joseph Blake, John Boone and James Moore, whose relations with Jamaica and Barbados were very close, became more active than ever in their Indian trade, making alliances even farther west than Woodward had gone. Savannah Town, modern Augusta, Georgia, was the most remarkable of Carolina-Indian towns, where representatives of the Cherokees, Creeks and half a score of smaller tribes exchanged their bear and deer skins, even furs, for British arms, gunpowder, rough cloth and gay decorations in great quantities. The Carolinians carried their goods on horseback overland or on boats up the rivers at lower

[21] McCrady, 240-45; Mr. S. S. Fraser, Georgetown, S. C., has kindly supplied excellent data.

prices than the Spaniards or even the French could offer; and when there were Indian captives to be sold they yielded £10 or £12 each. When the famous Jean Coutre, the French explorer and master of a half score of Indian languages, learned in 1688 that La Salle's settlement on the lower Mississippi had failed, he traded on his own account with natives in the Kentucky-Tennessee uplands, and even made the upcountry Marylanders uneasy about his Indian maneuvres. A little later he broke his relations with French frontiersmen in the Illinois region, became a partner of Joseph Blake, drew several Indian tribes on the lower Mississippi into the Carolina trade activity and himself became a citizen of Charles Town—one of the causes of Carolina success during the early eighteenth century against both French and Spanish hostility.[22] Nearly all the deputies of the proprietors, like William Dunlop, John Farr, Paul Grimball and Thomas Smith participated in this vast Indian trade and their descendants played prominent rôles later in the terrible Indian wars of the two Carolinas. The little colony was as secure as could be expected with 200,000 Indians surrounding them and the French beginning their thirty years war for the domination of Europe and at the same time organizing Indian tribes all the way from the American Great Lakes to the Gulf of Mexico, in the hope of preventing the English Protestants from crossing the Alleghany Mountains. Little Charles Town was carefully palisaded against Indian attacks; from the basements of a number of the larger houses fronting the navigable rivers there were underground tunnels through which families might escape to their boats; and there were five or six companies of the best trained soldiers in all the colonies. The Council and assembly leaders were aware of their dangers, and they managed, like Europeans, always to keep certain Indian tribes organized against other tribes and to help now one

[22] Crane, 42-44.

side, now another, with a view always to destroying the great multitude of native owners of the country.

This complex the proprietors only half understood and consequently nearly always lost the support of their landgraves and caciques before they had been on their lands a couple of years. The Earl of Shaftesbury had understood the distant problem fairly well, and he had devoted a great deal of his attention to Carolina problems. He had lost at least £20,000 on his lower Carolina adventure; but busy always trying to limit the arbitrary powers of Charles II, he never got a chance to settle on his Ashley River land, as the second Lord Baltimore had done in Maryland; and, like the Earl of Clarendon, the senior proprietor of the first Carolina organization, Shaftesbury was permitted to save his life for a few months by settling in Amsterdam. The other proprietors continued to lose their investments till they thought of surrendering their titles to their monarch. Neither of the Carolinas resembled Maryland except in their ideals and struggles for self-government and freedom of religion. The Charles Town settlement, still the smallest of all the southern colonies, was of the greatest strategic importance. Little North Carolina was in almost as dangerous a position, but nobody seemed to know it. Would these small farmer-trading colonies maintain their struggles for democratic governments?

Index

Accomac County, 59
Africa, Dutch slave zone in, 198
African Slave Co., 236. *See also* Royal African Co.
Albemarle (district), 215; population and living conditions, 229 ff.; assumes Virginian forms, 227; democratic character, 228; resists government from Charles Town, 280
Albemarle (ship), destroyed by storm, 257
Albemarle, Duke of (Monck), 163, 172, 174, 177, 196; Admiral, 168; death, 206 fn. *See also* Monck
Albemarle Sound, 19
Allen, John, 158; as frontier leader, 239
Altamaha River, 286
Amsterdam, Netherlands, 19, 73
Anabaptists, 32
Andrews, M. P., *Founding of Maryland,* 60 fn., 70 fn., 145 fn.; *History of Maryland,* 152 fn.
Andrews, C. M., *British Committees,* 174 fn., 176 fn.; *Colonial Period,* 256 fn., 283 fn.
Anne, Queen, 167
Appalachians, 3
Appomattox River, 105, 128
Apprentices, 50
Argall, Capt. Samuel, 26; sea rover in first slave trade, 51
Argyle, Duke of, 152; executed, 163
Arke (ship), 61, 159; arrives safe in Potomac R., 62
Arlington, Earl of (Henry Bennet), 170, 196, 236. *See also* Bennet, Henry
Arthur, Gabriel, 263
Ashe, S. A., *History of North Carolina,* 2 fn., 194 fn., 211 fn., 217 fn., 281 fn.

Asheville, N. C., 7
Ashley, Lord (Cooper), 177, 181, 196; becomes prime minister, 206. *See also* Shaftesbury
Ashley River, 6, 255
Audubon, John James, naturalist, 14
Augusta, Ga., 2
Axtell, Daniel, 267; "landgrave," 268

Bacon, Sir Francis, 28, 129
Bacon, Nathaniel, Sr., 129, 134, 187, 251; his "castle" captured by Berkeley, 249
Bacon, Nathaniel, Jr., 233, 235, 241; confers with friends (1676), 242; routs Indians, 242; elected burgess, 243; arrested, 243; commander-in-chief against Indians, 244; denounces opponents, 245, 246; marches on Jamestown, 246; destroys town, 247; seizes Greenspring Court, 247; rising hostility against him, 247; dies, 248
Ballads, 45. *See also* Firth, C. H.
Ballagh, J. C., *White Servitude in the Colonies of Virginia,* 44 fn.
Ballard, Thomas, 245, 247, 249, 251
Baltimore, beginnings of, 154
Baltimore, Lord, arrives at Jamestown (1629), 60; land grants to, 60; dies (1632), 61
Baltimore, Lord (II), 64, 69, 79, 123; presses union of Virginia and Maryland, 70; plans, 136; accepts Assembly's Acts, 141; challenge to Virginia, 144; last illness, 158; receipts from colony, 159
Baltimore, Lord (III), income, 184; violates Navigation Acts in Maryland, 278
Baptists, 135, 178, 184, 190, 256; in

299

INDEX

Maryland, 154; fines inflicted on, 191
Barbados, 84, 85, 88, 174, 195, 199; prosperity from sugar exports, 204; gets self-government charter, 211; bad times, 217; buccaneers, 276
Barbour, Viola, *Henry Bennet*, 170 fn.
Barlow, Philip, 21
Barlowe, Arthur, naturalist, 14
Bassett, J. S., *Writings of W. Byrd*, 242 fn.
Bazant, Jean, Huguenot, 273
Beaufort, S. C., 6
Beer, G. L., *Old Colonial System*, 121 fn., 134 fn., 174 fn., 278 fn.
Bennet, Henry (Earl of Arlington), 131, 166. See also Arlington
Bennet, Hugh H., *Soils and Agriculture of the Southern States*, 7 fn.
Bennet, Philip, 79, 144
Bennet, Richard, 78, 117, 118, 121, 141, 149, 185, 187, 210
Berkeley, Sir Charles, 170
Berkeley, Lord George, of Gloucester, 169, 176
Berkeley, Lord John, 155, 162, 169, 175-177, 198
Berkeley, Sir William, 76, 77, 78, 82, 107, 170, 177; author *The Lost Lady*, 75; appointed Governor of Virginia, 75; prescribes Church of England services, 79; banishes Puritan members, 79; leaves for England, 80; his resolute policy, 118; agreement with Dutch, 122; yields to Commonwealth, 122; succeeded by Bennet, 123; in retirement, 129; approached by House of Burgesses, 132; his reply, 132; salary as governor, 133; real programme, 134; visits England, 135; expels Boston preachers, 145; continues drastic policy, 147; becomes a Carolina proprietor, 182; directs public works, 193; marries, 203; visits Chowan Settlers, 214; speculation in land, 232; denies freedom of press or public education, 240; raises volunteers against Bacon, 244; captures Jamestown, 246; evacuates it, 247; removed from office, 253; ignores, then insults Commission, 253; leaves for England, 254; death, 254
Berkeley, Lady, marries Philip Ludwell, 285; richest woman in America, 285; political influence of, 285
Berkenhead, servant, reports planned rising, 195
Bermuda, 24, 25; buccaneers at, 276
Berry, Sir John, 250, 253
Beverley, Robert, 243, 248, 249; secretary of House of Burgesses, 252
Biggs, Timothy, Quaker leader, 280, 282, 283; escapes from Charles Town prison, 282
"Black Death," 18
Blake, Benjamin, 267
Blake, Joseph, 291, 295; partner of Jean Coutre, 296
Bland, Edward, 209
Bland, Giles, 233, 235; Va. Collector of Customs, 236; spurns duel challenge, 237; fined, 237; joins Bacon, 245; captured, 246; hanged at Greenspring, 251
Bland, John, 235, 238
Bland, Richard, 58
Bland, Theodoric, 187, 209, 235
Blok, P. J., *History of the People of the Netherlands*, 17 fn., 165 fn.
Blount, Richard, Jesuit, 138, 139, 140
Board of Trade and Plantations, 206, 236, 238, 240, 254
Bombay, 166
Bond, B. W., *Quit-rent System*, 45 fn., 191 fn.
Boone, John, 295
Boteler, John, 141
Bowdoin, Mordecai, 282
Bradshaw, John, 162
Brazil, 84
Breda, Peace of (1667), 202
Brent, Giles, 79, 80, 153, 188, 242, 251; acting governor in Maryland, 144; returns to Virginia, 146
Brent, Margaret, 146, 153, 188
Bristol, Eng., 3, 175
Brocas, William, 75
Brown, Alexander, *The First Republic in America*, 22 fn., 24 fn., 26 fn., 30 fn., 32 fn., 33 fn.; *Genesis*, 28 fn., 34 fn., 36 fn.,

INDEX

58 fn.; *English Politics in Early Virginia,* 54 fn.
Brown, W. H., *George and Cecilius Calvert,* 61 fn., 136 fn.
Browne, Henry, 76
Bruce, P. A., *Economic History,* 42 fn., 44 fn., 51-2 fn., 76 fn., 83 fn., 84 fn., 110, 111 fn., 188 fn., 195 fn.; *Institutional History,* 90 fn., 92 fn., 95 fn., 96 fn., 99 fn., 100 fn., 103 fn., 106 fn., 108 fn., 114 fn.; *Social Life of Virginia,* 129 fn.
Brunken, Ernest, *North American Forests,* 3 fn.
Buffaloes, 14
Bull, Stephen, 258, 259
Bunyan, John, 170
Burnet, G., Bishop of Salisbury, *History of Own Time,* 165 fn.
Byrd, Valentine, 227, 281
Byrd, William, 233, 236; frontier leader, 239; militia captain, 241; Indian trader, 241; withdraws support from Bacon, 245
Byrd family, 58

"Cabal," the, 168
Cabrera, Governor Juan, St. Augustine, 286; attacks Port Royal, 288; his ships wrecked, 288
"Caciques," "landgraves," made official names of palatinate court members in Charles Town, 281
Calvert, Charles, 156, 205; governor and lieut.-general in Md., 153
Calvert, George (Lord Baltimore), 59. *See also* Baltimore, Lord
Calvert, Leonard, 61, 64, 66, 79, 81, 136, 139; governor, Md., 62; sails for England, 144; retires, 146. *See also* Maryland
Calvert, Philip, 151, 153, 195
Calvin, John, 17, 18
Campbell, Thomas, 20
Cape Charles, 25
Cape Fear, 6
Cape Fear River, 9, 12, 181, 216; colony there abandoned, 220
Carolina, Puritans and Quakers in, 181; rivers explored, 255; early conditions, 259 ff.; a "land of Canaan," 260; Yeamans' claim to governorship, 261, 262; West re-appointed governor, 263; charter changed, 262; religious freedom denied, 262; renewed interest in colony, 264; difference of S. C. from Va. and Md., 274; religious denominations, 274; buccaneers swarm on coasts, 276; early N. C., 286; campaign against St. Augustine planned, forbidden, 290
Carolina (ship), 257
Cardross, Lord (Henry Erskine), 270 ff., 272; summoned before Carolina council, 272, 287; encourages Indian settlers, 286; aids William of Orange, 288
Carter, John, 129, 188
Carteret, Sir George, 155, 172, 174-176, 196, 198, 211, 232; Carolina grant, 168; loan to Charles II, 202; condemned for corruption, 206 fn.
Carteret, Peter, 226
Carver, Capt. William, 245, 246
Cary, Lucius (Viscount Falkland), 13
Cary, Miles, 134
Catawba Indians, 264
Catchmaid, George, 211, 215
Catherine of Braganza, consort of Charles II, 166
Catholics, hopes for colony damped, 61; English troubles of, 138; barred from London, 283
Cavendish, William, Earl of Devonshire, 21, 34
Cecil, William, Earl of Salisbury, 21
Charles I, 58, 59, 66, 68, 69, 72, 75, 79, 119; execution, 82
Charles II, 107, 120, 121, 135, 152, 164, 165, 237; lands at Dover, 130; secret treaty with Louis XIV, 206; commission to Virginia, 250
Charles V, 16
Charles Town, 255 ff.; founded (1680), 268; conditions, 268, 269, 286; palisaded, 296; strategic importance, 297; population, 293, 294; demands to govern all Carolina, 294
Charleston, 6
Charlotte, 3
Cheesman, Edward, 248, 249
Chesapeake Bay, 1, 4, 22, 57; rival

tobacco communities on, 125; Dutch warships enter, 206; buccaneers in, 276; war vessels stationed, 279
Chicheley, Sir Henry, 124, 188, 245; imprisoned by Bacon, 247
Chicheley, Sir Thomas, 188
Chickahominy River, 105
Chowan River, 210, 211; settlers on, 211, 212
Churches, 89, 90; importance in Virginia, British model followed, 189, 190
Churchill, Gen. John (Duke of Marlborough), 56, 57
Claiborne, William, 60, 64, 75, 80, 117, 118, 121, 122, 126, 132, 140, 149, 188, 249, 251; Indian trader, 66; naval battle with Marylanders, 68; treasurer of Virginia, 77, 144; secretary for second time, 123; in London, 125; removed, 134; outlawed by Maryland, 144
Clarendon, Earl of (Edward Hyde), 162, 167, 172, 177, 196; exiled, 178, 205; tried for treason, 205
Clarendon Code, 170, 178, 181, 256; reapplied in England, 265
Clark, G. N., *The Later Stuarts*, 166 fn.
Clergy, authority of, in colonies, 94, 95. *See also* Ministers
Clerks of Court, 100
Climate, 7 ff.; a 17th century storm described, 11
Cloberry and Co., 66, 70
Clothing, 29
Coke, Sir Edward, 30
Colby, Charles C., *Economic Geography of North America*, 7 fn.
Colleton, James, governor, Charles Town, 290; lofty behavior of, 291; arbitrary methods, 292; expelled, 292; banished, 293
Colleton, Sir John, 175, 177, 181, 211, 215
Colleton, Sir Peter, 218, 226; letter to Locke, 228
Colleton, Thomas, 257, 268
Columbia, S. C., 2
Commissioners of shires, later justices of the peace, 95; a typical library, 96

Committee of Trade and Plantations, 175, 176, 180, 185
Condé, Louis, 202
Connor, R. D. W., *History of North Carolina*, 212 fn.
Cooper, Ashley, 257. *See also* Shaftesbury
Cooper River, 6
Coosawatchie River, 6
Copley, Father Thomas, Jesuit, at St. Mary's, 138, 139; Indian grants to, 139
Coptank River, 157
Corbin, Gawin, 107
Corbyn, Henry, 195
Cornwaleys, Thomas, 136, 140, 141, 145, 151, 153; returns to London, 153
Cornwallis, Capt. Thomas, 68
Coroners, 100, 101
Cottington, Lord Philip, 134
Cotton, 10
Council, Governor's, combined functions, 102; personnel, attendance, 102; dress, procedure, 103
Councillors, precedence and powers, 108
County Court, procedure and functions, 97 ff.
County families, houses and living conditions, 110, 111, 112
Coutre, Jean, French explorer, 296
Cox, James, 119
Crane, V. W., *Southern Frontier*, 264 fn., 289 fn.
Crane, W. F., *Life of Robert Rich*, 79 fn.
Craven, A. O., *Soil Exhaustion, etc.*, 48 fn., 50 fn.
Craven, Earl of, 177, 226, 264
Crawford, William, 281
Creek Indians, 13, 286
Creighton, M., *The Age of Elizabeth*, 19 fn.
Crewes, James, 242; elected burgess, 243
Crimes and offenses, 96; punishments, 97
Crispe, Sir Nicholas, 175
Cromwell, Oliver, 121, 125, 162, 173; denounces Virginia Assembly, 120; sends commission to Virginia, 121; decides in favor of Baltimore,

INDEX 303

125; death, 129; rebuke to Bennet and Claiborne, 150
Cromwell, Richard, 129; resigns Protectorship, 212
Cruikshank, Gen., *Life of Sir Henry Morgan*, 196 fn., 277 fn.
Cullen, Thomas, 227; speaker of assembly, 281
Culpeper, Alexander, surveyor-general of Virginia and upper Carolina, 203
Culpeper, John, 226, 280, 283
Culpeper, Lord Thomas, 236; proprietor of Northern Neck, 203; protest against, 238
Cumberland Valley, 4
Curtis, Edmund, 122
Custis, John, 251

Dale, Sir Thomas, 26
Danby, Earl of (Sir Thos. Osborne), activities of, 240
Danville, Va., 3
Delaware Indians, 13
Delaware River, 155; Dutch and Swedes on, 232
De La Warr, Lord, 28
Denbigh, home of Samuel Mathews, 57; description, 58
Denman, Elizabeth, *Slave Trade to America*, 177 fn.
Dew, Thomas, 124, 128, 132
Digges, Edward, 187, 188; first "experimental farmer" in America, 125; elected governor of Va., 125
Digges, Mrs. Elizabeth, 129
Discovery (ship), 22
Dismal Swamp, 5
Doeg Indians, 158
Dove (ship), 61, 159; arrives safe in Potomac R., 62
Downing, George, 172, 174, 176; ambassador to Holland, 173; nephew of John Winthrop, favorite of Cromwell, 173 fn.; demands of, 197
Downing Street, London, 173
Drake, Sir Francis, 172
Drax, Sir James, 84
Drew, Capt., 248
Drummond, William, 194, 202, 233, 242, 245; governor of Albemarle, 215; hanged by Berkeley, 249

Drummond, Mrs., sues Lady Berkeley, 285
Dunkirk, 165, 167
"Dunkirk House," 167
Dunlop, Alexander, 270
Dunlop, William, 287, 291, 296
Durant, George, 210, 211, 215, 227, 280, 281, 284
Durant, John, 147
Durant, William, 119, 147, 210
Durant's Neck, 211
Dutch, last English war (1672-1674), 157; illicit trade with, 193

East India Company, 20, 21, 31
East Indies, 20
Eastchurch, Thomas, fails to become Carolina governor, dies, 280
Edenburgh, John, Indian trader, 287
Edisto River, 288
Edmundson, William, 157, 233
Eleanor, Ingle's ship, 145
Eliot, Sir John, 59
Elizabeth, Queen, 18
Elizabeth River, 128
Ellyson, Robert, 195
Ems River, Norway, 199
England, 17; "Virginia fever" in, 43; religious dictatorship, 69; second Dutch war (1665), 199; last Dutch war (1672), 206
England, Church of, as legal religious mentor, 89
English, William, 67
Erasmus, 17
Essex, Earl of, 21, 73
Europe, 16
Evelin, George, 70, 71

Fairfax, H., *Proprietor of the Northern Neck*, 236 fn.
Falkland, Viscount, 110
Falmouth, England, 24
Farr, John, 296
Fendall, Josias, 150 ff.; appointed governor by Baltimore, 152; varying fortunes, 152
Ferguson, I., *County Court in Virginia* (art.), 97 fn.
Ferrar, Nicholas, 32
Firth, C. H., *Ballads Relating to America*, 45 fn.
Fish, 15

304 INDEX

Fiske, John, *Old Virginia*, 57 fn., 68 fn., 246 fn.
Fitzhugh, William, 188
Fleete, Henry, 64-66
Florida, 12
Force, P., *Tracts*, 51 fn., 58 fn.; *Leah and Rachel*, 87 fn., 114 fn.; *Virginia's Cure*, 89 fn., 115, 116 fn.; *A Perfect Description*, 88 fn.; *Voyage to Virginia*, 107 fn.
Forman, H. C., *Early Manors of Maryland*, 184 fn.
Fort Comfort, 58
Fowke, Gerard, 195
Fox, George, Quaker, 157, 233; visits Maryland, 154
France, her ambition to dominate Europe and South America, 202
Freemen, personnel and status, 113; houses and living conditions, 114, 115; daily routine, food, dress, 115, 116
Fuller, Capt. William, 151

Gaillard, Richard, Huguenot, 273
Gallop, Capt. George, captures Dutch slave ship, 277
Gardiner, S. R., *History of England*, 73 fn.
Gates, Sir Thomas, 24
Geneva, 17
Georgia, 3
Germany, 17
Gillam, Zachariah, shipmaster, 233, 282; pays record customs duties, 230, 231
Gloucester County, executions in, 195
Godfrey, Capt. Daniel, 226
Goodspeed (ship), 22
Goose Creek, Car., 273
Goree Island (Afr.), 198
Goring, Lord, head of tobacco commission, 70, 71
Gosnold, Capt. Bartholomy, 22
Governors, functions and powers of, 55, 56
Grand jury, procedure, 98
Great Santee River, 12
Green, Roger, 210
Greenbrier White Sulphur Spgs., 3
Greene, Thomas, 81
Greenspring Court, mansion of Sir Wm. Berkeley, 186; seized by Nicholas Bacon, 247

Greenville, S. C., 3
Grimball, Paul, 291; secretary to Council, 292; imprisoned by people, 292; Indian trader, 296
Grinard, Jacob, 273
Grinnell, M. G., *Life of Admiral De Ruyter*, 200 fn.
Guale Indians, 286

Habeas Corpus, in both Carolina Constitutions, 294
Hailstorm, does immense damage to tobacco crop, 200
Hall, C. C., *Narratives of Early Maryland*, 62 fn., 64 fn., 149 fn.
Hamiltons, in lower Carolina, 270
Hammond, Col. Mainwaring, 105, 135; appointed general of militia, 132
Hampden, John, 31, 59, 72, 74
Hansford, Col. Thomas, 248; hanged, 249
Harlow, V. T., *History of Barbados*, 85 fn., 86 fn., 211 fn.
Harrison, F., quoted, 37 fn.; *Memoirs*, 110 fn.
Harrison, Thomas, 76, 81, 118, 119; gets message from Cromwell, 121
Hart, Oliver, quoted, 8
Harvey, John, planter, 211, 227
Harvey, Sir John, governor of Virginia, 55, 64, 66-70, 208; his tobacco control scheme, 59; methods, 65; ordered from Va., 68; returns to post, 71
Harvey, Thomas, governor of N. Carolina, 295
Hatcher, William, 97
Hawley, Jerome, 136, 139
Hazlitt, W. C., *Old English Plays*, 75 fn.
Heath, Sir Robert, 177, 209
Hendrick, B. J., *The Lees of Virginia*, 247 fn.
Hening, *Statutes at Large*, 35 fn., et passim
Henrietta, sister of Charles II, 164
Henrietta Maria, Queen, 59, 61, 69, 73, 138, 164, 176
Henrico, plantation, 31
Henry IV (of France), 164, 165
Henry VIII, 17
"High Sheriffs," 100

INDEX   305

Hill, Edward, 80, 81, 111; Speaker of House of Burgesses, 126
Hirsch, A. H., *Huguenots of South Carolina,* 273 fn.
Holden, Robert, 284
Holmes, Capt. Robert, 198, 199
Hot Springs, Va., 2
House of Burgesses, Virginia, 65, 102, 106, 107, 204, 237, 247; elected by freemen, 54; supreme power of, 109; characteristics of members, 109
House of Commons, 30
Howe, George, *History of the Presbyterian Church in South Carolina,* 294 fn.
Hudson River, 173
Huguenots, 272; many leave France, 272; reach Carolina, 273; settlement, 273; leading families, 273; increase of French and Swiss, 293
Hundred Years' War, 18
Hyde, Anne, daughter of Clarendon, 167; marries Duke of York, 164
Hyde, Edward, English statesman, 130; Earl of Clarendon, Chancellor, 131. *See also* Clarendon
Hyde, Lawrence, 180

Illegitimacy, 94
Illiteracy, 114
India, 20
Indian corn, 23, 24, 29, 39, 40
Indian Ocean, 20
Indian war, first (1675), 158
Indians, 2, 143; raid in 1622, 34; sell cleared ground to Maryland settlers, 62; trade with, 62; hostility, 79; new treaties, 128; danger in Carolina, 260; allies of Spanish, 272; many Indian captives enslaved, 274; organization by French, 296
Ingle, Richard, arrives St. Mary's, 80; captured, 80; depredations, called "pirate," 145, 146
Ireton, Henry, 162
Iroquois, 57, 64; fur trade, 125; raid rival natives in Susquehanna Valley, 237
Isham, Henry, 242
Isle of Kent, 57, 60, 64, 67, 70, 81, 125, 140, 154; Claiborne's occupancy, 64; uproar in Virginia over proposed seizure, 65. *See also* Claiborne
Isle of Wight, 67

Jamaica, 173, 181, 195, 196; prosperity of, 204; buccaneers at, 276
James I, 20, 30; issues *A Counterblaste* (1604), 27, 27 fn.; opposition to Sandys, quoted, 32; imposes tobacco duties, 33
James City (plantation), 31
James River, 5, 6, 9, 22, 56, 82
Jamestown, 23, 25, 26, 77, 185; protest, *Tragical Relation,* issued at, 35
Jarratt, D., *Memoir,* 116 fn.
Jarvis, Thomas, 281; governor of Albemarle, 285
Jeffreys, Herbert, 250; in charge in Virginia, 253
Jenkins, John, 211, 226; acting governor at Charles Town, 280; again, 284
Jennings, Peter, 102, 195
Jennings, William, 281, 282
Jesuits, 18, 142; hated in Virginia, 140
Jews, in Maryland, 154
Johnson, J., *Old Maryland Manors,* 137 fn.
Johnson, Alderman Robert, carries petition to King, 34
Justices of Peace, functions of, 96. *See also* Commissioners

Kecoughton, home of Claiborne, 57
Kemp, Richard, 65, 66, 69, 75, 78, 111; appointed secretary of Maryland, 67; governor in charge, 80
Kendall, George, 22
King Philip's War, 239
Kiowha Indians, 258
Knight, Sir John, 206, 230
Knoxville, Tenn., 3, 7
Kusso Indians, 261
Kyrle, Sir Richard, governor of Carolina, dies, 271

Lamb, Caleb, 282
Langford, John, 151
Larrimore, Capt., 253
La Salle, great North American plan of, 295
Latané, J. H., *Early Relations be-*

tween Virginia and Maryland, 79 fn.; *Johns Hopkins Studies,* 121 fn., 125 fn.
Laud, Archbishop William, 65, 69; as religious dictator, 74; committed to Tower, 74
Lauderdale, Earl of (John Maitland), 283; dictator of Scotland, 266
Laurence, Richard, 242, 243, 245, 249
Lawyers, distrust of, 126, 127, 225; act restraining, 127
Lecky, W. E. H., *England in the 18th Century,* 91 fn.
Lee, Richard, 107, 124, 129, 188, 251; attorney-general, 102; imprisoned by Bacon, 247
Legge, William, 176
Lewger, John, 136, 140; acting governor, 141
Lillington, Alexander, 281
Littleton, Nathaniel, 124
Lloyd, Edward, 153
Lloyd-Thomas, J. W., *Autobiography of Richard Baxter,* 178 fn.
Locke, John, 181; *Fundamental Constitutions,* colonial scheme, 221 ff.; rewrites charter, 256
Logwood, trade in 1670's, 277, 278
London, 19, 20, 175; plague of 1665, 199; great fire of 1666, 201; speculation, 213; colonizing enthusiasm, 218; recovery from plague and fire and the naval defeat of 1667, 226
London Company, 21, 25, 56
Lords of Plantations, 71
Louis XIV, 164, 165, 166, 200, 220; schemes, 202; secret treaty with Charles II (1670), 206; American dread of, 207; designs on Netherlands, 237; persecutes Huguenots, 272; his American plans feared, 295
Loyola, Ignatius, 78
Ludlow, George, 76
Ludwell, Philip, 246; governor of both Carolinas (1691), 295
Ludwell, Thomas, 11 fn., 107, 110, 129, 187, 195, 237, 238; appointed secretary of Virginia, 134
Lunsford, Sir Thomas, 102, 110, 124
Luther, Martin, 16
Lutherans, 16

Lynch, Sir Thomas, governor of Jamaica (1680), 279
Macaulay, T. B., *History of England,* 91 fn.
McCrady, Edward, *History of South Carolina,* 256 fn.
Magna Charta, 127, 140
Mahan, A. T., *Sea Power,* 173 fn.
Maltravers, Lord Henry, 209
Manhood suffrage, 117
Marcham, F. G., *Sir Edwin Sandys,* 31 fn.
Maria de' Medici, 164
Mary, daughter of Duke of York, wife of William of Orange, 266
Mary, mother of Prince of Orange, 165
Maryland, 3; Indians sell ground, 62; Council mostly Catholic, 62; quit-rents, 63; tobacco cultivation, 63; livestock, 63; relations with Virginia neighbors, 63, 64; improvement of agriculture, 84; Cromwell decides for Lord Baltimore after three years' delay, 125; manorial rules, 137; marriage, 137; union with Va. sought, 141; religious freedom, 142; land regulations, 142; early living conditions, 143; Puritans in Assembly (1649), 147; counties division, 148; after fall of Stuarts, 148; Catholic council, Puritan Assembly, at Saint Mary's, 149; "squatters" on frontier, 155; property rule for voters, 205; restlessness (1674), 237; frontier warfare, 239; remodeling, 239; resentment against Charles Calvert, 244; depression (1660–63), 256
Marshal, Ralph, 258
Marston Moor, 80
Mason, George, 158, 188, 189, 242; frontier leader, 239; assembly leader, 243
Massachusetts, 60, 212
Mastian, Nicholas, 67
Mathews, Samuel, 56, 57, 64, 67, 69, 70, 118, 124, 141, 243; succeeds Digges as governor, 125
Mathews, Thomas, 243
Meherrin Indians, 232
Menefie, George, 67, 69, 70

INDEX

Mereness, N. D., *Maryland as a Proprietary Province*, 82 fn., 185 fn., 205 fn., 244 fn.
Merriman, Roger B., *Rise of the Spanish Empire*, 18 fn.
Middleton, Sir Thomas, 28
Militia: make-up, compensation, officers, rules, discipline, 104 ff.
Miller, Thomas, denounces Charles II, 234; governor, 280; imprisoned at Charles Town, 282
Ministers: pay of, personnel, living conditions, 90-93
Modyford, Sir James, 176, 211, 213
Modyford, Sir Thomas, 180, 203, 218
Monck, George, Duke of Albemarle, 130. *See also* Albemarle
Montgomeries, in lower Carolina, 270
Montgomery, Earl of, 65
Moore, James, 295
More, Sir Thomas, *Utopia*, 17
Morgan, Sir Henry, 197, 204, 256; leading W. I. pirate, deputy governor of Jamaica, 277; retires from piracy, 279
Morton, Joseph, 267; "landgrave," 268; governor of Carolina, 269; demoted, 271
Moryson, Francis, 185, 238, 250, 253
Moryson, Richard, 73, 110; acting governor, 135
Moseley, Arthur, 243
Motley, Thomas, acting governor, Md., 253
Mt. Desert Island, French at, 26
Mt. Vernon, 82
Muddiman, J. G., *Trial of King Charles the First*, 119 fn.
Muschamp, Capt. George, 292, 293; sent to Carolina, 289; his difficult task, 290; arrests Scottish ship, 291
Muscovy, 20

Nansemond, 82, 221
Nansemond River, 187, 209
Nantes, Edict of, revocation by Louis XIV, 273
Naseby, 80
Navigation Act (1651), 123; amended, 134; Cromwell's policy in, 135; Acts of 1660 and 1663, 155, 256; difficulty of enforcement, 276

Neale, James, 153
Needham, James, 263
Negro slavery, in lower Carolina, 265
Nelson, Capt. Francis, 24
Netherlands, 16, 68, 69, 73, 76, 165, 172; Spanish, 166
Neuse River, 5
Nevis Island, W. I., 257
New Amsterdam, 57, 60, 199
New England, prosperity in, 175; trade interests and shipping, 179, 180; active in N. C. and W. I. trade (1670-90), 282
Newfoundland, 25, 60
Newport, Capt. Christopher, 22, 24
Nichols, Sir Edward, 170
Nicholls, Col. Richard, 198
Noell, Martin, 173, 174-76, 196
North Carolina. *See* Carolina
Northampton, Earl of, 73
Northern Neck, Va., 236
Norwood, Henry, 107
Nottoway River, 5
Nova Scotia, 173
Nugent, Nell M., *Cavaliers and Pioneers*, 186 fn., 189 fn.

Oates, Titus, 266
Opechancanough, Indian chief, 80; leads massacre, 80
Orleans, Duchess of, 176; Duke of, 164
Oyster Point (Charles Town), 268

Parliament (1661), 170
Patuxent River, 157
Peaks of Otter, 4
Pedeco River, 6
Pembroke, Earl of, 65; letter quoted, 34
Penalties, 99. *See also* Crimes and Offenses
Penn, William, 159, 160; buys N. J. rights of Sir George Carteret, 267; becomes Stuart champion, 267; gets vast grant, 267
Penn, Admiral William, conqueror of Jamaica, 166, 173
Penney, N., *Journal of George Fox*, 157 fn.
Pepys, Samuel, 181; *Diary*, 198 fn.
Perry, W. S., *Historical Collections*, 94 fn.

INDEX

Peters, Robert, 76
Peters, Thomas, 124
Petit, René, Huguenot, 273
Petit jury, procedure of, 98
Petition of Right (1628), 59, 68
Philip II, aids Jesuitism, 18
Philip IV, 166
Phillips, Ulrich B., *Life and Labor in the Old South,* 46 fn.
Phoenix (ship), Capt. Francis Nelson arrives at Jamestown on board, 24
Piracy, in Jamaica, 204; widespread activity in, 276; Virginia waters "infested," 278; pirates arrested, hanged, ships seized (1678-90), 279
Plague, of London, 198, 200
"Plantations," 31
Plymouth, Eng., 23, 175
Pollock, Thomas, 284
Port Royal, Jamaica, 197, 270
Port Royal (ship), wrecked near Bahamas, 257
Portugal, 73; King of, 166
Potapsco River, 159
Potomac River, 3, 9, 12, 82, 236
Pott, Francis, 67; imprisoned, 68
Pott, Dr. John, acting governor, 60, 67
Povey, Thomas, 173-176, 196
Powhatan, Indian chief, 24
Presbyterians, 256; Scotch P. persecuted, 265; in lower Carolina, 270
Preston, Richard, 151, 154
Privateers, Dutch, 155; in Virginia and Maryland, 194
Purchas, Samuel, *Pilgrimages,* 25 fn.
Puritans, 60, 89, 184, 194; reject loyalty to Stuarts, 120; clergy deprived, 170
Pym, John, 31, 59, 72, 74

Quaker, Capt. Allen's ketch, 230
Quakers, 89, 126, 131, 135, 178, 184, 194, 256; drastic statute against, 133; in Maryland, 154; fines imposed on, 190, 191
Quit-rents, 45, 63, 238, 292; refused in Albemarle, 280. *See also* Virginia, Maryland

Radcliffe, Capt. John, 22

Raleigh, Sir Walter, 2, 19, 21, 27; "lost colony" of, 208
Randolph, Edmund, sent out to make Colonial survey, 278; imprisoned in Boston and Bermuda, 279
Randolph, Henry, 185
Rappahannock River, 5, 66, 236
Read, Conyers, *Secretary Walsingham,* 19 fn.
Rebecca (ship), 253
Rebellion, "Bacon's" (1676), 233, 240 ff. *See also* Bacon, Nathaniel
Religion, conditions in England, 265-267
Religious liberty, greater in Colonies than in England, 126; conceded by Shaftesbury, Locke, and colleagues, 225
Riccard, Sir Andrew, 175
Rich, Henry, 73
Rich, Richard, 21
Rich, Robert, 21. *See also* Warwick, Earl of
Richmond, Va., 2
Rivers, of the South, 12
Rivers, W. J., *History of South Carolina,* 261 fn., 270 fn., 290 fn.
Roanoke River, 5, 77, 84, 215
Rolfe, John, sends first tobacco leaves to London, 27
Romney, Sir William, 20
Rotterdam, 73
Royal African Company, 155, 197, 277; aim at slave trade monopoly, 176; competitor of East India Co., 177; power, 180
Royal Exchange, 21
Rupert, Prince, 176
Ruyter, Admiral de, 198, 199; retreats, 200; again in Thames, 201; fails to capture London, 202

Sackville, Sir Edward, 34
St. Christopher, W. I., 85
St. Croix River, N. S., 26
St. John's River, 1
Saint Mary's, 62, 64
Salisbury, Earl of, 30
Salley, A. S., *Narratives of Early Carolina,* 258 fn.
Sanders, Richard, 281
Sandys, Sir Edwin, 21, 29, 34, 36, 54, 82; author *The Religious State of Europe,* 31; opposes the East India

Co., 33; elected to Parliament, 33; imprisoned, 33
Sanford, Robert, 219; explores Carolina coast, 219, 220; further explorations, 255, 256
Santa Lucia, W. I., 196
Santee River, 6, 273
Saponas Indians, 217
Saunders, W. L., *Colonial Records*, 210 fn.
Savannah, Ga., 6
Savannah River, 2, 3, 12, 255
Savannah Town (Augusta, Ga.), 295
Sayle, William, first governor of Carolina, 257, 258; dies 1671, 260
Scarborough, Charles, 251
Scarborough, Edmund, 187
Scotch settlement, Port Royal, Carolina, 270, 271; anxiety in Charles Town over, 287; settlement destroyed by Spanish-Indian attack, 288; few survivors, those absorbed elsewhere, 289
Scotland, 17
Scott, A. P., *Criminal Law in Colonial Virginia*, 94 fn., 97 fn., 99 fn.
Scott, W. R., *Joint Stock Companies*, 21 fn.
Searles, Daniel, 211
Seneca Indians, 157
Servants, indentured, 50, 51, 113; personnel and status, living conditions, 114, 115; work, food, dress, 115, 116; runaways, crime, 116; rules and penalties, 191
Severn River, 159
Severn Valley, 146, 147
Sewall, Henry, 153, 195
Shaftesbury, Earl of (Ashley Cooper), 170, 206, 240; loses Chancellorship, organizes dissenters, 240, 241; sent to Tower, 241; contemplates emigration, 263; escapes to Holland, 270; death, 270. *See also* Ashley, Lord
Shakespeare, 19
Shaw, Sir John, 175
Shenandoah, 3
Shipman, William, 28
Shipping, 178, 179; regulations and decrees, 121, 174; in Chesapeake Bay, 128
Silk, production ordered, 192

Six Nations, Indian tribes, 157
Slave trade, 51, 52, 176, 177; prices, 180; Barbados and Jamaica, 232; in Carolina, 274; between New England and West Indies, 277
Smith, Capt. John, 22-24, 29
Smith, Paul, 258
Smith, Preserved, *The Age of the Reformation*, 16 fn.
Smith, Richard, 188
Smith, Robert, 238
Smith, Thomas, Virginia trader, hanged, 141
Smythe, Sir Thomas, 20, 21, 29, 33, 34, 35; with Sir E. Sandys prepared first democratic constitution in North America, 31
Soane, Henry, 134
Sothell, Seth, Albemarle governor, 284; captured and imprisoned, 284; removed, 285; appears in Charles Town and is elected governor, 292, 293; goes to London, 295
South America, 180
South Carolina. *See* Carolina
Southampton, Earl of, 21, 32, 34
Spain, 68, 73; struggle with, 264
Spanish territory, in North America, grant of, 177
Spencer, Nicholas, governor, Virginia, 278
"Squatters," 209
Stanard, M. N., *Story of Bacon's Rebellion*, 242 fn., 245 fn., 249 fn.
Stanard, W. G., quoted, 37 fn.; *Colonial Virginia Register*, 76 fn.
Staples Act (1663), on shipping, 174. *See also* Shipping
Star Chamber Court, 68
Steinmetz, Andrew, *Tobacco*, 27 fn.
Stephens, Frances (Lady Berkeley), 107
Stephens, Samuel, governor of N. C., 107
Stephenson, N. W., on Sandys, 33 fn.
Stone, William, Maryland governor, 81, 82, 119, 146, 148; upholds Baltimore, 149; in semi-exile, 153; defeated in battle, 150; imprisoned, 150
Strafford, Earl of, impeached, 74
Strong, Leonard, writes *Fall of Babylon*, 150

INDEX

Stuart Town, Carolina, 272, 287; burned by Cabrera (1686), 288. *See also* Scotch settlement
Stuyvesant, Peter, 132, 198; letter from Berkeley to, 132
Sugar, customs duties, 175; fall in price (1664), 195
Sugar cane, 84
Surinam, 180
Susan Constant (ship), 22
Susquehanna River, 57, 142
Susquehannock Indians, attempt to settle in Virginia, 237
Swann, Thomas, 132, 245, 250
Switzerland, 16, 17

Tangiers, 166, 169
Tawney, R. H., *Agrarian Problems in the 16th Century*, 44 fn.
The Flying Horse (ship), 28
Thirteen Colonies, 19
Thirty Years' War, 59
Thompson, George, 151
Thoroughgood, Adam, 58
Thorpe, Otto, 245
Throgmorton, Robert, 110
Tobacco, 10, 11, 27; beginning of plantations, 36 ff.; valuable development, 42; insect enemies, 47; Spanish tobacco, 48; prices, 49, 76, 77, 79; harvesting regulations, 48, 49; first standardization, 49; King offers monopoly, 53; declined in part by Va., 54; price decline (1629-31), 61; in Md., 63; British abandon the business, 85; London trade, 85, 86; rivalry between Va. and Md., 86; as standard of value, 87; "stint" of 1663-64, 155; resented in Md., 156; "cessation" forbidden by King, 156; destruction by storms, 156; production about 1675, 159; royal revenue from, 160; customs duties, 175; reduction regulations, 192, 193, 195; hail damage, 200; upper Carolina output, 281
Trevelyan, G. M., *England under the Stuarts*, 69 fn., 74 fn., 131 fn., 172 fn., 199 fn., 202 fn., 232 fn.
Tromp, Admiral Martin, 73
Truman, Major Thomas, 151, 154, 158, 239

Turenne, Henri, famous French soldier, 202
Tuscarora Indians, 13
Tyler, L. G., *Early Virginia*, 32 fn.; *Cyclopædia of Virginia*, 64 fn.; *The English in America*, 80 fn., 83 fn.

United Netherlands, 18. *See also* Netherlands

Vandel, Joost, Netherlands poet, 200
Vane, Sir Henry, 124, 152; beheaded, 163
Vassall, Henry, 218
Vassall, John, 203, 218
Vestrymen, functions and powers of, 91, 92
Villiers, Barbara, 163
Virginia, 3, 21, 31; free distribution of land in, 31; legislature established, 31; controversies, 34; Assembly asserts taxing rights, 35; charter vacated (1674), 35; adverse report of Commission, 35; early conditions, livestock, agriculture, fences and cabins, 37-39; hogs, 40; diet, baking, "corn pone," "ash cakes," 40-41; titles in fee simple, 42; landlords, 43; immigrants bonded, 43; criminals, 44; indentured servants, 44; quitrents, 45; agricultural methods, 46; "plantation" becomes individual term, 50; "hundreds" and plantations organized like English counties, 54; the "parish," 54; Council first American supreme court, 56; issue with Md., 64; status of ministers, 77; trading with Dutch banned, 77; church matters, 78; increase of immigrants and population, 83; farm improvements, 84; tobacco for England, 85; financial returns, 88; horse-racing and betting, 111; burgess supremacy recognized, 123; title to Maryland argued, 124; exports, 128; population (1650-66), 128; penance for execution of Charles I, 135; Calverts ask union with Md. under Baltimore, 141; statutes revised, 185; sheriffs, 186; travel in later 17th

INDEX 311

century, 186; aristocratic society, 186; lumber, 188; conditions among leading residents, 186 ff.; character of colony, 189; preachers paid in tobacco, 190; recovery measures, 192; building, 192; Berkeley's reconstruction schemes, 193; limitation of suffrage (1670), 205; new regulations of Charles II, 214; restlessness in 1674, 237; frontier warfare, 239; remodeling colony, 239; manhood suffrage restored, 243; Bacon rebellion ends, 248; King's commission arrives, 250; attainder and confiscation, 252; Berkeley master, 252; depression (1660–63), 256; bad times in 1682, 278
Virginia Company, 29, 30

Ward, R. de C., *Climatology of the U. S.*, 10 fn.
Wardens, functions of, 91
Warner, Augustine, 132; Speaker of House of Burgesses, 252
Warwick, Earl of (Robert Rich), 34, 73, 144; sea rover, in slave trade, 51; Admiral-in-Chief and Colonial Governor-General, 78
Washington, John, 154, 158, 188, 189, 239, 242, 251
Water power, 15
Wentworth, Thomas (Earl of Strafford), 72. *See also* Strafford
Wertenbaker, T. J., *Virginia under the Stuarts*, 37 fn., 126 fn., 130 fn., 133 fn.; *Planters of Colonial Virginia*, 44 fn.
West, John, 58, 64, 67, 69, 75, 76, 80, 105, 124, 141, 251, 259; acting governor of Virginia, 68; property confiscated by Harvey, 71; exempted from taxation, 132; Carolina governor, 260; secretary, 262; reappointed governor, 263; retired, 269
West, Joseph, deputy for Duke of Albemarle, 258
West, M. D., *Virginia*, 58 fn.
West, Samuel, 258
West, Thomas, Lord De La Warr, governor, 25. *See also* De La Warr
West Indies, 22; blacks from, 52;
regulations, 196; Dutch in, 209, 211
Westo Indians, 257, 258, 286
Westover, 58
Wheat, 10
Wheeling, Va., 3, 7
White, Father, *Briefe Relation*, 62 fn.
Wild life, 14, 15
Wilkinson, Henry, Albemarle governor, 283; imprisoned, 284
William of Orange, 18, 75, 165, 291, 293
Williamson, Atkin, first Church of England pastor in Charles Town, 269
Willoughby, Lord Francis, 81, 85, 180, 211; governor of Barbados, 196
Willoughby, John, 226
Willoughby, Thomas, 69, 81, 187, 210
Wilmington, N. C., 6
Wingfield, Edward, governor, 22
Winslow, John, 282
Winthrop, John (Mass.), 79, 119, 145
Winthrop, John (Conn.), 198
Witt, Jean de, 165, 198, 200
Wood, Col. Abraham, 59, 106, 128, 187, 263
Woodhouse, Henry, 59
Woodward, Henry, explorer of Carolina, 255; captured, 256; escapes, 257; joins pirate ship as doctor, 257; escapes from pirates, 257; treats with Indians, 264; arrested by Cardross, 272, 287; strictures on Cardross, 288
Woodward, Thomas, Surveyor-General of Albemarle, 215, 216
Wormeley, Ralph, 110, 124, 129, 188, 251
Wyatt, Sir Francis, governor, 55, 71, 75

Yadkin Valley, 263.
Yamasee Indians, 286
Yeamans, Sir John, 203, 217, 257; wrecked at Cape Fear River, 219; claims governorship of Carolina, 261; rejected, 262; proclaimed governor by Shaftesbury, 262; distrusted, retires to Barbados, 263

Yeardley, Argal, 124
Yeardley, Francis, 210
Yeardley, Sir George, governor, 31
York, Duke of, 121, 130, 168, 172, 176, 198, 220; High Admiral, 131; annexes New Netherland, 155
York River, 56, 129

Zurich, Switzerland, 16
Zwingli, Ulrich, 17

CPSIA information can be obtained
at www.ICGtesting.com
Printed in the USA
BVHW060316230120
570202BV00004B/236